WITTGENSTEIN'S LATER PHILOSOPHY

Wittgenstein's Later Philosophy

Oswald Hanfling
Reader in Philosophy
The Open University

MACMILLAN

First published 1989 by
MACMILLAN PRESS LTD
Houndmills, Basingstoke, Hampshire RG21 6XS
and London
Companies and representatives
throughout the world

ISBN 0–333–47575–5

A catalogue record for this book is available
from the British Library.

10 9   8   7   6   5   4   3   2
04 03 02 01 00 99 98 97 96

Printed in Great Britain by
Antony Rowe Ltd
Chippenham, Wiltshire

Contents

Acknowledgements

The author and publishers wish to thank the following who have kindly given permission for the use of copyright material:

Basil Blackwell for extracts from 'What Does the Private Language Argument Prove?' from *Philosophical Quarterly*, 1984, 'Does Language Need Rules?' from *Philosophical Quarterly*, 1980, and from 'On the Meaning and Use of "I Know" ' from *Philosophical Investigations*, 1982, all by Oswald Hanfling.

Croom Helm Publishers Ltd, for extracts from 'Criteria, Conventions and Other Minds' by Oswald Hanfling, from *Ludwig Wittgenstein: Critical Assessments, Volume II*, edited by S. G. Shanker.

The author further wishes to acknowledge Justyn Balinski who compiled the indexes.

List of Abbreviations

BB   *The Blue and Brown Books.*
LK   *Logic and Knowledge*, Bertrand Russell (Allen & Unwin, 1956).
OC   *On Certainty* (Blackwell, 1969). References are to sections.
PG   *Philosophical Grammar* (Blackwell, 1974).
PI   *Philosophical Investigations* (Blackwell, 1958). References to Part I are by sections (e.g. PI 109) and references to Part II are by page numbers (e.g. PI p. 226).
PR   *Philosophical Remarks* (Blackwell, 1975).
RFM   *Remarks on the Foundations of Mathematics* (Blackwell, 1978).
WVC   *Wittgenstein and the Vienna Circle*, Friedrich Waismann (Blackwell, 1979).
Z   *Zettel* (Blackwell, 1967). References are to sections.

References are to page numbers except in the case of OC, PI Part I, and Z.

1

Introduction

This book was written to provide a general discussion of Wittgenstein's ideas, especially his influential later philosophy, rather than to put forward some new theme or thesis which had escaped previous commentators. In the course of writing, however, I found that one particular aspect of his thought seemed especially important; and I believe that various misunderstandings of his ideas, by professionals and ordinary readers, by those hostile and those sympathetic to his views, have stemmed largely from a failure to grasp, or come to terms with, this aspect of his thought.

Wittgenstein more than once expressed a fear that his work would be widely misunderstood. Sometimes the point at issue is straightforward enough, as in PI 307, where he anticipates that he will be regarded (wrongly) as a behaviourist – one who maintains that statements about the mind can be reduced to statements about behaviour. But the more difficult matter to grasp is that which he sometimes expresses by saying that his method is 'purely descriptive' (BB 125). 'We may not', he wrote in the *Investigations*, 'advance any kind of theory. . . . We must do away with all *explanation*, and description alone must take its place' (PI 109).

These remarks have not, of course, gone unnoticed. Nevertheless there is a continuing tendency to ascribe to him such and such a theory (of language, mind, knowledge and so on) and to assimilate his ideas to one of the traditional schools or '-isms'. I believe that this involves a failure to come to terms with the essential originality of his (later) ideas, and their discontinuity with what had gone before. Another source of misunderstanding has been the desire to ascribe to him hard-and-fast views or claims in place of what he actually says, which may be more tentative and qualified. A common pitfall here is to treat as obviously rhetorical some of his questions which were really intended as *questions,* and not to have 'obvious' answers supplied by the reader. Another is to resort to the cruder, more dogmatic statements that we sometimes find in his less finished drafts, or notes of lectures, to make up for what

1

seems to be (on this mistaken view) left unstated in his more authoritative works.

Wittgenstein was not a careless or obscure writer. He went to infinite pains in drafting and re-drafting his remarks until they would express exactly what he intended. There is no justification here, as there might be, say, in studying the writings of Locke, for supposing that though the author said X, we may as well take him to have meant Y or Z, or some more or less murky combination of these. Hence, when Wittgenstein does not draw what may seem to be an obvious conclusion, we should beware of thinking that we can clarify his meaning by doing so; and when he refrains from coming down neatly on one side or the other of a question, we should beware of doing so on his behalf. Wittgenstein sometimes said that the difficulty that people would have with his later ideas would be one of will rather than understanding.[1] This may seem a strange thing to say, but I believe there is a good deal of truth in it. Wittgenstein's message was not excessively complicated, and he was right to describe his work as one of 'assembling reminders' of things familiar to us. The difficulty lies in grasping the full import of his message and method, and in being prepared to open one's mind to the radical change of approach that this calls for.

In the chapters that follow (not including the first, which is about the 'early' philosophy) I sometimes present Wittgenstein's ideas by contrast with rigid or theoretical views that one may be tempted to ascribe to him (and which have often been so ascribed in the literature), contrary to his insistence on 'description alone', as quoted above. In Chapter 3, which is about his identification of the meaning of a word with its use in practice, I argue that this is not a *theory* of meaning, comparable with others that have been put forward; and I try to bring out the importance of this point. I also try to show that his refutation of his early philosophy is not as direct as has sometimes been thought; and how the new 'descriptive' approach is related to traditional problems of philosophy. In Chapter 4 I expound and defend Wittgenstein's slogan that 'explanations come to an end', and reject the view that his remarks about 'family resemblances' amount to a theory of meaning. Chapter 5 is about the celebrated 'private language argument', and here I try to show (among other things) that Wittgenstein's position was less rigid and more gradual than is usually thought. I also criticise the widespread idea that he used the term 'criterion' in a technical sense, for the purpose of laying down conditions of meaning. In Chapter 6 I discuss the question of concepts and practices in societies remote from ours. Here I defend the 'strange' imaginary examples introduced by Wittgenstein but try to show that his pluralism has limits, and that his position cannot be accommodated under such well-known dichotomies as that of 'realism' versus 'relativism'. I also argue against the idea that the concept of *following a rule* is central to Wittgenstein's account of language. Finally, in the discussion of Wittgenstein's notes *On Certainty*, in Chapter 7, I resist an excessively rigid interpretation of his remarks about the expression 'I know' (as in 'I know I have two hands' for instance). In this chapter, as elsewhere, I try to bring out the true significance of the descriptive approach.

Throughout the book I also discuss objections that may be, or have been brought against Wittgenstein's position on various matters. But this is not a book written by an uncommitted reader. For, as will become clear, I share Wittgenstein's views, as I understand them, to a very large extent. My aim, therefore, is not merely to present the views of a great thinker as clearly as possible, but to advocate and defend a philosophy of whose correctness and importance I am convinced.

My thanks are due to Peter Hacker and Godfrey Vesey for reading through an earlier draft of this book. Their helpful comments have enabled me to improve what I had written and avoid a number of mistakes.

2

The *Tractatus* and the 'Essence of Human Language'

A. THE CORRELATION THEORY OF MEANING

'What is the meaning of a word?' With this question Wittgenstein opened one of the first works of his 'later' philosophy, the *Blue Book* of 1933–4. How do words have meaning? What is the relation between them and what they are about? Why does language have the structure that it has? Such questions occupied Wittgenstein throughout his philosophical career. In his 'early' masterpiece, the *Tractatus Logico-Philosophicus*, he had answered them in one way; in the later philosophy he rejected this answer and put forward a different one. But the change was not merely between one answer, A, and another, B, to a given question; it was, as we shall see in later chapters, a more radical change, involving a different perception of the problem and of philosophical problems altogether.

The present book is mainly about Wittgenstein's later philosophy, as expounded in his most finished work, the *Philosophical Investigations*. In this work, as in others of the later period, he sometimes presented his new ideas by contrasting them with the old, occasionally referring to his early book by name and more often by implication. It is appropriate, therefore, to begin a study of the later thought with an account of the earlier; and this will be the object of the present chapter. I should say, however, that this will not be a full or balanced account of the *Tractatus*; it is far too short for that. My main aim will be to bring out aspects of the work which serve to highlight Wittgenstein's later thought, to which the rest of the book is devoted.

The *Tractatus* is a difficult and often obscure work. But behind the obscurity likes a conception of language and the world which may well strike the reader as attractive and plausible. It is that of a correlation between elements of language and elements of the

4

world. In the opening section of the *Investigations*, Wittgenstein gave a simple statement of this view, describing it as 'a particular picture of the essence of human language'.

> The individual words of language name objects – sentences are combinations of such names. – In this picture of language we find the roots of the following idea: Every word has a meaning. This meaning is correlated with the word. It is the object for which the word stands. (PI 1.)[1]

It may well be thought that there must be some such correlation between words and objects, language and reality. Otherwise, it may be thought, language would not be *about* reality; it would merely be some kind of game or ritual, in which sounds are exchanged according to agreed patterns or rules. The quoted account of language would also explain why language is the way it is – having the kind of structure and vocabulary that it has; for these would be determined by the reality to which language corresponds.

Now there are two ways in which language may be said to correspond with reality, that of word and object, and that of sentence and fact. Sentences, unlike words, have a 'truth-value' – they are either true or false. If I say that John Noakes lives at Slough, this will be true if there is a corresponding fact and false if there is not. But the relation between word and object is not one of truth-value, and words are not described as true or false. In making the above statement, the existence of the objects mentioned would be assumed but not stated; whereas the existence of the fact would be stated and not assumed: this would be the purpose of the statement.

How are we to conceive of the two kinds of correspondence? We might say that in the case of word and object it is one of meaning – the meaning of a word being 'the object for which the word stands'. But this cannot be so in the case of sentence and fact, for the meaning of a sentence leaves it entirely open whether there *is* such a fact. This meaning seems to depend, rather, on the meanings of the words making up the sentence. Moreover, facts do not *exist* in the same sense as objects; a fact is not a kind of object. A fact exists – there is such a fact – if objects are combined or related in a particular way, for example, if John Noakes is living at Slough. But how should we think of the correspondence between the sentence and the fact that would make it true? What is truth? The answer of the *Tractatus* is that a sentence (or proposition)[2] is true if the objects named in it are related to one another in the same way as are the words in the sentence.

When Wittgenstein was composing the *Tractatus*, he found an attractive example of this conception in a magazine article about a road accident. (Cf. *Notebooks*, p. 7.) At the court hearing a physical model of the situation was produced, with miniature vehicles and figures in the relevant positions. The figures in the model represented ('meant') the corresponding real figures; and the model would be *true* if the latter had been related in the accident in the same way as their counterparts in the model, false if they had not. In the *Tractatus* he spoke of propositions as being like a *tableau vivant* (*ein lebendes Bild* = a living picture).

> One name stands for one thing, another for another thing, and they are combined with one another. In this way the whole group – like a *tableau vivant* – presents a state of affairs. (T 4.0311.)

If the presented state of affairs exists, is a fact, then the proposition (or picture) is true; otherwise not.

We should not be deterred, says Wittgenstein, by the fact that 'at first sight a proposition – one set out on the printed page, for example – does not seem to be a picture . . . '. A piece of musical notation, he points out, does not 'seem to be a picture of music, nor our phonetic notation (the alphabet) . . . a picture of our speech'. Yet, he claims, they 'prove to be pictures, even in the ordinary sense, of what they represent' (T 4.011). This is hardly correct if it means that we would ordinarily *describe* them as pictures. But the essential point (and the essential conception of the picture theory of meaning) is that of the one-to-one correlation between elements of that which represents (picture, musical notation, proposition) and elements of that which is represented (the state of affairs, piece of music and so on). The 'depicting' relation can range, he said, over 'a gramophone record, the musical idea, the written notes, and the sound waves', all of these standing 'to one another in the same internal relation of depicting that holds between language and the world' (T 4.014).

He was able to claim that some sentences, of the form 'aRb', even strike us as pictures (T 4.012.). In this type of sentence, an object a (say a knife) is said to be in relation R with an object b

(say a fork). Now if this relation is that of 'being to the left of', then the correlation between sentence and state of affairs is obvious. It would of course be less obvious if the sentence said that *a* is to the *right* of *b*, for in that case the spatial arrangement of the sentence might seem to be the wrong way round. But it could still be regarded as depicting the state of affairs, though by a different convention; and its truth would still depend on the arrangement of its components. There are also, of course, many other kinds of relation besides the spatial, and it is far from clear how they might be 'depicted' in sentences. It may be replied that there are also many different relations in a piece of music, and yet they all seem to have counterparts in the musical notation, the gramophone record, and the 'musical idea'. But it is not clear how this analogy can be applied to sentences. In any case, as we shall see in the next section, the picturing relation was supposed to hold for 'fully analysed' sentences and not sentences as they ordinarily appear to us.

Wittgenstein also made the point that in the sentence-type '*aRb*', the inclusion of '*R*' is not in accordance with the picture theory. For while '*a*' and '*b*' have objects corresponding to them, there is no such object in the case of '*R*'. The state of affairs that is being depicted contains two objects (say a knife and a fork), and not three. (If *R* *were* an object, then we would need to say how this object is related to the other two, which would need a further relational term, and so on *ad infinitum*.) How then are we to account for the existence of three terms in the sentence when there are only two objects in reality? The answer is not to postulate a third object, but to regard the sentence as having, properly speaking, only *two* terms. We are not to say that '*aRb*' represents the state of affairs in which '*a* stands to *b* in the relation *R*', but: '*That* "*a*" stands to "*b*" in a certain relation says *that aRb*' (T 3.1432).[3] In other words, the sentence does its work, not by containing the term '*R*', but by a suitable relation existing between '*a*' and '*b*' in the sentence.

This is what we should expect, if the sentence is a kind of picture. For in a picture (model, map), *R* would not be depicted as a separate object. The picture would contain counterparts of the relevant objects, but the *relations* between the latter would appear from the way in which their counterparts are related in the picture. Hence the appearance of '*R*' in the sentence is misleading as to its true form.

So far I have spoken of pictures and sentences in physical terms.

But in fact the pictures that Wittgenstein had in mind were mental; he spoke of them as 'thoughts'. In a sentence, he said, 'the thought is expressed in a way that is perceptible to the senses' (T 3, 3.1). Thus the picturing relationship takes in three items: that which is depicted; the picture of it, which is a thought; and the expression of this in language. The thought, he said, 'can be expressed in such a way that elements of the propositional sign [that is, of the written or spoken sentence] correspond to the objects of the thought' (T 3.2); and this correspondence also, of course, reaches out to the depicted state of affairs.

Wittgenstein does not say very much about the mind in the *Tractatus*, but it is important that (like many others before and since) he regarded language as being fundamentally mental. The pictures (propositions) that we make ourselves of the world are, initially, in the mind, and it is only in order to make them 'perceptible to the senses' that we resort to their spoken or written counterparts. He seems to have taken it for granted that language is mental in this way; but in his later work, as we shall see, one of his main objectives was to overturn this conception of mental priority, which he came to regard as a source of deep confusion, in the philosophy both of language and of the mind.

The *Tractatus*, as we have seen, presents a certain account of the relation between language and reality, proposition and fact. But we are not to think of these as belonging to different realms – as if language were not part of reality, or as if a fact could be depicted by something *other* than a fact. If a proposition were something different from a fact, then the correspondence between them would not be perfect. But according to Wittgenstein, this is not so; for 'a picture is a fact' (T 2.141); and its expression, the 'propositional sign', is likewise a fact (T 3.14). He asks the reader to consider an arrangement of tables and chairs. Here we have a fact, which might be depicted by a corresponding proposition. But, says Wittgenstein, the arrangement of tables and chairs can itself be regarded as a proposition; we should indeed think of propositions in such terms.

> The essence of a propositional sign is very clearly seen if we imagine one composed of spatial objects (such as tables, chairs, and books) instead of written signs.
>
> Then the spatial arrangement of these things will express the sense of the proposition. (T 3.1431)

Thus the propositional sign may consist of spoken sounds, of written words or of tables and chairs. But in each case we have a *fact*, representing another fact.

B. ATOMISM AND 'THE SUBSTANCE OF THE WORLD'

The name-object conception of meaning may seem plausible if we think of the names of existing people, towns and other objects. But what if we are speaking of non-existent objects, or even, perhaps, objects that never existed? If the meaning of a word is 'the object for which the word stands', then these words must be literally *meaningless*. Yet we often speak of non-existent objects or objects of whose existence we are uncertain. (We may, for instance, *ask* whether such an object exists.) This brings us to one of the most important ideas of the *Tractatus* – that of 'simple' names which would not be exposed to the hazard of non-existent objects. The problem of non-existence was due, on the *Tractatus* view, to the *complexity* of ordinary words and objects. An ordinary name, such as John Noakes, stands for a complex entity whose existence depends on the *combination* of certain elements; and these elements may or may not be combined in reality. Now these elements might themselves be composed of yet simpler elements, but ultimately we must arrive at elements which are absolutely simple. These would not be capable of dissolution, and *their* names could not be meaningless. Wittgenstein held that there must be such simple elements behind the appearance of ordinary objects and names, and he reserved the terms 'object' and 'name' for these elements. In the *Investigations*, recapitulating his earlier views, he used as an example the word 'Excalibur', which, he pointed out,

> is a proper name in the ordinary sense. The sword Excalibur consists of parts combined in a particular way. If they are combined differently Excalibur does not exist. But it is clear that 'Excalibur has a sharp blade' makes *sense* whether Excalibur is still whole or is broken up. (PI 39)

Hence there must still be 'something corresponding to the words' of the sentence, which would account for its meaning. This something was to be reached by means of *analysis*. 'So the word "Excalibur" must disappear when the sense is analysed and its place be taken by words which name simples. It will be reasonable to call these words the real names'.

The criterion of a 'real name' is that it 'cannot be dissected any further by means of a definition: it is a primitive sign' (T 3.26). In another section of the *Investigations*, he quoted a passage from Plato, in which this idea was well expressed.

> there is no definition of the primary elements . . . out of which we and everything else is composed; for everything that exists in its own right can only be *named*, no other determination is possible. . . . [For a primary element] nothing is possible but the bare name; its name is all it has. But just as what consists of these primary elements is itself complex, so the names of the elements become descriptive language by being compounded together. For the essence of speech is the composition of names. (PI 46)

Such 'primary elements', he concluded, were what he had meant by 'objects' in the *Tractatus*, and what Russell (using similar arguments) had meant by 'individuals' (cf. *Tractatus* 2.02, 2.0201, 2.024).

It is not easy, however, to conceive of objects or names having the required simplicity. For is not every object capable of some description other than 'the bare name'? And does not every name have some descriptive implications? Bertrand Russell, whose arguments in 'The Philosophy of Logical Atomism' were similar to those of the *Tractatus*, concluded that it was indeed 'very difficult to get any instance of a name at all in the proper strict logical sense of the word' (LK 201). The only suitable candidates, he thought, were demonstratives which were bare of any descriptive content – 'words like "this" or "that" '. But even these would not have the required simplicity if they referred to times other than the present or involved persons other than the speaker. The 'this' in question must be used merely 'to stand for a particular with which one is acquainted at the moment'. It was part of Russell's theory of knowledge that each person is 'acquainted' with 'sense data' which are private to him, these being the source of all knowledge and meaning. Hence the 'this' in question would have 'a very odd property for a proper name, namely that it seldom means the same thing two moments running and does not mean the same thing to the speaker and the hearer'.

This was not, however, a conception of meaning to which Wittgenstein subscribed. As we shall see in a later chapter, the rejection of the view that meanings are 'private' was one of the main concerns of his later philosophy. And in the *Tractatus* he held that names (that is, the 'real' names) have a fixed and permanent meaning, not confined to the momentary state of a given speaker, the corresponding objects being similarly permanent. This brings us to one of the most remarkable doctrines of the *Tractatus*. It is that behind the shifting appearances of the world there is something eternal and unchanging – a world of 'objects' that remain always the same. These objects are 'the substance of the world', they are 'fixed and subsistent'; it is only their arrangement or 'configuration' that is 'changing and unstable' (T 2.021, 2.0271). Such a change would mean that a proposition which was true at one time would be false at another; but no such changes could occur within the elemental objects or their names.

When such names were combined into a proposition, the result was an 'elementary' proposition. It was, he claimed, 'obvious that the analysis of [ordinary] propositions must bring us to elementary propositions which consist of names in immediate combination'; and 'we know on purely logical grounds that there must be elementary propositions' (T 4.221, 5.5562).

What were these grounds? Consider again the statement that Excalibur has a sharp blade. There are two quite different ways in which it may fail to be true. One is that Excalibur does not have a sharp blade, the other that there is no such object as Excalibur. In the latter case, should we say that the statement is *false*? This would have an awkward consequence, as Russell pointed out (LK 251). For if the above statement is declared false because of non-existence, then the same reason must apply to its contradictory, 'Excalibur does *not* have a sharp blade', which must likewise be declared false. Yet it is a principle of logic that two contradictory statements cannot both be false. Russell's solution (using different examples) was that the appearance of 'Excalibur' as a name was misleading as to the true nature of these statements. What they are really asserting, besides the fact that something does or does not have a sharp blade, is that such and such a complex thing *exists* – that 'objects' are combined in such and such a way. This part of the statement is encapsulated in the word 'Excalibur'. Thus two component statements (at least) are contained in each of the original two; the first component, in each case, asserting the existence of 'Excalibur' (that is, that objects are combined in that way), and the second adding a point about the blade (that it is or is not sharp). But given that the first component is false, both of the original statements may be declared false without violating the principle of logic.

Is there an alternative to declaring them false? One might perhaps say that they are neither true nor false, but a kind of nonsense. (This would be more tempting, perhaps, in the case of one of Russell's examples, a statement about 'the present King of France'.) But in this matter Wittgenstein agreed with Russell: 'A proposition that mentions a complex will not be nonsensical, if the complex does not exist, but simply false' (T 3.24).

Wittgenstein, however, was more concerned about what he called 'determinacy of sense'. He held that we can fix the sense of a given proposition only by getting down to its constitutent elementary propositions, consisting of names. A proposition that mentioned a complex (for example, by using a name of the ordinary kind) would lack determinacy until this were done. That a complex is involved would, indeed, 'be seen from an indeterminateness in the proposition in which it occurs. In such cases we *know* that the proposition leaves something undetermined' (T 3.24).

If such complexes could not be analysed into simples, then, he argued, no ordinary propositions would ever have a determinate sense at all; we would not know what we were talking about. Therefore 'the requirement that simple signs be possible is the requirement that sense be determinate' (T 3.23). He believed, however, that this requirement can be met, at least in principle; and that each proposition has 'one and only one complete analysis' (T 3.25). Here we have part of what, in his Preface to the *Tractatus*, he described as 'the whole sense of the book': that 'what can be said at all can be said clearly' (p. 2).

In another section he put his argument in terms of simple objects (as opposed to their names). If there were no such objects, then, he said, 'whether a proposition had sense would depend on whether another proposition was true' (T 2.0211).[4] If there were no such objects, then all words would have to stand for complexes. But, given that words have meaning by standing for something, such a word *would* be meaningless if the corresponding complex did not exist; and so would the proposition in which it occurred (contrary to T 3.24, quoted above). We would not be able to rescue the word, so to speak, by reducing it to names of simples. Hence we would need to bring in another proposition, asserting that the complex does exist, before we could know whether the first proposition had meaning. But the second proposition could not be guaranteed to have meaning either, since its words too could only stand for complexes. And so the whole of language would remain self-enclosed, and there would be no way of talking about the world outside language.[5]

As we have seen, Wittgenstein did not follow Russell in regarding the fleeting 'this' as the fundamental name. In the *Investigations* he spoke of this view as 'a queer conception', pointing out that 'this' would not normally count as a name at all (PI 38–9). But what would he, when he wrote the *Tractatus*, have given as examples of names and objects? Here we come to a notorious and characteristic difficulty of the *Tractatus*. To Russell, who had enquired about the ultimate components of thought, he replied: 'I don't know *what* the constituents of a thought are but I know *that* it must have such constituents which correspond to the words of Language' (*Notebooks* 130). To Norman Malcolm, who in later years asked what he would have regarded as an example of an object, Wittgenstein replied that his thought at the time of the *Tractatus* had been 'that he was a *logician*; and that it was not his business, as a logician, to try to decide whether this thing or that was a simple thing or a complex thing, that being a purely *empirical* matter!' (*Ludwig Wittgenstein: A Memoir* (OUP, 1958) 86).

Here we have a fundamental difference between the *Tractatus* way of doing philosophy and the approach of the later Wittgenstein, which was to be 'purely descriptive'. The *Tractatus* tells us how language and the world *must* be; in the *Investigations*, by contrast, we are told to 'look and see' how language is actually used (PI 66). In the latter work, we are assured that what is relevant for philosophy is all on the surface; what is needed is only to look properly at what is before our noses. The *Tractatus*, however, gives us a *theory* of language, in which certain entities and relations are postulated as 'requirements'. This is regarded as necessary because the true nature of language and meaning is hidden from us.

> Man has the ability to construct languages capable of expressing every sense, without having any idea how each word has meaning or what its meaning is. . . .
> It is not humanly possible to gather immediately from [every-day language] what the logic of language is. (T 4.002)[6]

Language, he continued, 'disguises thought. So much so, that from the outward form of the clothing it is impossible to infer the form of the thought beneath it . . .'. This did not mean that I can find out 'how each word has meaning or what its meaning is', by attending to my thought (that is, to a proposition in its mental existence). For (as the reply to Russell shows) the difficulty about names and objects arises with the mental proposition no less than with the spoken one. By 'thought', he must have meant something deeper, more essential, than ordinary thought.

C. TRUTH-FUNCTIONS AND 'THE ESSENCE OF LANGUAGE'

If Wittgenstein was silent about examples of names and objects, he was explicit about the method of analysis that would lead to the relevant elementary propositions. The method was that of 'truth-functional' logic, nowadays regarded as a standard system, and used widely inside and outside philosophy (for example, in the construction of computers). Without going too much into the complications of the system (for which textbooks are available), I shall try to describe it sufficiently to give an account of the relations between analysis, simplicity, and the essential nature of language as Wittgenstein saw them in the *Tractatus*.

Consider a proposition p (for example, 'The book is on the table') and another proposition q (for example, 'It is raining'). From these we can build the conjunctive proposition 'p and q'. It will be seen that the truth of the latter depends on the truth of the conjuncts p and q. If one of them is false, then 'p and q' will be false; if both are true, then 'p and q' will be true. Now consider the disjunction 'p or q'. For this to be true, only one of the components needs to be true. For example, if p is false, 'p or q' may still be true (that is, if q is true). But if both components are false, then, of course, the disjunction 'p or q' will be false.

We saw earlier how, according to the picture theory, the truth of a proposition depends on whether the names in it are combined in a way corresponding to a combination of objects. But the dependence just described is of a different kind. The way in which the truth of 'p and q', for example, depends on the truth of its conjuncts, is not that of the picture theory. Its truth is said to be a 'function' of theirs; and such propositions as 'p and q' are said to be 'truth-functions' of their component propositions. Wittgenstein believed, however, that the truth-functional analysis of any given proposition would lead ultimately to elementary propositions standing directly in the picturing relationship with a state of affairs. The term 'proposition' could, indeed, be defined in this way. 'A proposition is a truth-function of elementary propositions' (T 5). (This would also include the elementary propositions themselves, since, according to Wittgenstein, 'an elementary proposition is a truth-function of itself' (T 5).)

Here again, however, the sentences we actually find in language are merely an 'outward clothing'; for a proposition may be a truth-function of others without appearing in any such form as 'p and q' or 'p or q'. The logic of the sentence may be disguised, for example, by the use of a word such as 'Excalibur'. This appears as a name, but really represents an assertion, or set of assertions, about combinations of objects, involving conjunctions, and perhaps disjunctions, of elementary propositions.

In the *Investigations*, Wittgenstein used a different example to illustrate the method of analysis (this time for the purpose of criticism).

When I say: 'My broom is in the corner', – is this really a statement about the broomstick and brush? Well, it could at any rate be replaced by a statement giving the position of the stick and the position of the brush. And this statement is surely a further analysed form of the first one. . . . If the broom is there, that surely means that the stick and the brush must be there, and in a particular relation to one another; and this was as it were hidden in the sense of the first sentence. (PI 60)

What we have here, however, would only be the beginning of an analysis, since 'stick' and 'brush' (and also 'corner') are still complex. Perhaps further analysis will contain disjunctions – 'p or q' or 'p or q or r' – since such an object may be made in more than one way. Again, we must not assume that the analysis would remain in the physical realm, for we cannot be sure that the ultimate objects, 'the substance of the world', are physical. (One proposal, but not the only one, put forward by commentators, has been to treat the particles of theoretical physics as *Tractatus* objects.) In any case, many of the things we ordinarily talk about do not have an obvious breakdown into parts, as in the case of the broom.

(The term 'corner' is an example.) Thus the application of the method of analysis – how to proceed from the outward clothing to the essence – remains unclear.

Two other terms, of the system need to be mentioned. One of these, written $\supset$, corresponds roughly to the implicative 'if . . . , then . . . ' of ordinary language. Thus '$p \supset q$' (for example, 'the book is on the table $\supset$ it is raining') may be rendered as 'If the book is on the table, then it is raining'. This rendering is only approximate, however. The term in question is defined in such a way that '$p \supset q$' is *false* in the case in which p is true but q is false (in this way resembling the 'If p, then q' in ordinary language); but *true* in the other three possible cases (p and q both true, p and q both false, p false and q true). The ordinary 'If p, then q' would not, however, be described as true in all these cases. (Its logic is more complicated, and less easy to define than that of $\supset$; and the same is true of the 'and' and 'or' of ordinary language, as opposed to their truth-functional counterparts.)

Finally there is negation, written $\sim$ in the *Tractatus* notation. Thus '$\sim p$' may be rendered as 'not-p', and similarly with '$\sim(p$ or $q)$'. Not-p counts as a truth-function of p, since its truth-value depends on that of p. (The *Tractatus* notations for 'and' and 'or' have not yet been given; they are a dot '.' for 'and', and 'v' for 'or'; for example $p.q$, p v q.)

The idea of truth-functional analysis leads to a more precise definition than has been given so far of the elementariness of elementary propositions, and the simplicity of the relevant names and objects; for Wittgenstein defined these notions in terms of deduction and non-contradiction, these relations being understood in truth-functional terms.

'It is', said Wittgenstein, 'a sign of [a] proposition's being elementary that there can be no elementary proposition contradicting it' (T 4.211); and 'One elementary proposition cannot be deduced from another' (T 5.134). These criteria are really interchangeable, but it will be convenient to start with the second. According to a well-known principle of logic, the deduction of one proposition from another is valid only if the former is already 'contained' in the latter; there must not be more in the conclusion than there is in the premise. 'If p follows from q, the sense of "p" is contained in the sense of "q" ' (T 5.122). Now this notion of 'containing' is given precise expression by the truth-functional method. For if p follows from q, then the analysis of q would reveal

p as one of its truth-functional components. For example, (q) 'My broom is in the corner' might be analysed into two component propositions, one (p) about the stick and the other (o) about the brush. And in that case, of course, each of the propositions p and o would be deducible from the proposition q. But such deduction can only take place if the latter proposition is composite and *not* elementary. Hence 'one elementary proposition cannot be deduced from another' (T 5.134).

The point about non-contradiction (T 4.211) is essentially the same; for if one proposition (p) is in contradiction with another (q), this means that the *negation* of p is deducible from q (and vice versa). Hence not-p must be 'contained' in q (and not-q contained in p), and this would be revealed by analysis. And then, again, the propositions would be composite and not elementary.

But are there really elementary propositions of the required kind, satisfying the criterion of logical independence? Russell had proposed 'This is white' as an example of a 'simple fact'; it was, he claimed, 'about as simple a fact as you can get hold of' (LK 198). Questioned about simple and complex by one of those attending his lectures, he reaffirmed his belief that 'complexes are composed of simples', but confessed that for all he knew 'analysis could go on forever' (LK 202). But this standpoint was not acceptable to Wittgenstein. He insisted, as we saw, that analysis must terminate in simples; if this were not so, then there could be no 'determinacy of sense', and all our words would lack definition.

The example of colour-words does, however, bring out a general difficulty about the programme of analysis. Such propositions cannot be elementary according to the *Tractatus* criterion, since (for example) 'This is red' entails 'This is not green' (not blue, not white and so on); and yet these negative propositions could hardly be given as part of an *analysis* of 'This is red'. Here we have a complexity that appears to be different in kind from that of the broom. (The question of colours is raised at T 6.3751, and appeared as a major difficulty in Wittgenstein's Lecture of 1929, in which he modified the requirement of logical independence.)[7]

The truth-functional conception of language may be described as an ideal, whereby the multifarious phenomena of language, as actually used, are to be reduced to a smooth and well-ordered system. This is also evident in the definitions of the truth-functional 'and' and 'or' as opposed to their counterparts in ordinary language. Take, for example, a proposition of the form 'p or q'. This, as we saw, will be true if either p or q is true. But what if I knew both to be true? Then it would be misleading for me to say 'p or q', for this would imply that one or the other may be false for all I know. Should the analysis of 'p or q' therefore include an item about the speaker's state of knowledge, as one component? This would clearly be a different sort of component from the items 'p' and 'q'. Unlike the latter, it would make the truth of 'p or q' relative to a given speaker at a particular time. Another example, involving conjunction, is the statement 'He pressed the button and there was an explosion'. In this case there is an implication that the two conjuncts are temporally and causally related; and this is not captured by the truth-functional analysis, which treats the two components in isolation. And in general, the meanings of 'and' and 'or' in actual usage are context-dependent and complicated in various ways that cannot be captured by a uniform system of analysis. But in the truth-functional system these complications are smoothed out by definition. Thus the symbol 'v' (corresponding to 'or') is defined in such a way that 'p v q' counts as *true* if both components are true; and the symbol for conjunction is defined purely in terms of component propositions, without regard to other considerations. It is part of the *Tractatus* view that, in the final analysis, all these complications *can* be reduced to simple truth-functional relations as defined in the system.

A further and final step in the ideal of reduction was taken with the introduction of the 'Sheffer stroke', written '$p \mid q$', the meaning of which may be rendered as 'neither p nor q'. It had been shown, prior to the writing of the *Tractatus*, that the truth-relations expressed by the four constants mentioned above ($.$, v, $\supset$, and $\sim$) could all be reduced to the single one. According to Wittgenstein, this means that the true nature of such relations 'is masked . . . by our mode of signifying' (T 5.1311). (Here again the essence is being concealed by an 'outward form of clothing'.) Take, for example, the argument from 'p v q' and '$\sim p$' to 'q', which would be expressed thus: $((p \text{ v } q) . \sim p) \supset q$. (If '$p$ or q' is true, and 'p' is not true, then q is true.) Using the Sheffer function, Wittgenstein writes:

> If instead of 'p v q' we write, for example, '$p|q.|.p|q$', and instead of '$\sim p$', '$p|p$' ($p|q$ = neither p nor q), then the inner connexion becomes obvious. (T 5.1311)

What this means is that instead of 'not-p' ('$\sim p$'), we are to write 'neither p nor p' ('p|p'); and instead 'p or q', 'neither: neither p nor q, nor: neither p nor q'. This (according to the definition of the stroke) means that 'neither p nor q' is being *denied*, which is equivalent to *affirming* 'p or q', as in the original. Similar conversions are possible for other formulae, but these will not be explored here.

To a reader not familiar with such manipulations, the word 'obvious' will hardly seem appropriate. But the important point to bear in mind is that there *is* a way of operating the whole system by a single function, suitably defined. Again, to express truth-relations in this way is very cumbersome, as the above example shows; and it might be said that these relations are 'masked' by the new function rather than by the original four. But Wittgenstein's concern was with essential and not apparent simplicity. What is revealed by the new function, and concealed by the original four, is that the latter are inter-definable – they are all aspects of a single relation.

Thus it turns out, if Wittgenstein is right, that behind the apparent complexity and diversity of propositions there lies an orderly and uniform structure of truth-functional relations; and these can all be reduced to a single constant. This is what all propositions have in common; here lies their essence.

> One could say that the sole logical constant was what *all* propositions, by their very nature, had in common with one another.
> But that is the general propositional form.
> The general propositional form is the essence of a proposition. (T 5.47, 5.471.)

Moreover, given the correspondence between language and world, Wittgenstein's conclusion applied also to the latter. Thus

> To give the essence of a proposition means to give the essence of all description, and thus the essence of the world. (T 5.4711; see also 4.5 and 6ff.)

But, as we have seen, the essential structure, with all that it involves, was postulated rather than discovered. The analysis into elementary propositions, and the identification of simples, remained a programme that was never carried out. There was more, however, to Wittgenstein's conviction than the arguments that have been given; he also had a *feeling* that this kind of approach must be on the right lines; and in this, as he pointed out, he was not alone.

> Men have always had a presentiment that there must be a realm in which the answers to questions are symmetrically united – *a priori* – to form a self-contained, regular system.
>
> A realm subject to the law: *Simplex sigillum veri*. (T 5.4541.)

This presentiment has been a powerful ingredient in the history of human thought – in philosophy, science and elsewhere. In science, especially, it has led to many important insights and discoveries. But in his later writings Wittgenstein rejected it, at least as far as philosophy was concerned. This was a fundamental change in his approach to the subject.

There is yet another aspect of the reductionism of the *Tractatus*, which is of great importance. In section 5.541 Wittgenstein considered one apparent counter-example to the truth-functional account of language. 'At first sight', he said, 'it looks as if it were also possible for one proposition to occur in another in a different way' than by being a truth-functional component of it. This occurs in the case of propositions about beliefs, for example – as when we say of some person A that he believes that p. What, in this case, is the relation of 'A believes that p' to the component 'p'? It is not the truth-functional one, for the truth-value of the larger proposition is not affected by the truth-value of p. If the former is true – if A has that belief – then it is so regardless of whether p is itself true or not. Or to put the point in another way, we could not *deduce* that p is true from the fact that A has this belief. But what, in that case, is the correct analysis of this fact according to the *Tractatus*?

The answer, and the solution of the difficulty according to the *Tractatus*, is to eliminate the reference to A. The appearance of a relation between p and A is, we are told, only 'superficial'. The real meaning of 'A believes that p' is nothing more than ' "p" says that p' (T 5.542). There is no relation between a proposition p and an object A, but only 'the correlation of facts by means of the correlation of their objects' – that is, the fact of the picture (proposition, thought) contains elements which are combined in the same way as those of a corresponding state of affairs.

According to Wittgenstein, this solution also shows that 'there is no such thing as the soul – the subject, etc. – as it is conceived in the superficial psychology of the present day' (T 5.5421). But (whatever may be meant by the qualification about pyschology) this way of disposing of the difficulty hardly does justice to the role of *human beings* in any account of language. If all we are given is ' "p" says that p', then there would be no difference between a *person* saying (believing, doubting and so on) that p and the existence of a piece of paper or other material on which this proposition is written. Now we might indeed say of such an inscription that 'it says' that p. But this use of 'it says' is parasitic on that in which a *person* says something. The inscription says what it does in virtue of the intention of someone who wrote it; and if we did not know that intention, then we would not know how to understand the inscription (whether, for example, as an assertion, a speculation, a wish, a command, or an idle playing with words). And if the human context were lacking altogether, then nothing (no inscription, sound, picture) would say anything. If a space-traveller came upon what appeared to be arrangements of elements, he would not be able to tell from them alone whether anything was being said or depicted. This would be so even if the arrangements corresponded with one another, in the *Tractatus* sense. As far as the example goes, they might all have been produced by some natural process, such as the formation of fossils.

There is no place in the *Tractatus* for the fact that language is *used* – used by people for various purposes, in connection with a variety of human needs and interests. A human being makes certain signs (in speech or writing) for the purpose of communicating a fact, asking a question, telling a story and so on; and others *react* in suitable ways if they have understood him correctly. Again, a person is *responsible* for what he says; he may have to answer the question 'Why?', or to accept blame if he said something wrong. These aspects of language are omitted and, indeed, as we have seen, eliminated from the *Tractatus*. The result is a *de-humanised* account of language. Here is one of the main differences between the *Tractatus* and the later approach, as we shall see in subsequent chapters.

D. WHAT CANNOT BE SAID

I

One of the most famous statements of the *Tractatus* is its final
proposition: 'What we cannot speak about we must pass over
in silence'. Wittgenstein's fascination with the unspeakable had
already been expressed in certain passages in the *Notebooks*. 'But
might there not be something which cannot be expressed by a
proposition . . . ?' '*Is there no domain outside the facts?*' (*Notebooks*
51–2). In the *Tractatus* he identified 'the inexpressible' with 'the
mystical' (T 6.522). He also spoke of ethics and 'the meaning of
the world' in this connection. There are various fascinating and
difficult remarks in this part of the *Tractatus*; but one line of
argument is clear enough. The meaning of the world (assuming
there is such a meaning) could not be part of the world; for if it
were, then we could ask what was the meaning of the whole
including that part. Again, given the strict correspondence between
language and world, word and object, there can be no propositions
about anything beyond that.

But Wittgenstein's notion of what cannot be said has an application that is more specific to the *Tractatus*. This is clear from
the penultimate section (T 6.54), in which it turns out that the
propositions of the *Tractatus* do not themselves belong to the realm
of what can be said. They will have served their purpose if 'anyone
who understands me eventually recognises them as nonsensical'.
This paradoxical conclusion – the subject of many a witty remark –
is important to a correct understanding of the *Tractatus*. (It also
has wider implications, as we shall see.) The point is that the
account of language given in the *Tractatus* cannot be applied to
that account itself. If language is as the *Tractatus* describes it, then
the propositions of that work are not themselves examples of
language.

In the *Tractatus* we are told that propositions have a certain
'logical form', in virtue of which they are able to depict facts. A
name means an object; an elementary proposition is a combination
of names, corresponding to a combination of objects; if objects are
combined in that way, the proposition is true, and so on. But these
statements cannot themselves have meaning in that way; the truth
of 'a name means an object', for example, cannot be said to depend

on a combination of objects, and the meaning of 'object' cannot be an object. 'Propositions', wrote Wittgenstein,

> can represent the whole of reality, but they cannot represent what they must have in common with reality in order to be able to represent it – logical form.
>
> In order to be able to represent logical form, we should have to be able to station ourselves with propositions somewhere outside logic, that is to say outside the world. (T 4.12).

The point can also be made in terms of pictures, in the ordinary sense of the word. A picture can be used to represent a fact, for example that *a* is to the left of *b*; but the relation between picture and fact, whereby this is achieved, cannot itself be depicted. 'A picture cannot . . . depict its pictorial form'; it cannot 'place itself outside its representational form' (T 2.172, 2.174).

A similar point may be made about the *existence* of simple objects. As we have seen, this is presupposed in the use of corresponding names. But we cannot *say* that such an object exists. We cannot do it by saying that an object of such and such a description exists, for if we could, the object would not be simple. Nor could we do it by simply using the name, as in '*a* exists'. For this statement would be either meaningless (if *a* did not exist) or redundant (if *a* did exist). There cannot be any *question* whether *a* exists; its existence must be, so to speak, already given before we attempt any such statement or question. The world, the speakable world, has certain limits, coinciding with the limits of language. '*The limits of my language* mean the limits of my world'; its logic 'pervades the world'. Hence

> we cannot say in logic, 'The world has this in it, and this, but not that'.
>
> For that would appear to presuppose that we were excluding certain possibilities, and this cannot be the case, since it would require that logic should go beyond the limits of the world; for only in that way could it view those limits from the other side as well. (T 5.6, 5.61.)

The demarcation of sense from nonsense, of what can be said from what cannot, was regarded by Wittgenstein as one of his main objectives. The task of philosophy was 'to set limits to what can be thought; and, in doing so, to what cannot be thought. . . . It will signify what cannot be said, by presenting clearly what can be said' (T 4.114–15). But is it correct, after all, to describe the propositions of the *Tractatus* as nonsense? They are not so according to the ordinary meaning of this word. Someone who reads the work may properly say that he *understands* what it is saying, at least to some extent. And though it may be hard to make sense of some of its propositions even after careful study, it would be absurd to describe the whole work as unintelligible. However, the point may still be made that the *Tractatus* account of language, of how words and sentences have meaning, is not applicable to that account itself. This would not mean that the latter is nonsense; it would mean, rather, that that account is incomplete, since it does not allow for propositions of that kind. Instead of the claim about 'nonsense', we might prefer to conclude that there are two types of meaningful language: one *described* in the *Tractatus* and the other *used* in that work. But this would still leave us with an important distinction.

This distinction, and the difficulties connected with it, are not peculiar to the *Tractatus*. It has often been pointed out that the propositions of philosophy, quite generally, have a special character, though a good deal of argument has taken place about what this is. The same may be said about the later Wittgenstein's 'descriptive' method of philosophy, based on descriptions of the actual uses of words. The logical status of such descriptions (for example, of how we use the word 'know') has been the subject of much debate, for it is not clear whether, or in what sense, they might be regarded as a priori, empirical or normative.

The problem of reflexivity (whether a given account is applicable to itself) is also not peculiar to the *Tractatus*. A well-known example is the 'verification principle' of the Logical Positivists, according to which 'the meaning of a statement is the method of its verification'. As was pointed out soon after its introduction, this statement is not itself amenable to verification (nor is it true by definition). The same problem arose for the related 'criterion of verifiability', which says that a statement is meaningful only if it can be verified. For how is this statement itself to be verified? In reply it was claimed that, despite appearances, these statements were really 'proposals' or 'recommendations', and therefore not covered by the criterion or principle. But, needless to say, this solution has not satisfied everyone.[8]

Another example is the empiricist claim about knowledge, as put forward, for example, by Locke in the seventeenth century, according to which all knowledge is based on sense-experience. Here again we may ask whether the statement itself is, or could be, known in that way. Locke thought he could prove his case if he 'should only shew (as I hope I shall in the following Parts of this Discourse), how Men, barely by the use of their Faculties, may attain to all the Knowledge they have' (*Essay Concerning Human Understanding*, 1.2.1). But such a demonstration could never prove that there are no other sources of knowledge. The empiricist claim about knowledge cannot itself be known to be true in the empiricist way.

Finally, there is Wittgenstein's identification, in his later philosophy, of the meaning of a word with 'its use in practice' (which will be more fully discussed later). According to this, the meaning of a word is to be ascertained from the way it is actually used. But how is this claim to be proved? It might be replied that it is confirmed by the *use* of the word 'meaning' itself; for we would say of someone that he knows the meaning of a word if, and only if, he knows how to use it in practice. But to argue in this way would be begging the question. The question is whether the meaning of a word does consist in its use, and it cannot be answered by consulting the *use* of the word 'meaning'. The claim about meaning and use must stand outside the discourse to which it is applied, and its justification (if any) must be sought elsewhere.

II

There was another kind of proposition that Wittgenstein described as 'senseless' (as distinct from the 'nonsense' of philosophy). Consider again the example on p. 18, of arguing from '*p* or *q*' and 'not-*p*' to '*q*'. Now the proposition that *q* follows from these premises remains true whatever may be the case regarding *p* and *q*. We may not know whether both or either of the premises are true or false, but we know that *if* they are true, then the conclusion must be true also. Wittgenstein spoke of such propositions as 'tautologies', and of their negative counterparts as 'contradictions'. A contradiction would be obtained if, in the example just given, we wrote 'not-*q*' for the conclusion, instead of '*q*'. In this case, we know that if the above premises are true, then the conclusion 'not-*q*' must be *false*. Thus a tautology 'is unconditionally true; and a contradiction is true on no condition'. Such propositions, says Wittgenstein, 'lack sense'; they cannot tell us anything. 'For example, I know nothing about the weather when I know that it is either raining or not raining' (T 4.461). (Thus '*p* or not-*p*' is a tautology.) They are, however, 'part of the symbolism, just as '0' is part of the symbolism of arithmetic' (T 4.4611). Such propositions 'have no "subject-matter" '; nevertheless they 'describe the framework of the world, or rather they represent it' (T 6.124); they show 'the formal – logical – properties of language and the world' (T 6.12), being part of the overall system which contains 'the essence of all description, and thus the essence of the world' (T 5.4711).

The 'senselessness' of tautologies and contradictions is connected with Wittgenstein's position regarding the meanings of logical terms ('constants'), such as 'and' and 'or'. Such words, he held, do not represent objects; they do not have any meaning in that sense. 'The "logical constants" are not representatives; . . . there can be no representatives of the *logic* of facts' (T 4.0312). Russell had thought that we are 'acquainted' with 'logical objects', so that their names would have meaning in the same way as names of other, more ordinary objects. But Wittgenstein rejected this view. 'There are no "logical objects" . . . (in . . . Russell's sense)' (T 5.4).

Wittgenstein illustrated his denial by reference to negation. 'Nothing in reality', he declared, 'corresponds to the sign "∼"' (T 4.0621). 'The propositions "*p*" and "∼*p*" have opposite sense, but there corresponds to them one and the same reality.' A proposition '*p*' asserts the fact that *p*; and if *p* is not a fact, then '*p*' will be false (and '∼*p*' will be true). But this does not mean that, corresponding to the negative proposition, there must be a negative fact – one that includes an object whose name is '∼'. We are not to think that the world contains negative facts as well as ordinary (positive) ones, disjunctive facts, and so on. There are only, so to speak, plain facts, consisting of combinations of objects.

Wittgenstein pointed out that facts could be multiplied indefinitely if the opposite view were taken. For example, '*p*' is equivalent to 'not not-*p*' – the double negative bringing us back to the original 'sense' of '*p*'. A third negative would again reverse the sense, and so on. But do such logical manipulations represent the real world?

it seems scarcely credible that there should follow from one fact
p indefinitely many *others*, namely ~~*p*, ~~~~*p*, etc. . . .

But in fact all the propositions of logic say the same thing, to
wit nothing. (T 5.43).

But is it true, after all, that the propositions of logic (tautologies)
say nothing? To answer this question adequately, we must bring
in *human* considerations, of a kind not represented in the *Tractatus*.
I have already made the point (p. 21) that saying is done primarily
by *people*, and only in a secondary sense by propositions or pieces
of paper. But if we ask whether a tautology can or cannot be *used*
(by someone) to say something (to another person), then the
answer will depend on the hearer's state of knowledge.

Some tautologies are such that one could not fail to be aware of
their truth. Wittgenstein's example 'It is either raining or not
raining' is of this kind. Someone who understands the *meanings* of
these words could not fail to be aware of the truth of the statement;
and therefore it could not say anything to anyone. But this is not
so with more complicated tautologies. Such, for example, are the
exercises in textbooks of logic, in which one is presented with a
complicated string of propositions and connectives, with questions
about what does or does not follow. In this case the learner may
well wonder what the correct answer is, even though it will be a
tautology in Wittgenstein's sense. The same distinction exists in
mathematics. (According to the *Tractatus*, 'mathematics is a method
of logic', and its propositions are self-evident (T 6.234, 6.2341).)
Now someone who knows the *meaning* of 'Two plus two equals
four' cannot be in doubt as to the truth of this statement; hence it
cannot serve to 'say' to anyone that two plus two equals four. But
other propositions of mathematics are far from self-evident; and
one may know what they (or the component words) mean without
knowing whether they are true or false. Hence, again, such a
statement may serve to convey information, even it is classified
under 'methods of logic'. But the *Tractatus* demand for uniformity,
and the consequent abstraction of language from its human context,
leads to the elimination of such distinctions and such uses of
language.

III

A proposition tells us that something is the case. But for this to be possible, we must know what the proposition means; and this is not stated by the proposition itself. It can, however, be stated by means of other propositions. According to the system of the *Tractatus*, its meaning would be explained by giving an analysis. If *this* were not understood, then its terms might be subjected to further analysis; and so on until the ultimate elementary propositions are reached. Thus 'the introduction of elementary propositions provides the basis for understanding all other kinds of propositions' (T 4.411). But might one not fail to understand an elementary proposition? No; according to the *Tractatus*, there must be a basic understanding which is not subject to further explanations; it is the means by which all other understanding is to be acquired. In *this* case – of elementary propositions – 'I understand the proposition without having had its sense explained to me' (T 4.021). This sense is something that 'shows itself', as distinct from being 'said'.

> A proposition *shows* its sense.
> A proposition *shows* how things stand *if* it is true. And it *says that* they do so stand. (T 4.022).

The distinction between showing and saying is absolute: 'What *can* be shown, *cannot* be said' (T 4.1212).

A similar point applies to the explanation of words and simple names. An ordinary word can be defined by analysis: the word *w* means *a*, *b* and *c*-or-*d*; and these terms may be defined in their turn. But ultimately we shall arrive at simple names, and there is no going beyond them. 'A name cannot be dissected any further by means of a definition: it is a primitive sign' (T 3.26). If I tried to explain such a name (or its sign), I would have to use that very sign in the explanations; hence these could 'only be understood if the meanings of those signs are already known' (T 3.263).

But how is the basic understanding, of names and elementary propositions, to be accounted for? Can there be a proposition that 'shows its sense' in the sense that no misunderstanding is possible? As we have seen, Wittgenstein regarded propositions as pictures; such a picture, he said, 'is *essentially* connected' with the corresponding situation (T 4.03). But is there only one way of understanding a picture? In his later writings he gave an example of a picture 'representing a boxer in a particular stance'. This, he pointed out, might be used to convey how one should stand or should not stand, how someone did stand on a particular occasion, and so on. In another picture we see a man walking up a steep hill. But 'might it not have looked just the same if he had been sliding downhill in that position? Perhaps a Martian would describe the picture so' (PI pp. 11, 54).

The *Tractatus* is remarkably silent about the representation of time and motion. But the problem of more than one meaning can also be illustrated by the picture of a cube which appears at T. 5.5423.

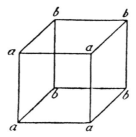

As Wittgenstein pointed out, 'there are two possible ways of seeing the figure': one can see it so that 'the *a*'s appear to be in front', or so that the *b*'s appear in front. But this means that 'we really see two different facts'. Hence the picture could not be one of those (elementary) propositions that 'shows its sense', so that no question about its sense could arise. The relation between an elementary proposition and its sense must be somehow more intimate than that of any ordinary picture and its sense. Otherwise the meaning of the proposition would not be determinate, and this would undermine the determinacy of language that Wittgenstein insisted on. It may be doubted, however, whether any proposition or picture could conceivably supply what was required.

In his later writings Wittgenstein had a good deal to say about *mental* pictures or images. It has often been thought that meaning and understanding (recognising, remembering and so on) are brought about by means of such images; and one may be tempted, in this connection, to attribute to the mental image a kind of determinacy that no ordinary picture could achieve.

'The [mental] image must be more like its object than any picture. For, however like I make the picture to what it is supposed to represent, it can always be the picture of something else as well. But it is essential to the image that it is the image of *this* and of nothing else.' Thus one might come to regard the image as a super-likeness. (PI 389).

This super-likeness is required by the theory of the *Tractatus*. There must be, according to that theory, a kind of picture (proposition) which 'shows its sense' in a way that is beyond explanation and beyond misunderstanding. But according to the later Wittgenstein, the idea of such a picture, mental or otherwise, is an illusion.[9]

3
Meaning and Use

A. THE *TRACTATUS* VERSUS THE LATER PHILOSOPHY

Wittgenstein's dissatisfaction with his earlier views is evident from the first fifty-odd pages of the *Investigations*. This is not a systematic criticism, and Wittgenstein was not concerned to discuss the earlier views point by point. Moreover, the 'particular picture of the essence of human language', which forms the starting-point of the later work, is attributed there to St Augustine rather than to the author of the *Tractatus*. Here, as in his quotation from Plato (see p. 10 above), Wittgenstein was aware that his earlier views were typical of perennial tendencies of human thought. There are also, however, many passages in which he alludes or refers specifically to his earlier book.

What is the relation between the two works? How does the Wittgenstein of the *Investigations* criticise his earlier views? He draws attention to the uses of words in various practical situations, contrasting these with the abstract and uniform model of *Tractatus*. Having described the 'particular picture' of human language (which is essentially that of the *Tractatus*), he immediately gives an example of someone asking for 'five red apples' in a shop, and points out that each of these words has to be acted upon in a different way. To comply with the word 'apples', the shopkeeper opens a drawer marked 'apples'; for the word 'red', he looks (rather improbably, it must be said) at a colour-chart; and in the case of 'five', he says the numbers from one to five, taking out an apple for each number (PI 1). This diversity of use is to be contrasted with the uniformity of the 'particular picture' of human language. Wittgenstein then proceeds to pose what may be called the 'meaning question', choosing for this purpose the word 'five'. 'But what is the meaning of the word "five"?' (PI 1). One may be inclined to think that there must be an object of some kind, corresponding to the word 'five', in virtue of which it has meaning. Some philosophers have indeed held that there are special 'mathematical objects', corresponding to such words, while others have maintained that the relevant objects are nothing other than the numerals as they appear on paper or in speech. According to the *Tractatus*, 'a number is the exponent of an operation' (T 6.021). What is the answer in the *Investigations*? What, according to it, is the meaning of the word 'five'? Here (in PI 1) the question is simply brushed aside. 'No such thing was in question here, but only how the word "five" is used.'

In the ensuing sections Wittgenstein takes his stand on the actual use of language, contrasting this with the *Tractatus* account. He draws attention especially to the *practical* aspects of language (describing words as 'tools'), and to the *variety* of words and sentences.[1] To the question 'How many kinds of sentence are there?' he replies that they are 'countless' (PI 23). He introduces the term 'language-game' to 'bring into prominence the fact that the *speaking* of language is part of an activity, or of a form of life'; and gives a long list of examples of different 'language-games', including: giving orders and obeying them; reporting; speculating; singing; making a joke; translating; asking, thanking, cursing, greeting, praying (PI 23). He then invites the reader to compare 'the multiplicity of the tools in language and of the ways they are used . . . with what logicians have said about the structure of language (including the author of the *Tractatus Logico-Philosophicus*)'.

In other sections he compares the usage of key words in the *Tractatus* with their use in actual practice. The word 'name', he points out, is used in a variety of ways; and therefore it is a mistake to look for a unique relation between names and that which is named (PI 38). The word 'meaning' is being used 'contrary to language' (*Sprachwidrig*) if it is used 'to signify the thing that "corresponds" to the word' (PI 40). In the *Tractatus*, as we saw, he had stated: 'A name means an object. The object is its meaning' (T 3.203). But now he points out that the name 'Excalibur' has meaning even when the thing that 'corresponds' to it no longer exists (PI 39); and 'when Mr N. N. dies one says that the bearer of the name dies, not that the meaning dies' (PI 40). He also points out that if the meaning did 'die' – if the name became meaningless – then 'it would make no sense to say "Mr N. N. is dead"'; but obviously this does make sense.

A key notion in the *Tractatus* was that of simples. But, Wittgenstein now observes, the word 'simple' is used 'in an enormous number of different . . . ways' (PI 47e).[2] What are the simple parts of a chair? 'The bits of wood of which it is made? Or the molecules, or the atoms?'

> Is the colour of a square on a chessboard simple, or does it consist of pure white and pure yellow? And is white simple. . . ? Is this length of 2 cm. simple, or does it consist of two parts, each 1 cm. long? But why not of one bit 3 cm. long and one bit 1 cm. long measured in the opposite direction? (PI 47e)

Simple and complex are, says Wittgenstein, relative to particular language-games (PI 47d). 'It makes no sense', he concludes, 'to speak absolutely of the "simple parts of a chair"' (PI 47a).

Again, 'when I say: "My broom is in the corner", – is this really a statement about the broomstick and the brush?' (PI 60). According to the *Tractatus* notion of analysis, we might say that the latter is 'a further analysed form' of the former. Should we say that it is closer to the real – fully analysed – meaning of the statement? This is not what we would normally say. If we asked the speaker what he meant, 'he would probably say that he had not thought specially of the broomstick or specially of the brush at all'. And if,

> instead of saying 'Bring me the broom', you said 'Bring me the broomstick and the brush which is fitted to it', – isn't the answer: 'Do you want the broom? Why do you put it so oddly?'

What are we to make of these remarks about the ordinary usage of words? So far, one might almost think that their author had not read the *Tractatus*, or not read it with sufficient understanding. Of course the Wittgenstein of the *Tractatus* was not basing his ideas on ordinary usage. How then can a description of this serve to refute what he said there? Nor is it likely that the earlier Wittgenstein was *unaware* of the ordinary usage. He was surely aware, for example, of the difference between his use of 'name' and the ordinary one (or ones). When he used the word 'name', however, he did so in a sense suitable for his purpose: not to mean ordinary names, like the names of people, but for those simple elements of language which would appear in the final analysis. And the simple 'objects' named by these names were held to be (as we saw) 'fixed and subsistent'; unlike 'Mr N. N.', they were *not* exposed to the hazard of death or disintegration. Thus, in stating that the meaning of a name is an object, Wittgenstein was not trying to follow or give an example of ordinary usage, but making a claim about the relationship between names and objects in his special sense of these terms. What if we had pointed out to him that when someone dies his name does not become meaningless? We may be sure that this had not escaped the earlier Wittgenstein's notice; it was merely one of the ways in which the names of the *Tractatus* differed from ordinary names.

The fact that 'simple' and 'complex' are normally context-dependent seems similarly beside the point. In the *Tractatus* these terms had been given a sense that was not thus dependent, and it was claimed that there must be names and objects which are *absolutely* simple in that sense. Again, the fact that one might be puzzled if one were asked to bring a broom in the 'further analysed' wording of PI 60 would hardly have come as a surprise to the author of the *Tractatus*. His claims about the ultimate meanings of propositions were obviously not claims about ordinary usage and ordinary reactions.

Again, what is the point of comparing the variety of sentences and language-games with what 'logicians . . . including the author of the *Tractatus*' have said about language? This comparison should not embarrass the logicians or the author of the *Tractatus*, since they were talking about the underlying structure as *distinct* from the various uses of language of which we are aware in ordinary experience.

In his critique of the *Tractatus*, Wittgenstein seems merely to be opposing one standpoint to another. It is true and hardly surprising that from the standpoint of ordinary usage many of the *Tractatus* claims are seen to be false and perhaps even ridiculous. But why should this standpoint be preferred? Is there to be nothing more to philosophy than descriptions of ordinary usage? In section 65 of the *Investigations* an imaginary objector puts it to Wittgenstein that he has merely abandoned the difficult questions.

> You take the easy way out! You talk about all sorts of language-games, but have nowhere said what the essence of a language-game, and hence of language, is. . . . So you let yourself off the very part of the investigation that once gave you yourself the most headache, the part about the *general form of propositions* and of language. (PI 65).

Wittgenstein's reply is to admit the charge. 'This is true. – Instead of producing something common to all that we call language, I am saying that these phenomena have no one thing in common which makes us use the same word for all. . .' (PI 65). He then makes a similar claim about the word 'game' and challenges the reader to produce a set of conditions that is common to all games, in virtue of which they are called games. But if, as Wittgenstein predicts, the reader is unable to meet the challenge, what will this prove? As a number of critics have pointed out, the fact that something has not been found does not prove that it does not exist. The author of the *Tractatus* can still maintain that a proposition containing the word 'game', for example, must be analysable, like every other, in the way described in that work. And he may continue to believe, contrary to the later Wittgenstein's assertion, that the propositions of language do all have something in common, this being the 'general form' described in the *Tractatus*. Wittgenstein admonishes the reader (in discussing the word 'game'), not to say 'There *must* be something common', but to '*look and see* whether there is' (PI 66). But this advice, again, would not be applicable to the author of the *Tractatus*. For as we saw (pp. 13–14), it was part of the latter's thesis that the true logic of language is hidden from us. That language does not *appear* to us as described in the *Tractatus* is not at issue; how then can the advice to 'look and see' help us to evaluate the *Tractatus* position?

To get at the real issue between the old and new philosophies we must look deeper. Now an important ingredient of Wittgenstein's philosophising, early and late, is about the nature of philosophy itself; about the logical status of its propositions and 'solutions', and about what does and does not fall within its province. This is especially true of his later writings, and what he says here about philosophy is essential to a proper understanding of his treatment of particular issues.

'It was true to say', he writes in PI 109, 'that our considerations could not be scientific ones'. Here he alludes to T 4.111: 'Philosophy is not one of the natural sciences'. The *Tractatus* did, however, have a good deal in common with scientific theories. It is typical of such theories that a range of phenomena, apparently diverse or disconnected, is unified, and in that sense explained, by postulating some underlying principle (process, force, concept). This has happened, for example, in the case of phenomena of chemical change, of animal life, and of economic and cultural activity. It is characteristic of such theories that the principle in question is *postulated*, rather than being amenable to direct observation, as the phenomena are. We may be told that there 'must be' such and such an entity or process, if the phenomena are to be accounted for.

These features, as we have seen, are also present in the theory of meaning expounded in the *Tractatus*. Now there *can* be scientific theories of meaning, or at least language, but they are not what we find in the *Tractatus*. For example, discoveries or assumptions about the larynx or other organs might serve to explain the production of various linguistic sounds (cf. PI 376). Or there may be a law (for example, Grimm's Law) which imposes an orderly pattern on the development of a group of languages through the ages. But theories of this kind, with their reliance on empirical data, fall outside the a priori reflections of the philosopher. And it is clear enough that Wittgenstein was not advancing this kind of theory in the *Tractatus*. His theory, as the name of the book – *Tractatus Logico-Philosophicus* – implies, was intended to be logical and not scientific. And the prominent use of a logical system (of truth-functions) seems to confirm that it was a logical theory.

But how can the logic of language, or of particular words and sentences, be hidden from us? The difficulty is not merely that of verifying the theory by producing examples of names and objects; it is about making sense of the concepts of logic, analysis and meaning that are supposed to be involved here. This may be illustrated by taking some ordinary word for which a truth-functional analysis is readily available – say the word 'aunt'. We can say that the truth-value of the proposition '*A* is an aunt' will depend on the truth-values of certain other propositions, containing words like 'son' and 'sister', arranged in suitable ways with the connectives 'and' and 'or'. But where did we get our analysis from? Such an analysis will be an expression of the *use* of the word 'aunt' in actual discourse. It will be based on the kind of reasons that are given for describing someone as an aunt, or for challenging that description. Thus the analysis will have a normative aspect, for these reasons would be used in *justifying* (or challenging) the use of the word. It would also be normative in a forward-looking sense, for it would tell us how the word is *to be* used – under what conditions its use would be *correct*. (These aspects are also there in the case of dictionary definitions, which tell us how a word is *to be* used, but on the basis of what is regarded as justified in actual usage.) In this respect an analysis of meaning is different from, say, a chemical analysis, which would not have these normative aspects. The analysis of water into H_2O, for example, tells us nothing about the correct use of water, or anything else.

But the *Tractatus* analysis, while not scientific, does not have the normative function either. Hence it is not clear what is meant by 'analysis' when, in the *Tractatus*, it is claimed that words and sentences are to be analysed in such and such a way. Even if examples of names and elementary propositions could be given, they would not amount to an analysis of *meaning*, unless they were actually available to us for the purpose of justifying our uses of words. The logical conditions of a word must 'lie open to view'; it is this that makes them suitable for their normative role – and, at the same time, for the a priori reflections of the philosopher. 'Philosophy', wrote the later Wittgenstein,

> simply puts everything before us, and neither explains nor deduces anything. – Since everything lies open to view there is nothing to explain. For what is hidden is of no interest to us. (PI 126)

The conditions of the *Tractatus*, however, do not lie open to view, and are not part of the understanding of the actual users of the language. In what sense, then, can they be regarded as *logical* conditions? If they were logical conditions in the normal sense, then they would be about *correct* uses of words, as known to speakers of the language; and they would be able, on the basis of their knowledge, to evaluate what is said about these conditions. And in this case there might be a direct engagement between what the *Tractatus* says about such words as 'name' and 'meaning', and the later Wittgenstein's denials. But, as we saw, there is no such engagement. The fundamental issue, and Wittgenstein's fundamental change of mind, is about whether the meaning of a word – unlike its use – can be hidden from us, and thus a matter of theory as opposed to mere 'description'. 'We must not', he wrote in the later work,

> advance any kind of theory. . . . We must do away with *explanation*, and description alone must take its place. . . . The problems are solved, not by giving new information, but by arranging what we have always known. (PI 109)

In the *Tractatus* he did advance a theory – one that would explain how language works and how 'the requirement that sense be determinate' is satisfied. It is satisfied, according to that theory, by a correlation of names and objects, propositions and states of affairs. But how does the later Wittgenstein deal with this requirement, if the theory is given up? In the example of PI 1 we had a case in which the sense of what was said was determinate by normal standards. The purchaser asked for five red apples, the shopkeeper supplied them. Here is an example of successful communication, without any lack of determinacy. And, in spite of occasional unclarity and misunderstanding, the sense of what people say is, in most cases, perfectly clear. But how did the shopkeeper know what to do? 'Well, I assume he *acts* as I have described. Explanations come to an end somewhere '(PI 1). This may sound as if Wittgenstein is merely abandoning the chase. Of course the fact – the truism – that explanations must end somewhere does not entail that they must end *here*, right at the start of the enquiry. Wittgenstein believed, however, that as far as philosophical theories were concerned, one might as well end here, since their explanatory promise was an illusion. He argued this mainly in connection with mental theories (that meanings are 'in the mind'), as we shall see in the next chapter. But the same criticism may be made of the theory of the *Tractatus*. Its explanation of determinacy of sense can throw no light on how the *users* of language determine the sense of a proposition (or other speech-act), given that the relevant analysis is not available to them; nor can it tell us *how* an elementary proposition 'shows' its sense (as discussed on p. 28).

The aim of the later Wittgenstein is, in a sense, more modest than that of his earlier self. He will not offer another, superior theory; instead of trying to do better what he had previously attempted, he will 'do away with all explanation' and confine himself to 'description alone'. This 'modesty' also affects the meaning of 'determinate'. Consider again the case of the shopper. Was the sense of his statement really determinate? After all, no precise shade of red was specified, and the word 'apples' covers a considerable variety of fruit. According to the *Tractatus*, the statement would be determinate because, contrary to appearances, it would have 'one and only one complete analysis' (T 3.25) – an analysis terminating in a strict and absolutely unambiguous correlation of elements. But according to the later Wittgenstein, this is only one 'ideal of exactness' (PI 88), and there are others.

'Exact' and 'determinate' must be understood according to their function in a given context.

'Inexact' is really a reproach, and 'exact' is praise. And that is to say that what is inexact attains its goal less perfectly than what is more exact. Thus the point here is what we call 'the goal'. Am I inexact when I do not give our distance from the sun to the nearest foot, or tell a joiner the width of a table to the nearest thousandth of an inch? (PI 88)

Again, if I tell someone to 'stand roughly here', is what I say inexact? In a sense, yes. 'Only let us understand what "inexact" means. For it does not mean unusable' (PI 88). The person to whom I say this (given a suitable context) would have no reason to *reproach* me for being inexact; he would know perfectly well what I mean, and what he has to do to satisfy my request. Thus what is required for determinacy of sense is not conformity to a universal standard or model (such as that of the *Tractatus*), but an understanding of what is needed by those concerned in a given context.

It may be objected that in arguing in this way Wittgenstein is again helping himself to the ordinary usage of words in opposing the claims of the *Tractatus*, which were not meant in that way. But the philosophical theorist cannot cut himself off from ordinary usage altogether. He may be allowed to use certain terms, for example 'name' and 'simple', in a special way, but there are limits to his redefinitions. If the problem he addresses only *arises* from a technical or idealised usage, then it may not deserve to be called a problem. Thus if he asks how language can be determinate, meaning 'determinate' in a technical sense, then we may reply that even if language cannot be 'determinate', it can still be determinate; and if there is a question about the latter, then he has not yet addressed it.

A common source of dissatisfaction with Wittgenstein's position is what he described as 'the craving for generality' (BB 17) – in this case, for some general, uniform account of meaning. Whereas in the *Tractatus* he had offered an account of 'the essence of a proposition', and hence 'the essence of all description and thus the essence of the world' (T 19), he now tells us: 'There are *countless* kinds' of sentences and words (PI 23); their functions being as diverse as those of objects in a tool-box: 'a hammer, pliers, a saw, a screw-driver, a rule, a glue-pot, glue, nails and screws' (PI 11). Now it would be satisfying if we could reduce this apparent diversity to a single type or model, as has often been done to advantage in science and mathematics. This would give us a sense of progress and achievement, unlike a philosophy that merely 'leaves everything as it is' (PI 124). But, says Wittgenstein, a philosopher should resist the temptation to emulate the aims and methods of science. 'It can never be our job to reduce anything to anything', and 'elegance is *not* what we are aiming for' (BB 18–19). Nor should we regard logic as 'something sublime', that tries to 'see to the bottom of things' (PI 89) in the hope of discovering the essence of meaning.

The motivation described here by Wittgenstein may be compared to the quest for 'the meaning of life'. There are various ways in which a person's life, or episodes in it, might ordinarily be described as meaningful or meaningless. But sometimes these piecemeal descriptions strike us as superficial; we find ourselves asking whether there is not something at the bottom of it all – a kind of essential meaning of human life in general, behind the appearance of episode and diversity. This may lead us to postulate a supernatural realm, the repository of a meaning that is beyond human understanding. And this in turn may lead to difficulties (of a kind familiar to theologians) about connecting this meaning with the world of experience in which we actually live. Wittgenstein's point was, of course, about logic and not theology; but it was, so to speak, a *theological* conception of logic that he rejected.

The satisfaction of seeing 'to the bottom of things' that may be obtainable, in different ways, in science and religion, is not obtainable in the case of logic, if Wittgenstein is right. What we must do is not to go on looking for an underlying essence, but to cure ourselves of the craving for this kind of satisfaction. Our task is 'to *understand* something that is already in plain view' (PI 89). He was aware that his approach might seem 'only to destroy everything interesting, that is, all that is great and important . . . (as it were all the buildings, leaving behind only bits of stone and rubble)'; but, he replied, he was destroying 'nothing but houses of cards' (PI 118).

Now it may be thought that the task of understanding what is 'already in plain view' cannot amount to very much; and that, at least as far as intellectual challenge is concerned, the new way of doing philosophy will be a poor substitute for the old. Surely, it may be said, to understand and describe what lies plainly before us must be an easy and perhaps even trivial undertaking. This view was expressed by Bertrand Russell in his autobiography, in which he bitterly denounced his former pupil and friend. 'The later Wittgenstein', he complained, 'seems to have grown tired of serious thinking and to have invented a doctrine which would make such an activity unnecessary' (*My Philosophical Development*, 161). But he (Russell) could not believe 'that a doctrine which has these lazy consequences is true'.

Now the last point is not strictly relevant, for a doctrine may be true even if, for one reason or another, its consequences are unpalatable. Thus if it turns out that there really is nothing for philosophers to do that involves 'serious thinking', then this result, if properly established, must be accepted. This would be an important result of philosophising about philosophy, and might well be described as a milestone in the history of human thought. The truth is, however, that Wittgenstein's 'doctrine' does not have this consequence; for what 'lies open to view' – our own, familiar uses of language – is, in certain ways, far from easy to comprehend; and much thought and insight may be required in order to view them correctly.

This may seem a paradoxical state of affairs. How can it be a matter of difficulty to see what lies open to view? Wittgenstein sometimes spoke of his investigations as being about 'grammar' – using this word in a rather special sense. But it may be helpful to approach the question by reference to grammar in the ordinary sense. Do the rules of grammar lie open to view? Anyone who has studied the subject will know that it may be very difficult to state them correctly, and some people never manage it, even after considerable study. Moreover, the very idea of rules of grammar may be absent from a given culture; and its introduction can be regarded as a great achievement in the history of ideas. But does this mean that those who lack this idea have no knowledge of grammar? There is a sense in which they do have it, even though they cannot formulate the rules. For where do the rules of grammar come from? They are systematic formulations of knowledge that the speakers exhibit in their linguistic behaviour. Someone who speaks German, for example, will know that it is wrong to use the article 'der' for the accusative, and he will correct the child or foreigner who makes this mistake, even though he may be quite unable to state the rule and may never have heard of the term 'accusative'. Now someone who learns such a rule will recognise it as an expression of what (in another sense) he already knows perfectly well; but this does not mean that learning it will be an easy or trivial matter.

The same point may be made about 'grammar' in Wittgenstein's sense. He was not concerned about the grammar of particular languages (like the example just given), but about logical features of what may be called *human* language (or human thought). When he says, for example, that 'the grammar of the word "know" is evidently closely related to that of "can" and "is able to"' (PI 150), he is not talking about the English word as such, but about the concept of knowledge as shared by mankind in general. (His aim in this passage is to challenge the tendency to think of knowledge as a 'state of consciousness'.) Now the question 'What is knowledge?' has been a long-standing subject of philosophical enquiry, and not everyone would agree that it is to be settled by investigating the use of the relevant word or words. But even if this *is* agreed, it will not follow that the investigation must be easy and the answer quickly obtained. For the truth is that it may be very difficult to give a correct account of the use of this word, and of others that have troubled philosophers. And, strange as it may seem, those who use the words straightforwardly in ordinary discourse (that is, the ordinary speakers of a language) may be mistaken or confused when it comes to *describing* that usage. Wittgenstein spoke in this connection of 'the bewitchment of language' (PI 109); we must endeavour, he said, to 'reject the grammar which tries to force itself on us' (PI 293) when we think about certain concepts that lie at the heart of philosophical perplexity.

B. MEANING AND USE

In his later writings Wittgenstein identified meaning with use. 'The meaning of a word', he wrote, 'is its use in the language' (PI 43); 'the use of the word *in practice* is its meaning' (BB 69). This is connected with the emphasis on 'description alone', for the use of a word is something that is *available* for description; it is not an entity or process that is hidden from us, as were the 'meanings' (that is, objects) of the *Tractatus*.

If we approach the matter without preconceived theories in mind, then the claim that meaning and use are identical, or at least closely connected, may strike us immediately as plausible. It may seem obvious that in describing how a word is used, we describe its meaning; and that *knowing* what it means is the same as knowing how to use it. When lexicographers give the meaning of a word, their criterion must be the way it is used; and this would be our criterion in *evaluating* their definitions. 'Is this a correct definition?' would mean: 'Does it conform to the way this word is used?' These and similar observations readily support the later Wittgenstein's views.

Wittgenstein's position has, however, been misunderstood in a number of ways. Some commentators, disregarding his explicit rejection of 'theory', have ascribed to him a theory of meaning (the 'meaning-as-use' theory, the 'rules-of-use' theory and so on). Some have complained that Wittgenstein nowhere says exactly what he means by 'use', so that his 'theory' is not clear. Finally, the fact that in PI 43 he seems to limit his claim about meaning and use to 'a large class of cases' has been taken to throw doubt on its scope.

No doubt the word 'theory' can be used in a broad sense, to include remarks of the kind made by Wittgenstein. It is, however, liable to be misleading in this context. For in the sense in which there have been theories of meaning, Wittgenstein's account is not a theory. In theories of this kind it is claimed that there is something other than words, which bestows meaning on them (and does so in a uniform way). In the *Tractatus*, as we saw, this role is played by the corresponding 'objects'. According to the 'verification principle' of the Logical Positivists, it was the 'method of verification' which constituted the meaning of any given statement. (cf. p. 24.) Another, common view has been that meaning is bestowed by something in the speaker's mind – a thought or image, perhaps.[3] Finally, according to the recently advocated 'scientific realism', the meaning of a word depends, in a large class of cases, on the 'real nature' of a corresponding kind of thing or substance, this being a matter for scientific enquiry. (This theory will be discussed shortly.) In all these cases the meanings of words or sentences are to be fixed by something outside language. But Wittgenstein's 'use' is not anything outside language. 'The meaning of a word is its use *in the language*'. It is the *meaningful* use of words that he is talking about (and not, say, their use in elocution lessons). Hence he is not 'explaining' what meaning is, by reference to something other than meaning. It is not, he remarks, as if we could say 'Here the word, there the meaning' – as one might speak separately of 'the money, and the cow that you can buy with it' (PI 120f). The meaning of a word and its use should rather be compared with the value of money and its use. Money (or, let us say, paper money) has value, within a given community, because of the way it is used. Thus we might say that 'the value of money is its use'. But the use in question is the use of it *as money* – as having such and such an accepted value within that community.

It is sometimes complained that Wittgenstein did not specify (or specify further) what he meant by 'use'. But this is hardly surprising, given his rejection of the idea of an 'essence of language'. The meaning of 'use' will be as multifarious, and as resistant to definition, as the various uses of language are. Similarly, it is a mistake to look for definitions of his terms 'language-game' and 'form of life'. It is sometimes asked what exactly Wittgenstein meant by these, whether one is reducible to the other and so on. But the meanings of these terms, like others, will depend on the *use* he makes of them in particular contexts. (In PI 7 he states that he is going to use 'language-game' in a number of related ways.)

When Wittgenstein speaks of 'use', does he mean *ordinary* use? Wittgenstein is known as an 'ordinary language' philosopher, for he proposes to 'bring words back from their metaphysical to their everyday use' (PI 116). Now it may be objected that the words just mentioned ('language-game', 'form of life') are themselves not examples of everyday use. But Wittgenstein is not committed to excluding non-ordinary uses from the category of 'use'. In the *Blue Book*, for example, he condoned the practice of psycho-analysts in speaking of unconscious thoughts, volitions, and so on. However, what he says about meaning and use will apply also to non-ordinary uses. Thus if a philosopher uses such words as 'knowledge', 'being', 'object' and so on (PI 116) in peculiar ways, then his *usage* will show what he means by them. The purpose of bringing these words 'back to their everyday use' is to remind ourselves that they *have* such a use, and to contrast this with the philosophers' use, avoiding the temptation to regard the latter as giving the 'real' meaning.

The identification of meaning with use was expressed by Wittgenstein in various ways – sometimes just by running the two words together, as when he speaks of 'the use – the meaning – of [a] word' in PI 30. But in one place there is a statement which has caused misunderstandings.

For a *large* class of cases – though not for all – in which we employ the word 'meaning' it can be explained thus: the meaning of a word is its use in the language (PI 43).[4]

Why only for a large class of cases? Are there others in which meaning and use are, after all, distinct? And is the word 'explain', in this passage, compatible with the descriptive method?

This – admittedly rather tricky – passage is not meant to *state* the identity of meaning and use, nor to put forward a general explanation of meaning. It is about how the word 'meaning' might be explained in a particular case. Sometimes ('for a large class of cases') one would do it in terms of use. For example, if someone asks for the meaning of 'traumatic', then we may take it that what he wants to know is how this word is used, and explain it accordingly. But another possibility is mentioned in the next sentence of PI 43: 'And the *meaning* of a name is sometimes explained by pointing to its *bearer*.' Asked whom I mean by 'Robinson', I might reply by pointing to the bearer of that name, and not by describing its use (though this would not entail that meaning and use are *distinct* in the case of this word). Wittgenstein may also have had in mind what he called 'experiencing the meaning' of a word, as discussed in Part IIxi of the *Investigations*; or he may have been thinking of non-linguistic uses of 'meaning', as when we ask what is the meaning of a certain medical symptom. But however this may be, the passage should not be taken to undermine the identification of meaning with use, or to hint at some mysterious qualification of it.[5]

But is it true, after all, that meaning and use are identical? We sometimes speak of a conflict between the usage of a word and its 'true meaning' (as given by the dictionary, perhaps). Nowadays, for example, the word 'refute' is commonly used to mean 'express disagreement with', but it may be said that this use is contrary to the true meaning of the word. Whether such verdicts are in order has been a matter of dispute among linguists, and some would claim that there is no sense in invoking a 'true meaning' by reference to which an actual usage can be criticised. But in any case, the reference to such a meaning would not go against Wittgenstein's account. For this 'true meaning' would still have to be found in the word's use – if not the present or majority use, then the use as it was 'originally', or among 'educated' people, however these terms might be understood. Thus the conflict would not be between meaning and use, but between different uses.

Another way in which meaning and use have been thought distinct is that of 'scientific realism'. According to this, the meaning of certain words depends, not on their use as known to speakers of the language, but on the ultimate nature of the things or substances referred to, which may be far beyond the speakers' knowledge. When people in ancient times used the word 'gold', for example, they did so in accordance with the criteria then available; and these were different from those available today, which depend on modern science (for example, atomic weight). We may assume, accordingly, that some of the substance described in ancient times as 'gold' was not gold by modern scientific standards (or, we might say, was not really gold). Yet it may also be claimed that the *meaning* of the word has not changed, since the ancients, like ourselves, meant to describe as 'gold' only what is really gold; and presumably the translation of the ancient Greek word for 'gold' is not in dispute. But how is the continuity of meaning possible, given the discontinuity in the conditions of use? The answer, according to the new theory, is that meaning is tied to the 'real nature' or 'essence' of the thing or substance referred to, and *not* to the use of the word; and because the former is unchanging (gold remains gold), the meaning too remains the same. Thus 'when Archimedes asserted that something was gold (χρυσός), he was not just saying that it had the superficial characteristics of gold. . . . ; he was saying that it had the same *hidden structure* (the same "essence", so to speak) as any local piece of gold' (H. Putnam, *Mind, Language and Reality* (Cambridge University Press, 1975) 235). Archimedes had of course to use the word in accordance with the characteristics known at that time, but his meaning (according to this view) went beyond that – reaching out, so to speak, to the characteristics recognised by today's science; and beyond that again, to such characteristics as are not yet recognised but may be so by the science of future ages.

This conception of meaning has the remarkable consequence that no-one can ever be sure of *knowing* the meaning – the true meaning – of the word 'gold' and others. (The scope of the theory has been a matter of discussion among its advocates. Initially it was thought to apply to the names of 'natural kinds' – roughly, all the kinds of substances and beings that are found in nature – including plants and animals, for example. But Putnam claimed that it was also true of other kinds, including human artefacts.)

For as we have seen, beliefs about the true nature of gold – and, therefore, about the true meaning of 'gold' – are always liable to revision. And even if they were not – if the science of this subject had, so to speak, come to an end – one would still not be in a position to *know* that it had.

In this respect the new realism is remarkably similar to that of the *Tractatus*. In each case the true meaning is hidden from us and lies beyond the conditions of use as known to speakers of the language. ('The essence is hidden from us', as Wittgenstein comments in PI 92.) Contrary to the later Wittgenstein's account, meaning and use are distinct.

But is the new theory acceptable? It does not accord with what we normally mean by 'meaning' and 'knowing the meaning'. For we would normally say of a person who uses a word in accordance with the current criteria that he knows its meaning – even if these criteria turn out later to be unsatisfactory. This is true even of today's layman who uses the word 'gold' without resorting to the current scientific criteria. Such a person may be told that a piece of metal described by him as gold is not really gold; but then his error would be one of fact and not meaning. Similarly, someone who uses the word 'electricity' in a normal way in speaking about electric light, electricity bills and so on, may be said to know the meaning of this word, even though his knowledge of the nature of electricity may be very defective.

It may be objected that in arguing from the normal use of the word 'meaning (pointing out that this is contrary to the new realism), I have begged the question. For according to the new theory the appeal to use is not decisive; and this must apply also to the use of 'meaning'. Now it is true that I have produced no independent argument for the appeal to use. But how else are such questions to be decided? Of course anyone can *stipulate* that a word (such as 'meaning') is to have such and such a meaning. But this would not amount to a claim about the *truth* of the matter – about what meaning really is, and whether meaning and use are really distinct. This view of the matter is, moreover, confirmed when we turn to the actual arguments of advocates of the theory. For what we find here are constant appeals to 'what we would say'. The reader is presented with some imaginary example, and invited to agree that he would describe it in such and such a way – that is, he would *use* the relevant words in that way; and this is taken to support some claim about meaning.[6] But if this way of arguing is allowed (and it is hard to see what other is available), then it must be likewise for the word 'meaning' itself.

But, returning to the examples of Archimedes versus modern science, what are we to say about the apparent discrepancy between meaning and use – sameness of meaning in spite of difference of use? Was the ancient meaning really the same as ours, in spite of that difference? It is not clear that we must answer 'yes' to this question. But if we do, it will be because there is a sufficient *overlap* between the ancient and modern meanings (and similarly, between those of the layman and expert today). It is, in any case, misleading to speak of *the* meaning of a word, as if meaning remained uniform regardless of context, and of the interests of those concerned. (Thus the 'expert' might be either a scientist or a jeweller, and their usages would not necessarily coincide.) One may be tempted to think of 'the' meaning as the scientific one, and it is true that, sometimes at least, the scientific meaning (supposing there is only one) is regarded as authoritative. Yet this fact may itself be embraced by the layman's meaning. For it may be part of that meaning – part of his conditions of use – that he will defer to the expert in the case of certain words (such as 'gold').

Thus, in one way or another, the identity of meaning and use is preserved; and there is no need to postulate a meaning – 'the' meaning – lying beyond the knowledge of those who actually use a given word.[7]

C. 'WHAT WE SAY' AND THE PROBLEMS OF PHILOSOPHY

I

The identification of meaning with use is important, not only for the philosophy of language, but for the treatment of philosophical topics in general. Some of these are brought together in a passage in the *Investigations*.

> When philosophers use a word – 'knowledge', 'being', 'object', 'I', 'proposition', 'name', – and try to grasp the *essence* of the thing, one must always ask oneself: is the word ever actually used in this way in the language in which it is at home? (PI 116)

According to Wittgenstein, the use of a word, and hence its meaning, depends on the situation in which it is used; and it is a mistake to assume that its meaning – the 'true' or 'essential' meaning – is fixed by a corresponding entity. Hence, in investigating the above topics, and others, we can do no better than to examine the actual use of the words in question.

What is knowledge? What is being? What is the self? What is a number? What is time, consciousness, happiness? Such questions have baffled thinkers through the ages. Like the question 'What is meaning?' itself, they 'produce in us a mental cramp. We feel that we can't point to anything in reply to them and yet ought to point to something' (BB 1). We may feel that if we cannot do so, then 'the essence of the thing' has eluded us, and our understanding of it is deficient. In the case of knowledge, for example, philosophers have long tried, and failed, to define its essence. In view of this we may be tempted to conclude that 'we don't know what it means, and that therefore, perhaps, we have no right to use it' (BB 27). According to Wittgenstein, however, 'there is no one exact usage of the word "knowledge"'; but this does not prevent us from using the word correctly, or from understanding what we are talking about when we do so. (He quotes a famous passage from Augustine: 'What, then, is time? I know well enough what it is, provided that nobody asks me; but if I am asked what it is and try to explain, I am baffled' (*Confessions* XI/14, Penguin, 264).)

In another passage he considers the self or 'I'. Is there an essential 'I', which is what the word stands for? If so, we may ask whether it is a physical or a mental thing. Taking the latter view 'creates the illusion that we use this word to refer to something bodiless, which, however, has its seat in our body' (BB 69). Descartes, who took this view (and identified the 'I' with the mind) was well aware of its difficulties. But what is the alternative? If 'something bodiless' is not the answer, must we embrace materialism? 'Is there then no mind, but only a body?' The solution, according to Wittgenstein, lies in rejecting the name-object conception of meaning, which seems to force this choice on us. 'Answer: the word "mind" has meaning, i.e., it has a use in our language' (BB 69–70). The meaning will consist in the work that the word is doing in a given context, and not in a corresponding entity.

What is thinking? Is there an essential thing or process of which 'thinking' is the name? If so, 'let us watch ourselves while we think: what we observe will be what the word means!' (PI 316; cf. 327–8). (The published translation has: 'we watch ourselves' etc. and is misleading.) But, comments Wittgenstein, 'this concept is not used like that'. Thinking, he writes in another passage, is 'a widely ramified concept. A concept that comprises many manifestations of life' (Z 110).

Can machines think? Do animals think? Wittgenstein replies by reference to 'what we say'. Thus 'we only say of a human being, and what is like one, that it thinks' (PI 360; cf. 281). The word 'think', like others, is used when there is a point in using it; it serves a need. 'Look at the word "think" as a tool!' (PI 360). But when there is no use for the word, no work for it to perform (other than philosophical speculation), then we may question what, if anything, it means. If the machine or animal is, in relevant ways, like a human being, then there *will* be a use for the word, and we shall find ourselves using it in a meaningful way. Now animals are, to some extent, like ouselves in the relevant ways; but there are limits. Of a dog we may say, 'He believes his master is at the door'; but, adds Wittgenstein 'can he also believe that his master will come the day after tomorrow?' (PI p. 174). There is a use, a need, for the first statement, and we can easily imagine the kind of case in which it would be made, and understand it accordingly. But this is not so with the second. Perhaps we could construct an example in which this statement too would have a use – a real use, as opposed to the idle philosophical one. But unless and until this is done, its meaning must remain in doubt. Again, we often have occasion to say of an animal – one that is sufficiently like a human being – that it is in pain. But can we suppose that a stone is in pain? What would this mean? In what circumstances, real or imaginary, would there be a use for such talk? (PI 283–4).

Another concept that has fascinated and troubled philosophers and others is that of consciousness. What is consciousness? Is possession of it confined to human beings? Or may other creatures, or artefacts, have it too? If so, what would theirs be like? We may be tempted to think of consciousness as some ethereal and elusive substance or process, perceptible, perhaps, to an 'inner eye' (cf. PI 417); and then these questions will appear mysterious and intractable. Such a view seems to be taken by Thomas Nagel in his essay 'What is it like to be a bat?'. 'Consciousness', he writes, 'is what makes the mind-body problem really intractable' (*Mortal Questions* (Cambridge University Press, 1979) 165). According to

Nagel, 'there is something that it is like to be a bat' (168); but our limitations as human beings prevent us from grasping this something. Now it might be thought that the question 'What is it like to be a bat?' can be treated in a straightforward way, in terms of what we know about a bat's life – their ways of flying, catching insects and so on. This would be a normal way of taking the question. But Nagel is careful to exclude this. What he wants to know, he says, is 'what it is like for a *bat* to be a bat' (*Mortal Questions*, 169). It is this intractable question that fascinates and mystifies him. But the difficulty of this question springs from an abnormal use of words, and not from some mysterious quality of consciousness (or the 'something that it is like to be. . .'). We can see the abnormality of Nagel's usage if we turn the question on ourselves: What is it like for a human being to be a human being? (Or: for me to be me?) These are baffling questions, to which one's first response would probably be: what do you mean? Nagel does indeed claim that 'we know what it is like to be us' (*Mortal Questions*, 170); but how are we to understand this? What is the use of this statement, and what is supposed to be conveyed by it? The difficulty is not that 'being us' is such a very familiar experience that the truth of the statement must be obvious to everyone: for there is no such experience as 'being us'. Nor is it that 'being us' is some ineffable or hard-to-describe experience (like being in love, or hearing a particular piece of music). It is that the expression 'what it is like' is not at home in this context. Someone who tells us that he knows what it is like to be in love would readily be understood, even if he could not describe the feeling. But someone who told us that he knew what it was like for him to be him would not. And the same difficulty arises with Nagel's (alleged) problem about the bat. 'Philosophical problems', wrote Wittgenstein, 'arise when language is *idling*' (PI 38).

This is not to deny that there are real and profound questions about 'what it is like'. I might, for example, wonder what it is like to be a woman, or a black man in the Deep South; or what it would have been like to live in the eighteenth century. These questions may call for a considerable effort of insight and imagination (as well as factual knowledge), but they are not puzzling in the philosophical way. We know what to do with such questions, even if we find them hard to answer. Language is not idling in these cases.

Wittgenstein also appeals to 'use' in dealing with the sceptical

problem of 'other minds', expressed by his imaginary interlocutor
as follows: 'Only I can know whether I am really in pain; another
person can only surmise it' (PI 246). It has been thought that in
order to *know* whether another person is in pain (thinks, etc), we
would need somehow to 'get inside his mind'; and that, being
unable to meet this condition, we can 'only surmise' from his
behaviour that he is in pain, but can never attain knowledge in
this matter. But Wittgenstein points out that this is contrary to the
normal use of the word 'know'. 'If we are using the word "know"
as it is normally used (and how else are we to use it!), then other
people very often know when I am in pain' (PI 246). Since the
sceptic uses the word differently, he cannot *mean* by 'know' what
we normally mean by it in this context.

It may be objected that the sceptic does not intend a different
meaning, but is using words with the *same* meaning, in order to
deny what is commonly assumed. Of course we must not conclude
that his meaning is different merely because he disagrees with us –
as if every case of disagreement entailed a difference of meaning.
The sceptical case is, however, special; it should be contrasted with
normal cases of disagreement, such as that in which two people
are disputing whether a particular person is really in pain or merely
pretending, with reasons given on both sides. The sceptic's case
is different, because he would deny knowledge in *all* cases –
including those in which there is (by ordinary standards) every
reason to say we know, and *no* reason for doubting, that someone
is in pain. Such cases are the paradigms whereby the meaning of
'knowing he is in pain' is established, and to deny them this role
is to alter the meaning of these words.

It is sometimes alleged that Wittgenstein made the mistake of
arguing from linguistic premises to ontological conclusions, 'from
words to world'.[8] On this view, Wittgenstein's argument, in the
example just considered, runs as follows: The sentence 'I know he
is in pain' has a use; therefore one sometimes knows that others
are in pain. (This in turn would entail that others really are,
sometimes, in pain.) But Wittgenstein is not arguing in this way.
his point is the 'purely descriptive' one, that we normally use the
word 'know' in the way described. This is the end and not the
beginning of his argument. 'Philosophy simply puts everything
before us, and neither explains nor deduces anything' (PI 126;
cf. 599). Used in that context, the word 'know' is a 'tool' that serves
a purpose in our lives; and we use it, and need it, accordingly.

Wittgenstein's question 'How else are we to use it? is important in this connection. In another passage he imagined the objector saying 'I can only *believe* that someone else is in pain, but I *know* it if I am'. He replied: 'Yes; one can make the decision to say "I believe he is in pain" instead of "He is in pain". But that is all. . . . Just try – in a real case – to doubt someone else's fear or pain' (PI 303). If we made such a change of terminology – if, say, a law were enacted which prohibited the use of 'know', then we would need new terminology to do the work of the old; another word or expression would come to have the use, the meaning, that 'know' has in human language.

Wittgenstein's challenge has had a revolutionary effect on traditional ways of doing philosophy. He questioned whether his own work should even be described as 'philosophy', rather than 'one of the heirs of what used to be called "philosophy"' (BB 28). Yet it must be admitted that, to a considerable extent, the impact of his message has been dissipated. Many philosophers have, in recent times, returned to the old questions and puzzles, often treating them as though Wittgenstein had never existed. But for them, as for others, his challenge remains valid. If these questions, claims and counter-claims are couched in abnormal language, using words out of their normal contexts and contrary to normal usage, then what – if anything – do they mean?

II

Wittgenstein's way of dealing with age-old problems about thought, knowledge, consciousness and so on is linguistic. He is not, he says, 'analysing a phenomenon (for example thinking) but a concept (e.g. that of thinking), and therefore the use of a word' (PI 383). Now it may be thought that this approach must pass by the great, important questions, which are not about words but about the reality behind the words – not, for example, about the *word* 'think', but about thinking itself. But this is a false dichotomy.

When Socrates posed the question 'What is courage?' (*Laches*, 190e), was he asking about courage or about the word 'courage'? The dialogue between Socrates and his colleagues follows a typical course. A definition of courage is put forward; it is opposed by counter-examples (examples of courage that do not fit the definition), and so on. It may be said that this was a discussion about the use of the word 'courage'; but it would be absurd to infer from this that it was not (as Socrates and his colleagues intended) about *courage*.

The tendency to separate words like 'thinking' and 'courage' from thinking and courage 'themselves', may itself be due to a mistaken conception of language – 'the idea that language always functions in one way' (PI 304). In the case of words like 'apple' or 'water', there is a valid distinction between word and thing (or word and substance). If we ask, for example, 'What is water?', then the question may be taken in a linguistic or a non-linguistic sense. What we want may be a chemical analysis of water, and not an account of how the word 'water' is used. But this is not so in the case of the words we are considering. Thinking, courage, knowledge – these are not kinds of stuff; and when we ask 'What is courage?', we are not asking about the chemical composition of a kind of stuff, but about the circumstances under which we would *describe* an act, or person, as courageous. Similarly, when sceptics have doubted whether we can really have knowledge, their doubt has not been about the existence of a kind of stuff (as one might) doubt the existence of an 'ether' pervading the universe).

The linguistic approach may seem to devalue the deep, important questions, transforming them into something 'merely verbal'. But this is a false impression. In asking about the conditions under which we would use words like 'courage', 'thinking', 'knowledge' and the rest, we *are* dealing with the deep and important questions. And if Wittgenstein is right, this is the only proper way to deal with them.

4

'Explanations Come to an End'

A. OSTENSIVE EXPLANATION: THE STEP 'OUTSIDE LANGUAGE'

We have seen (p. 32) how Wittgenstein disposes of the question 'But what is the meaning of the word "five"?' in the opening section of the *Investigations*. Another question was: 'But how does he know where and how he is to look up the word "red" and what he is to do with the word "five"?'. Wittgenstein replies: 'Well, I assume that he *acts* as I have described. Explanations come to an end somewhere' (PI 1).

One explanation that might be offered here is that the man was *taught* how to use the words, in the course of learning his native language. We can sometimes explain a person's ability by reference to what was explained *to him*. For example, he may be told that 'il pleut' means 'it is raining', and this would explain his ability to use the French expression. But can we similarly explain how he knows the words of his native language? Well, he might be taught the meaning of, say, 'deciduous', by having it explained to him; and this again would explain his subsequent ability to use this word. But these explanations will only work if at some stage the words are related to something other than words. A person who has learned that 'il pleut' means the same as 'it is raining' would not know the meaning of either of these expressions unless he was able to apply them to non-linguistic facts. And how is this ability to be explained?

This question occupied members of the Vienna Circle, with whom Wittgenstein had conversations in 1929–32. In the 'Theses' of Friedrich Waismann, we are told of two ways of giving meaning to a sign. There is the method of definition in terms of other signs, and the method of 'ostension'. The latter is done 'by constructing various propositions by means of that word [the word that is being defined] and each time pointing to the fact in question'. The former kind of definition 'remains inside language', whereas the latter 'steps outside language and connects signs with reality' (WVC 246).

It may be thought that without this step 'outside language', human speech would be mere sound and fury, signifying nothing. Or it might be a kind of game, in which sounds are exchanged in accordance with certain rules, but without being *about* anything, in the way that language is. Again, any *explanation* of meaning, or of knowledge of meaning, might be regarded as incomplete if it remained at the verbal level, without the backing of the other sort of explanation.

> The verbal definition, as it takes us from one verbal expression to another, in a sense gets us no further. In the ostensive definition however we seem to make a much more real step towards learning the meaning (BB 1).

It was thought that verbal definition proceeds by *analysing* a word (in the manner of the *Tractatus*) into simpler terms, the 'connection with reality' being made at the final stage of simplicity. This would fit in with the *Tractatus* conception of meaning. If it is true that 'a name means an object', then we should be able to *give* the meaning – the whole meaning and nothing but the meaning – by producing or indicating the object. And then the non-fundamental, verbal kind of definition could be given by combinations of names, whose meaning had already been established.[1] Moritz Schlick, leader of the Vienna Circle, saw the matter in terms of what could be learned from a dictionary. One might, he said, find the definition of a word in the dictionary, then look up the words of that definition, and so on. But finally, he claimed, 'you will arrive at very simple terms for which you will not find any explanation'. At that stage there would have to be 'some act, some immediate procedure', which would *show* what was meant; for example, pointing to a sample of what is meant by 'yellow' (*Philosophical Papers* I, 219–20). Did Schlick mean that the dictionary would have *no* entry for 'yellow'? This would obviously be incorrect. What is true, however, is that the entry would refer the reader to examples of yellow objects which he would have to see (or have seen) for himself.

A similar conception of meaning appears in the writings of John Locke in the seventeenth century, although in his case the relevant objects were mental entities – 'ideas'. Words, according to Locke, 'signify nothing but the ideas that are in the mind of the speaker' (*Essay Concerning Human Understanding*, 3.2.4). Some words, he said, are capable of definition by other words, and so on; but this could not go on indefinitely. 'For if the terms of one definition were still to be defined by another, where at last should we stop?' There is, he maintained, a class of *simple* ideas, whose names 'are incapable of being defined' (*Essay* 3.4.5, 3.4.7). This did not mean, of course, that these names were meaningless; the point was that one would have to know their meanings simply by *having* the corresponding ideas. Whereas, in the later account, ostensive definition is achieved by correlating words with objects, the correlation in Locke's account is between words and 'inner' objects. It might be described as a matter of 'inner ostensive definition'.

The ostensive method of definition is also invoked to explain how infants begin to learn their native language, before there is any possibility of verbal definition. 'The part of language that we learn first must be learned ostensively, thus not depending on other language-learning' (W. V. Quine and J. S. Ullian, *The Web of Belief* (New York: Random House, 1970)). 'It is a simple matter of learning to associate the heard words with things simultaneously observed – a matter, as modern psychologists put it, of conditioning' (pp. 13–14).

But to what extent can meaning, and the learning of meaning, be accounted for by ostensive definition? Does this kind of definition enable us to break out of the circle of language? Wittgenstein argues that it cannot perform this role – cannot make up for the (alleged) shortcomings of verbal definition. The latter was thought to 'get us no further', because it presupposes an already existing knowledge of words. But, if Wittgenstein is right, something similar is true also of the ostensive method. The learner must be in possession of a certain understanding or know-how, if he is to learn anything by this method.

In the *Blue Book* he introduced an imaginary word, 'tove', and supposed that someone pointed to a pencil, saying 'This is tove'. What would a learner make of this? He might, says Wittgenstein, take 'tove' to mean 'a pencil'; but he might equally take it to mean 'round', 'wood', 'one', 'hard', or various other things (BB 2). In the *Investigations* he pointed out that someone who is taught 'That is called "two"' by means of two nuts, may think that 'two' is a name given to this particular group of nuts. Conversely, if he *were* given the name of a particular group, he might mistake this for the name of a numeral. 'And he might equally well take the name of a person, of which I give an ostensive definition, as that of a colour, of a race, or even a point of the compass.' Thus, concluded Wittgenstein, 'an ostensive definition can be variously interpreted in *every* case' (PI 28). The obvious remedy would be to augment the ostensive definition by a verbal addition: 'This *number* is called "two"'. But, observes Wittgenstein, 'this means that the word "number" must be explained before the ostensive definition can be understood' (PI 29).

That the 'ostensive definition can be variously interpreted in every case' is due in part to the irreducible complexity of things, the fact that anything we can point to can be described in an indefinite number of ways. It would be different if we could point to objects which were 'simple' in the *Tractatus* sense. In that case there would be ostensive definitions that could not be misunderstood as referring to one aspect of a thing rather than another. This is not, however, the only way in which an ostensive definition might, conceivably, be misunderstood. Suppose the definition is given by *pointing* to a relevant object. Then the act of pointing must be understood correctly by the learner. We can imagine a person 'who naturally reacted to the gesture of pointing by looking in the direction from finger-tip to wrist' (185) – or, as a dog would, by looking at the hand. And while it is easy enough to think of examples of ostensive teaching by means of pointing, it is not clear how the meaning of pointing itself could be taught by this method. A similar difficulty arises about the teaching of words like 'this' and 'here' – words that may be used (or may have to be understood) in giving an ostensive definition.

There are various other words for which the idea of ostensive definition does not seem plausible even at first sight. The examples 'today', 'not', 'but', 'perhaps' and 'number' are mentioned in the *Blue Book* (1, 77). There is no obvious method of pointing or showing in these cases, as in the case of colours or an object on the table. Nor can such words be analysed into simpler components which would be amenable to this method. Could we, for example, teach the meaning of 'past' by this method? An obvious difficulty here is that the past is never, so to speak, present; it is never *there*, for the method of ostension to be applied. But in any case, the idea of pointing to an aspect of time is obscure. It has been claimed, nevertheless, that this concept can be acquired by the perception of instances. Thus 'a man can acquire the notion of pastness in precisely the same way as he acquires the notion of red, viz.

empirically, by seeing an instance of it'.[2] But when we turn to the details of this and similar claims, we find that the learner is assumed to be already in possession of temporal notions such as 'before', 'duration', 'event'. It is with the help of these that he is supposed to acquire the notion of pastness. But how did he learn these notions? And if he is assumed to have these, must he not have the notion of pastness too? These notions are all interwoven, and the idea of learning them one at a time is an illusion.

It is true that we might *convey* the notion of pastness, as distinct from teaching or defining it, by an ostensive method. (The same is true of the other words mentioned above.) Imagine a party game in which various objects (calendars, old objects, pictures of people from the past) are presented, and after a while the person 'in the middle' tumbles to the fact that what is meant is 'the past'. This would not, however, be a case of teaching or defining the concept; it is, on the contrary, because he already has the concept that the person concerned can guess what is meant.

The words 'past', 'not' and so on should not be regarded as merely 'awkward exceptions' to the method of ostension, for it cannot be assumed that the rest of language is independent of them. It is, for example, essential to an understanding of 'yellow' and 'pencil' that one should be able to say what is *not* yellow, and *not* a pencil; and essential to understand that 'pencil' means an *enduring* entity, one that has a past and future.

Another aspect of language that is sometimes overlooked concerns the point and purpose of using it. Wittgenstein frequently spoke of words as 'tools', to be used in various ways and in a variety of language-games. Someone who merely uttered words when in the presence of a corresponding object would hardly be thought to have mastered the use of language. Russell claimed, on the contrary, that the use of language is essentially a matter of habit. A child 'frequently hears the word "dog" uttered while his attention is fixed upon a dog', and this causes him to form 'two habits': the appearance of a dog 'gives him an impulse to say "dog", and hearing the word "dog" makes him expect or look for a dog'. When these habits have been acquired, says Russell, the child 'can speak correctly' (*My Philosophical Development*, 108–9). But this takes no account of the *purposes* for which this word, and others, are used, in a variety of language-games. Thus if one heard the word 'dog' in the course of a report, speculation, hypothesis, story, play, riddle, joke or curse (cf. PI 23) one would not 'expect or look for a dog', if one understood these language-games correctly. On the other hand, if someone had an impulse to say 'dog' whenever he saw a dog, this would be evidence of some strange psychological condition, rather than of competence in the use of language.

Now this aspect of language, again, cannot be accounted for by the ostensive method, for the situation in which such teaching is done is necessarily *different* from those in which the word is to be used thereafter. 'Ostensive explanation is, we might say, a language-game on its own' (PI 27). In this game we might, for example, tell someone 'This is a dog' when a dog is plainly in view; but there would be no point in doing this (and one would not do it) outside the teaching situation. But how does the person who learns the word in this situation know how it is to be used in other, non-teaching situations? This is not to be explained by the ostensive method or the inculcation of a habit.

Wittgenstein's critique of ostensive teaching is sometimes greeted with disbelief, as if he were denying something that obviously takes place. Parents reading his discussion may recall, perhaps fondly, how they taught their children words like 'red' and 'teddy bear' by pointing to suitable objects and saying these words. But Wittgenstein is not denying any of this. Ostensive teaching works in practice, because the required abilities to 'catch on' to what is meant, and to master other aspects of language, can normally be taken for granted.[3] The point is, however, that these abilities cannot themselves be explained by reference to ostensive teaching.

It is easy to overlook these abilities, because we who consider the matter are so familiar with them that they escape our notice. We notice the act of teaching, but not the immense framework of skills that must be there, or (in the case of the child) must be developed, if the teaching is to work. Here it is useful to contrast the learning of language with the learning of *another* language. In the latter case, the framework is already in place; the learner is in possession of a full range of concepts, and competent in the use of words in various language-games. Now it may be tempting, in trying to explain the learning of *language*, to suppose that the same kind of knowledge is already present, in the child's mind, before the process begins. In the *Investigations*, Wittgenstein ascribed such a view to Augustine. Having quoted the latter's account of language-learning at length, he comments:

> Augustine describes the learning of human language as if the child came into a strange country and did not understand the

language of that country; that is, as if it already had a language, only not this one. Or again: as if the child could already *think*, only not yet speak. And 'think' would here mean something like 'talk to itself'. (PI 32)

Someone who already has a language will be able to fit the sounds of the new language to concepts he already has; he is not learning new *concepts*. Thus, if he hears the expression 'il pleut', he will be able to consider whether its use coincides with that of 'it is raining'. And if people in the 'strange country' teach him, or seem to teach him, words by an ostensive method, then he will try to understand this by means of knowledge of similar practices in his own language. But learning one's native language is not like this. There is no way of 'translating from reality' into English, as there is from French into English; nor is the learner in possession of a prior language. Hence one cannot *teach* language, in the sense in which one can teach a second language. 'In a certain sense', wrote Wittgenstein, 'the use of language is something that cannot be taught, i.e. I cannot use language to teach it . . .' (PR 54).
* Some philosophers, unwilling to give up the quest for explanation, have defended the kind of view that Wittgenstein ascribes to Augustine, maintaining that there must indeed be a pre-existing language or 'code' in the infant's mind. According to Zeno Vendler, it would be 'clearly absurd' to think that an infant could catch on to the 'immensely complex "game"' of language without this.

> The most reasonable explanation is that a child must learn his native tongue in a way similar to the way one learns a second language. He must have, in other words, a native equipment that codes the fundamental illocutionary, syntactic and semantic features of any possible human language. (*Res Cogitans*, 139–40).[4]

What are we to make of this 'reasonable explanation'? One way in which it differs from the case of the second language is that the infant's 'equipment' or 'code' are merely postulated; they are not observable, as is a person's knowledge of English or French. Now it may be thought that this is merely a contingent matter. According to Vendler, we may suppose that there is a '"code", as yet unknown, operating in the human nervous system', the 'decipher-

ing [of which] remains a scientific possibility' (*Res Cogitans* 142).
But could such an equipment in the nervous system provide the
required kind of explanation? An equipment is of no value unless
someone is able to *use* it. Would the child who learns his native
language be able to use the supposed equipment in his nervous
system? How is this to be conceived? Does he look up a configuration of his nervous system as one might look up words in a
dictionary? Are the patterns of his nervous system available to him
in the sort of way in which the logic of our native language is
available to us when we learn a second language? These questions
will have to be dealt with before we can try to model the learning
of language on 'the way one learns a second language'. Suppose,
however, that we can, somehow, conceive of the learner as
consulting patterns of his nervous system in the sense in which
one might consult a dictionary. This still leaves us without any
explanatory advantage. For the question will now arise, how are
we to explain *this* ability? If the idea that one can acquire one's
native language without such equipment is 'clearly absurd', then
the same must be true of the ability to use the inner equipment. It
is true, as Vendler says, that human language is 'immensely
complex'; but the postulated equipment will have to be no less
complex. Must we not, then, postulate a further equipment, to
explain our ability to use the one already postulated?

It may be tempting to reply that in the case of the latter, one
'just knows' how to use it, that this ability is 'innate'. But then the
same can be said about the facts that are open to view – the natural
behaviour of children in picking up their native language. Either
way, 'explanations come to an end'.

But is that really the end of the matter? Wittgenstein's attitude
may strike the reader as negative and defeatist. As we saw in the
last chapter, he denies that behind the actual uses of a word there
is something (a 'meaning') that unifies and explains these uses.
And now he seems to be denying that there can be any explanation
of the *learning* of language. But if some theories are inade-
quate, are not others possible? In any case, isn't the question one
for empirical research, for scientists rather than philosophers?

Wittgenstein's enquiry is logical and not scientific. Of course
there can be scientific theories by various kinds (psychological,
physiological, social, evolutionary), but Wittgenstein is not concerned with these. His concern is about what I shall call 'justifying'
explanations. A justifying explanation (unlike the causal
explanations offered by scientists) can be used by a person to

justify what he is doing or saying. In the case of the teaching situation, for example, the learner will be able to justify (to explain, in that sense) his action or use of language by reference to what he was told. Thus if a person has been taught that a certain colour is called 'sepia' (PI 30), then he will be able to justify his subsequent use of it by reference to this teaching. By contrast, one could not justify a use of language by reference to, say, a state of the nervous system or a process of conditioning. These might be given as reasons why a person does X; but they would not be reasons *for doing* X.

Causal explanations are a matter of discovery. A person may *wonder* whether his behaviour or use of language is due to such and such causes; and it may be rash for him to predict that a causal explanation, perhaps of a kind he has never contemplated, will not be forthcoming. But this is not so with justifying explanations. If my reason for describing a colour as 'sepia' is that this is what I was taught, then I cannot be ignorant that this is my reason. If it is a justifying reason, then it must be one that I am able to give. 'If I need a justification for using a word, it must also be one for someone else' (PI 378).

Justifying reasons give a kind of satisfaction that is lacking from explanations of the causal kind. Now it may be thought that the ostensive teaching theory, whereby the learning of language is wholly accounted for by reference to corresponding objects, would also provide a justifying explanation of the nature of language itself. For, by 'getting outside language', as in the ostensive act, we would show, and see, that our language is the *right* one, and not merely one that comes naturally to us. But if Wittgenstein is right, this idea is an illusion. There are justifying explanations within language, but language as a whole cannot be justified.

B. VERBAL EXPLANATION: 'SEEING WHAT IS COMMON'

The ostensive method, as we have seen, was supposed to establish the vital link between language and reality, showing that language has a foundation in the non-linguistic world. Verbal definition could not have this fundamental role, since it merely 'takes us from one verbal expression to another' (BB 1). On the other hand, by staying 'inside language', it would not be exposed to the ambiguities and possible misunderstandings of ostensive definition. Sometimes, indeed, the latter can be cleared up by resorting to verbal explanation, as when we explain, in words, that the word 'tove', for example, should be applied to such and such an aspect (colour, shape, number and so on) of the object before us. But is verbal definition itself foolproof? Obviously there are possibilities of misunderstanding here too. But, it may be said, where the verbal method is applicable, words *can* be given a precise and unambiguous definition. Thus if the word W can be analysed into the terms x, y and z, and if the learner knows the meanings of the latter, then the definition 'W = x, y and z' will convey the meaning of W to him precisely and unambiguously.

But to what extent are words amenable to this kind of definition? One example considered by Wittgenstein was the word 'language' itself, as we saw earlier (pp. 34–5). Whereas in the *Tractatus* he had put forward a definition of 'the essence of language', he now rejected this idea, claiming instead that 'these phenomena have no one thing in common which makes us use the same word for all, – but that they are *related* to one another in many different ways' (PI 65). He illustrated this by reference to the word 'game'. This word can of course be explained, at least to some extent, by reference to characteristic features of games. But is there a definite set of features, x, y and z, in terms of which the word can be defined? What do all games have in common, in virtue of which we call them 'games'? According to Wittgenstein, the meaning of the word cannot be captured in this way; and we should not assume that such definitions are either available or needed. 'Don't say: "There *must* be something common, or they would not be called 'games'" – but *look and see* whether there is' (PI 66). He gave instances of various games (chess, football, patience, Olympic games, children's games), and pointed out that features that are important in one instance are lacking from another, and so on. The conclusion was that 'we see a complicated network of similarities overlapping and criss-crossing', but no essential set of features in virtue of which they are all games. The situation was that of a 'family resemblance'. Among the members of a family, some have the same build, others the same eyes or gait; but there is no need to postulate a set of features that all the members, and only they, have in common.

Wittgenstein's choice of the word 'game' as an example is particularly interesting, since, as we saw, he invites us to regard language itself as a game or set of games (sometimes the one, sometimes the other); but of course what he says here is meant to apply much more generally to the words of our language. He is opposing a widespread assumption that the meanings of words are fixed by some essential feature, or set of features, that all the instances have in common. It may be thought that this must be so, and that otherwise there could be no communication – or no unambiguous communication – between one speaker and another. But this assumption is rejected by Wittgenstein.

The issue between Wittgenstein and his 'essentialist' opponent may be illustrated as follows. Let us use letters for the various instances of games (chess, football etc.) and numbers for the features associated with games (competition, skill etc). Then Wittgenstein's position may be shown as follows. (The lines represent features that games have in common. For example, feature one is common to games A, B, E and G.)

GAMES

		A	B	C	D	E	F	G
F	1	———————				———		———
E								
A	2		———————			———		
T								
U	3		———		———————			
R								
E	4	———	———			———		
S								
	5		———————			———————		

It will be seen that no set of features is common to all the instances of games (shown as A–G), but they are related by various overlaps in the features 1–5. This way of displaying Wittgenstein's position fits in with another passage, in which he spoke of a concept being held together like a thread composed of many fibres: 'And the strength of the thread does not reside in the fact that some one fibre runs through its whole length, but in the overlapping of many fibres' (PI 67).

To illustrate the opposite, 'essentialist' view, we might divide the features 1–5 into two categories, essential and non-essential. The latter would be distributed in some random way (they contribute nothing to the meaning), but the former would be filled in for *every* instance of a game – failing which it would not be a game. (Thus there *would* have to be 'one fibre', – or one set of fibres – running through the whole length.)

Was Wittgenstein right? Innumerable writings have been provoked by his challenge. Some have claimed to identify features, different from those mentioned by Wittgenstein, which do, after all, satisfy the essentialist demand; while others have pointed out that even if the challenge has not been met so far, this does not mean that it never will be. Now it must be admitted that Wittgenstein's treatment is short and sharp, and hardly amounts to an *argument* for the fibre-to-fibre conclusion. He evidently thought, here as elsewhere, that his role was merely to *remind* the reader of something that, in a sense, he knew already. Having read the passage, the reader would exclaim 'Yes, of course, that's how it is' (cf. WVC 183) – in spite of the fact that he may have approached it with an unquestioned assumption of the opposite view. But is this plausible?

We must notice that the opposite view is very stringent and may itself seem far from plausible when spelled out. The view in question is not merely that all games have something in common. For example, Wittgenstein himself speaks of games as 'proceedings' and he would not deny that *this* is something they have in common. But this would obviously fall far short of a definition, since there are many other kinds of proceedings besides games. What is at issue is a condition, or set of conditions, that games and *only* games have in common – in other words, a set of necessary and sufficient conditions, which 'makes us use the same word for all' (PI 65).

We can see how implausible *this* view is if we consider how concepts develop in the course of time. Suppose we *introduced* a word *W* into the language with an essentialist definition. This can of course be done. But sooner or later we shall come across instances, not thought of at the time, which we now find it natural to call '*W*', even though they lack one of the defining features; and others that we shall *not* want to include, even though they have them. (In the meantime other features have come to seem more important and some of the original ones less so.) And so 'we extend our concept . . . as in spinning a thread we twist fibre on fibre. . . .' (PI 67).

This process can indeed be observed in the past and present development of familiar words. An interesting example was given by Tolstoy. In the Russian language of his day there was, apparently, no word corresponding to the English 'beauty'.

In Russian, by the word krasotá (beauty) we mean only that which pleases the sight. And though latterly people have begun to speak of 'an ugly deed', or of 'beautiful music', it is not good Russian.[5]

Here we see a new fibre being added (or, depending on how the metaphor is taken, an old one being removed). Perhaps those who used the word in the new way would have justified their extension by saying that what beautiful music had in common with a beautiful object of sight was more important than what separated them; and similarly with 'an ugly deed'. Yet they may have *refused* to apply these words to other pleasing or displeasing objects.[6]

The same process can be seen at work in legal and other official definitions. A regulation is introduced with a strict definition of some class of goods. Then an example turns up, which, though covered by the definition, is thought by a judge not to be fit for inclusion – this being 'not in the spirit' of that regulation. The Common Law has developed through the ages largely in such ways. (In these cases, however, the legislators will always try, in the interests of equity, to devise a new definition which will capture the concept as it now stands.)

But what if, after all, Wittgenstein turned out to be wrong about the word 'game'? What if some ingenious philosophers succeeded in meeting the challenge? It is sometimes thought that this would inflict a crucial blow to Wittgenstein's position; but this is a mistake. The crucial issue is not whether words have (or are likely to have) an essentialist definition, but whether they *must* have one, in order to function as words. It is the second claim that Wittgenstein denies. We can, if we like, '*draw* a boundary' round the word 'game', to make it conform to the essentialist view; but 'does it take that to make the concept usable? Not at all!' (PI 69).

In spite of his rejection of theory, Wittgenstein's position is sometimes described as a 'family resemblance theory'; and it may seem as if he intended to *explain* why we have the concepts we have, in the same way as traditional theories. Why, for example, do we have the concept 'game'? Does it conform to something we find in reality? A traditional answer has been that we notice the possession of a common feature, or set of features, by a group of objects; and that is why we apply a common word to them. In this way the existence of the concept is explained and justified (and at the same time, we have a method of explaining its meaning to a learner). It may be thought that Wittgenstein's 'theory' performs a similar role, but in terms of overlapping features rather than essential ones; but this would be a mistake. 'It might be said', he wrote, 'that the use of [a] concept-word or common noun is justified . . . because there are transitional steps between the members'. But to this he immediately objected that 'a transition can be made from anything to anything' (PG 75–6). The existence of transitions or overlaps does not *explain* why we have the concepts we have; why, so to speak, we prefer one arrangement of overlaps to others.

Again, Wittgenstein's metaphor of 'family resemblance' has sometimes been taken to imply a theory about 'ancestral connection'. Such a connection does of course exist in the case of members of a family, and can serve to *explain* the resemblances between them. Was not Wittgenstein hinting at something similar in the case of words and concepts? According to a recent commentator, it was part of 'Wittgenstein's theory' that 'something must link the resemblances through time' (David Bloor, *Wittgenstein: A Social Theory of Knowledge* (London: Macmillan, 1983), 32). One might also refer, in this connection, to the work of linguists and lexicographers in tracing the development of words through the ages (as presented, for example, in the Oxford English Dictionary). But these researches, interesting as they are, take us beyond the *logic* of our concepts, which, if Wittgenstein is right, is the philosopher's only concern. This logic is something that lies open to view, and is not a matter for research or theory. To know the logic of the word 'game', for example, is to know what is involved in using it correctly; and this does not presuppose any knowledge of the word's ancestry. Nor was the metaphor of 'family resemblance' meant as a theory about the ancestry or development of our concepts.

II

I have tried to show that, although Wittgenstein presents his fibre-to-fibre account with a sense of challenge, it can be made plausible enough by spelling out the alternative view. However, Wittgenstein's originality did not lie merely in drawing attention to this aspect of language. In this matter he was, in any case, anticipated by at least a century. In J. S. Mill's *System of Logic* of 1843, there is an excellent description of it, presented without any sense of challenge. 'Names creep on', writes Mill, 'from subject to subject, until . . . the word comes to denote a number of things not only independently of any common attribute, but which have actually no attribute in common; or none but what is shared by other things to which the name is capriciously refused' (*Logic*, 24). Mill quotes from another philosopher, Alexander Bain, who had provided an excellent example of 'family resemblance' (though not, of course, under this name). 'Take the familiar term Stone [writes Bain]. It is applied to mineral and rocky materials, to the kernels of fruit, to the accumulations in the gall-bladder. . . ; while it is refused to polished minerals (called gems) [etc. etc.].'

Wittgenstein's achievement did not lie in noticing something that no-one had noticed before, but in seeing its significance in a new way. In this respect there is a striking difference between him and philosophers like Mill. According to the latter, the usage in question was an aberration – a 'perversion of . . . language from its purpose', which rendered it 'unfit for the purposes of accurate thinking' (*Logic*, 24). But according to Wittgenstein there is no standard, beyond actual usage, by reference to which such judgements could be made. If we were to 'draw a boundary' round the concept 'game', this would not serve to 'make the concept usable', nor would it produce a *better* way of doing the job than is done by the existing word.

To the objection that one might describe the pre-boundary concept as 'inexact', Wittgenstein replied: 'Very well, it was an inexact one. – Though you still owe me a definition of exactness' (PI 69). The last sentence is not merely an *ad hominem* flourish. It shows that the issue goes deeper than merely the use of words like 'game' and 'stone', affecting the very words in which the issue is stated – words like 'accurate' and 'exact'. According to Wittgenstein, as we saw earlier (p. 39), such words have no meaning in the abstract, but must be understood according to the context in which they occur. What is meant by 'exact' will depend on *what* is being described, and for what purpose. For some purposes, for example, a drawing would be described as exact only if there were a high degree of correspondence, one to one, between its details and those of the object depicted. But in other cases this is not so. A person may say of a drawing of a piece of ground covered with plants: 'it looked *exactly* like this'. But 'were just *this* grass and *these* leaves there, arranged just like this? No, that is not what it means' (PI 70).

To the theorist who tries to explain our concepts by reference to similarities between instances, Wittgenstein replies: 'We use the word "similar" in a huge family of cases' (BB 133). And if it is claimed that the instances are 'the same', then he will point out that *this* expression functions in different ways 'when applied to colours, lengths, directions etc.' (BB 141), and in other ways still when we are speaking of 'the same note again' (that is, the octave) (BB 141) or 'the same feeling' (cf. PI 350).

> Perhaps a logician will think: The same is the same – how sameness is established is a psychological question. (High is high – it is a matter of psychology that one sometimes *sees*, and sometimes *hears* it.) (PI 377)

These remarks bring out something of the scope of Wittgenstein's claims about family resemblance – or, to put it more generally, the resistance of words to explanations in terms of 'what they have in common'.

It is sometimes thought that in speaking of family resemblance Wittgenstein had in mind a rather special class of concepts ('family resemblance concepts'), which are characterised by a certain vagueness or 'open texture'. Words like 'art', 'science', 'revolution' and 'romanticism' come to mind as ideal candidates for the fibre-to-fibre conception. And this conception has, indeed, been influential in recent discussions of such questions as 'What is Art?'[7] But to view the matter in this way is to underestimate the scope of Wittgenstein's remarks. Wittgenstein himself spoke of 'family resemblance' (or used similar expressions) in regard to a number of words, including 'game' (PI 67), 'number' (PI 67), 'good' (PI 77) 'sentence' and 'language' (PI 108), 'reading' (PI 164), 'comparing' (BB 87) and 'chair' (PG 118). But the reader can easily test the scope of Wittgenstein's claim by trying to find necessary and sufficient conditions for any given word, and then looking for counter-examples. (For example, the definition of 'chair' as 'separate seat for one' is not sufficient – something may satisfy the definition and yet not be a chair. It will be found that attempts to make it sufficient by adding further conditions will result in a definition that is not 'necessary' – something may be a chair without satisfying it.)

However, it is not merely a question of how many words are covered by the family resemblance relation. There is also the point that this relation affects a given concept several times over, so to speak. Consider the features mentioned by Wittgenstein in connection with games, such as amusement, skill, and luck. It is true, of course, that many games have these features in common, and they may indeed be given as reasons for calling something a game. But we must also remember that these features, in their turn, are characterised by family resemblance. Thus Wittgenstein reminds us of 'the difference between skill in chess and skill in tennis' (PI 66). Suppose that, contrary to Wittgenstein's claim, the concept 'game' could be wholly analysed into components such as skill, luck and amusement. We would still be left with the question: what do skill, luck and amusement in one game have in common with skill, luck and amusement in another? (As before, they will, of course, have something in common, but there will also be differences; and no set of features will be both necessary and sufficient.) What is involved in skill or amusement will depend on *which* game is being described.

A similar point arises in speaking of games versus activities other than games. Wittgenstein mentioned winning and losing as one of the characteristics of games (though not shared by all). But these features, again, must be understood in a sense appropriate *to games*. Losing a game, for example, is not like losing an umbrella or losing one's temper; and winning a game is not like winning a court case or winning someone's confidence. Hence, if the word 'game' were to be analysed into winning and losing (and other components), it would have to be stipulated that these must be understood in the sense appropriate to games.

A similar point may be made about colours. Whether we describe something as red, for example, will depend on *what* is being described; it cannot be decided by reference to an abstract colour sample. Thus 'Ginger Rogers has red hair. [Yet] if there were a coat of exactly the same shade of colour as Ginger Rogers' hair it would not be a red coat.'[8] And similar points may be made about 'white coffee, white wine, black grapes, red cows, auburn hair, yellow hair, white men'.[9]

Family resemblance is only one of a number of relationships that are contrary to the essentialist model. (We might say that these relationships are themselves related by family resemblances.) In the *Brown Book* Wittgenstein posed the question: 'What do light blue and dark blue have in common?' (BB 134). What makes us apply the same word ('blue') to these distinct shades of colour? This is perhaps a more striking illustration of the point that 'explanations come to an end', than the example of the word 'game'. Someone who is asked why he describes certain activities as games will not, after all, be stuck for an answer. He will mention appropriate features that are recognised as reasons for calling something a game. (This is not to say that he would produce necessary and sufficient conditions.) But what is he to say when faced with the question about light blue and dark blue? The word 'blue' is not associated with appropriate features, as the word 'game' is. It is true that there are intermediate shades between light blue and dark blue, but these do not constitute a 'network of overlapping similarities' (PI 66), as in the case of family resemblance. In this case, it seems, explanations do not even begin; we cannot begin to explain why we use one word ('blue') just for *this* range of colour, and, in general, why our colour concepts are grouped as they are.

Another remarkable feature of language is that of which the word 'high' is an example. Wittgenstein, as we saw (p. 70), pointed out that this may refer to an object of hearing (high notes) as well as an object of sight; but, we may wonder, what do high notes and high buildings have in common? Such uses of words are extremely common. The word 'sweet', for example, is used of various objects other than foods (for example, a sweet child). A knife may be sharp or blunt, and what someone says may be sharp or blunt (but in the latter case the terms are not opposed as in the case of knives). Some of these usages are shared by different languages, others are not. (The French 'doux', 'doucement' is an interesting example.) Wittgenstein also mentioned 'a *deep* sorrow, a *deep* sound, a *deep* well' (BB 137); and in another passage he imagined someone saying 'I heard a plaintive melody', and posed the question: 'Does he hear the complaint?' (PI p. 209). In one of his lectures he told an amusing story which shows that he was struck early by this aspect of language.

> When I was a boy I was bothered in listening to birds, because it obviously isn't *singing*. Finally someone said to me, 'All right, don't call it singing, call it something else'. And soon I could listen to birds and enjoy it. (*Philosophical Investigations*, 1984, p. 104).

However, as he came to see later, it is not a trivial, 'verbal' matter that we use these words as we do. The word 'singing' is the one we *want* to use in speaking of the calls of birds (or rather, some birds); and similarly with the other examples. And yet one might have thought that the differences between the instances are far greater than any similarities that could be mentioned.

Among the examples I have given, there is considerable variety, and a good deal more might be said about these and other examples. They are all, however, cases in which 'explanations come to an end'; and from an essentialist point of view, they are even more baffling than the case of family resemblance. These uses of language should not be confused with metaphors, of the kind for which there is a ready explanation and a 'literal' substitute – such as 'sift' in 'sift the evidence' or 'head' in 'the head of the company'. There is no way of replacing, say, the words 'high' or 'plaintive' by 'literal' equivalents, in the examples given above; nor are they to be *explained*, as in the case of the metaphors.

This assertion is sometimes greeted with incredulity; it is thought that there *must* be an explanation, that otherwise these words could not be used as they are; and one may feel a strong urge to produce such explanations. Thus it is sometimes claimed that a plaintive melody resembles the voice of a person who complains. But really the resemblance (where it exists at all) is no better than that between, say, a person singing and a chaffinch 'singing'. It would be just as reasonable to say that there is *no* resemblance, and perhaps a Martian would be baffled by our usage. Similarly, I have heard it said that an object dropped into a deep well would make a deep sound, that someone in deep sorrow would speak with a deep voice, and so on. But it is easy in all these cases to produce counter-examples, or alternative 'explanations' that would support a contrary usage.

The point of these examples (as in the case of family resemblance) is not to deny that there may be historical or psychological explanations of these usages, which might perhaps be unearthed by linguists or other scientists. Our issue is about the 'justifying' kind of explanation that belongs to the *logic* of our language. It is a question of whether someone who uses words in these ways must be able to justify his usage by producing explanations. It is in this sense that, if Wittgenstein is right, 'explanations come to an end'.

C. VERBAL EXPLANATION: A MATHEMATICAL INSTRUCTION

How, asks Wittgenstein, 'should we explain to someone what a game is?' He replies: 'I imagine we should describes *games* to him, and we might add: "This *and similar things* are called games." And do we know any more about it ourselves?' (PI 69). But this method will only work if the learner understands the word 'similar' in the right way – so as to include, more or less, what most people would regard as games, and exclude what they would not. And this understanding is not itself explained by the explanation he has been given.

The use of language, Wittgenstein reminds us, is not like 'operating a calculus according to definite rules' (PI 81). But what if it were? Wittgenstein's remarks about language are often interwoven with remarks about the operation of rules in mathematics. In PI 185 he considers the case of a learner who has been taught the meaning of '+2', with examples and tests up to 1000. He is now asked to continue the series '+2' beyond this number. To our surprise he writes: '1000, 1004, 1008, 1012'.

> We say to him: 'Look what you've done!' – He doesn't understand. We say: 'You were meant to add *two*: look how you began the series!' – He answers: 'Yes, isn't it right? I thought that was how I was *meant* to do it.' – Or suppose he pointed to the series and said: 'But I went on in the same way.' (PI 185).

The case of continuing a series 'according to definite rules' is not, after all, so different from understanding the instruction 'and similar things' in the case of games. In each case we rely on an understanding that should come naturally to the learner, as it would to ourselves; an understanding that is not itself explained by the explanation that has been given to him.

Commentators on this and similar passages have pointed out that some mathematical formula can always be found for a series of numbers, however irregular it may appear to be. Thus it might turn out that the learner in Wittgenstein's example went on 'in the same way', in accordance with an unexpected formula. In that case the misunderstanding might be removed by a more exact specification of the formula that was intended. But Wittgenstein's point is not about mistaking one formula for another; it is about what is involved in understanding any *one* formula. In the quoted section he supposes simply that it 'comes naturally' to the learner to understand the instruction '+2' in the way he did; as it might come naturally to someone, unlike ourselves, to react to the gesture of pointing 'by looking in the direction from finger-tip to wrist' (PI 185).

It may be thought that the instruction could be made foolproof by using a suitable formula. According to Michael Dummett, it would make all the difference if 'the training was not given only by example, but made use also of an explicit formulation' (Michael Dummett, *Truth and Other Enigmas*, 171). But this reaction is anticipated by Wittgenstein in the very next section, in which an explicit formulation is put forward. 'What I meant', he has his bewildered interlocutor say, 'was that he should write the next but one number after *every* number that he wrote'; and from this all the subsequent steps should follow. 'But', comments Wittgenstein,

> that is just what is in question: what, at any stage, does follow from that sentence. Or, again, what, at any stage, we are to call 'being in accord' with that sentence (PI 186).

It may be thought that the word 'every' ('after *every* number') must exclude any possibility of misunderstanding. But this word itself has to be learned in particular situations, and its application in other contexts is not determined in advance – except in so far as the learner catches on to what will be expected of him in using this word. We, no doubt, would find it absurd to think that what 'follows from that sentence' is that one should write '1000, 1004, 1008' and so on. But that we find it absurd is a fact that is not explained by the sentence. A formula does not explain why we react to the formula as we do.

Again, it may be thought that Wittgenstein's example is inconceivable because the intended numbers would follow, as we might say, in a 'purely mechanical' way, so that only one outcome would be possible. 'A machine can follow this rule; whence does a human being gain freedom of choice in this matter which the machines does not possess?' (Dummett, 171–2). But Wittgenstein is not saying that we have freedom of choice in this matter. Of course, if I am told to 'write the next but one number after every number', then I must write '1000, 1002 . . .', and not behave like the man in the example. But Wittgenstein's concern is about the nature of this 'must'.

It is true that a machine can be programmed to follow the instruction '+2'; and then we would expect it to write '1000, 1002. . .', just as a normal person would. But this result would not daunt the man in Wittgenstein's example, for he would reply that the machine *ought* to be writing '1000, 1004. . .'! Perhaps he would ascribe its 'failing' to a mechanical fault or a fault in the programme; and he might assure us that if *he* were in charge, these faults would be corrected.

Asked why I am writing '1000, 1002 . . .', I can justify what I do by reference to the instruction I was given. But what if I were asked *why* I interpret the instruction in that way and not the way described in Wittgenstein's example (or some other)? Perhaps I could justify my interpretation by appealing to some further rule or principle. But what if the same question were raised about my interpretation of the latter?

> If I have exhausted the justifications, I have reached bedrock, and my spade is turned. Then I am inclined to say: 'This is simply what I do'. (PI 217).[10]

D. MENTAL EXPLANATION: 'THE MYTH OF MENTAL PROCESSES'

I

It may be thought that the person in Wittgenstein's example was wrong because what he did was contrary to what the teacher *had in mind* when he gave the instruction. 'But I already knew, at the time when I gave the order, that he ought to write 1002 after 1000' (PI 187). 'Certainly', replies Wittgenstein, 'and you can also say you *meant* it then; only you should not let yourself be misled by the grammar of the words "know" and "mean"'. These words may seem to imply that the correct answer was already in existence, in the teacher's mind, when he spoke. But was it?

> you don't want to say that you thought of the step from 1000 to 1002 at that time – and even if you did think of this step, still you did not think of other ones. When you said 'I already knew at the time . . .', that meant something like: 'If I had then been

asked what number should be written after 1000, I should have replied "1002"' (PI 187).

A similar point is made in the *Brown Book* about what someone meant when he made a remark.

> Someone says 'Napoleon was crowned in 1804'. I ask him 'Did you mean the man who won the battle of Austerlitz?' He says 'Yes, I meant him'. – Does this mean that when he 'meant him', he in some way thought of Napoleon's winning the battle of Austerlitz? (BB 142)

At first sight it may seem inconceivable that one could have *meant* such and such a thing unless something to that effect had been in one's mind at the time. But this becomes less plausible when we consider that one would answer 'yes' to an indefinite variety of questions of the form 'Did you mean . . .?'. For any belief, however trivial or remotely connected, that I happen to have about Napoleon, would lead me to answer 'yes' to this question. And while I may perhaps have been thinking about the battle of Austerlitz when I spoke, I can hardly have been thinking of all those other beliefs when I spoke – any more than the man in the previous example can have been thinking of all the steps that followed from '+2'. We must also consider negative beliefs. In another of Wittgenstein's examples, 'someone says to me: "Show the children a game"', and I teach them to gamble with dice (PI Part I, p. 33). The other person says 'I didn't mean that sort of game'. But 'must the exclusion of the game with dice have come before his mind' when he made his request? The statements 'When I spoke, I meant X' and 'While I spoke, X was in my mind' are statements of very different kinds; and each may be true without the other. Hence it is a mistake to think that what a person meant by a word or an instruction depends on what was in his mind at the time of speaking.

But what makes the difference between meaning and merely saying, understanding and merely hearing? What is it that makes certain sounds or marks on paper into language? How does a person mean one thing rather than another? It has been thought that these and similar questions must be answered by reference to mental entities or processes occurring at the time of speaking, hearing or reading.

'I am not merely saying this, I mean something by it.' – When we consider what is going on in us when we *mean* (and don't merely say) words, it seems to us as if there were something coupled to these words, which otherwise would run idle. (PI 507)

The earlier Wittgenstein, as we saw in Chapter 2 (p. 8), held that language is used for the expression of thoughts (though he did not enlarge on this). Thomas Hobbes had declared, much earlier, that 'the general use of speech, is to transfer our mental discourse, into verbal; or the train of our thoughts, into a train of words' (*Leviathan*, (Fontana, 1962) 74). And according to Locke, 'words in their primary and immediate signification stand for nothing but the ideas in the mind of him that uses them' (*Essay*, 3.2.2).

These mental theories have implications for the *justification* of speech – for what it is to speak correctly and honestly. If speech is the expression of something existing in the mind, then the standard of correctness must lie there. Hence, 'when anyone uses any term', he would be well advised to keep the 'idea, which he makes it the sign of . . . , steadily annexed during that present discourse' (Locke, *Essay*, 'Epistle to the Reader'). Locke's successor, Berkeley, agreeing with him in regarding ideas as the primary materials of thought and knowledge, resolved, when he was engaged in serious thinking, to do without words (or 'names'), and think directly in ideas. 'I shall endeavour to take them bare and naked into my view, keeping out of my thoughts, so far as I am able, those names which long and constant use hath so strictly united with them' (*Principles of Human Knowledge*, Introduction). In our own time, one of the great advocates of good writing advised those who would follow his example to 'let the meaning choose the word, and not the other way about' (Orwell, *Collected Essays*, Secker & Warburg, 1961, 366). One should 'get one's meaning as clear as one can through pictures or sensations', after which 'one can choose . . . the phrase that will best cover the meaning'.

Wittgenstein attacked the mental theory in a number of ways. He reminds us of what actually happens when we speak and listen; draws attention to logical discrepancies between meaning and mental processes; brings out implausible consequences of the theory; and shows that its explanatory force is an illusion.

It is sometimes thought that Wittgenstein was trying, like thinkers of a behaviourist persuasion, to deny or question the reality of mental processes.[11] But this is far from the truth. He was, on the contrary, fascinated by these phenomena, and explored them in detail in many of his writings, notwithstanding his attack on what I have called 'the mental theory'. One case to which he drew attention was that of 'trying to find the right expression'. In such cases we may well feel – in accordance with Locke's and Orwell's conception – that there is *something there*, prior to the word, and that this something is what we really mean. But how are we to understand these cases?

> What happens when we make an effort – say in writing a letter – to find the right expression for our thoughts? This way of talking compares the process to one of translating, or describing: the thoughts are already there (perhaps were already there in advance), and we are merely looking for their expression. . . . But so many different things can happen here! – I surrender to a mood and the expression *comes*. Or: a picture occurs to me and I try to describe it. Or: an English expression occurs to me and I try to think of the corresponding German one. . . . (PI 335)

These and other things may be going on in my mind in such a case. (If the search is difficult, then I may be conscious of a feeling of *tension*, more than anything else.) But what is needed to support the mental theory is the existence of something *suitable* in my mind – something to which the right expression, when I find it, will correspond. Now it may be thought that the thing in question would be a suitable *thought* (or 'mental discourse', as Hobbes put it). But Wittgenstein asks: 'What did the thought consist in, as it existed before its expression?'. If the thought consisted in words, then we must ask how *these* words have meaning. If the meaning of spoken words requires explanation at a deeper level, must not the same apply to the meaning of the thought words?

Another view is that what exists prior to the expression is an image or set of images – these being wordless. 'A picture occurs to me', as Wittgenstein put it. But can a picture (or mental image) be, or be equivalent to, the meaning I express in words? As we saw in Chapter 2, one of the difficulties of the picture theory of language was that pictures are not determinate in the way that sentences are. A picture of a boxer standing in a particular way may be taken to mean how one should stand, how someone did stand, and so on (p. 29). And, in general, any given picture, or set of pictures, could be taken to correspond with any number of different sentences. Hence, even if there is a picture in my mind, this could not account for what I express when I use language; and even 'if God had looked into our minds, he would not have been able to see there whom we were speaking of' (PI 217). There is nothing 'there', in my mind or anywhere, that constitutes my meaning.

It might be thought that in this matter mental pictures are different from physical ones – so that the former *can*, somehow, represent one and only one meaning. 'Thus', as Wittgenstein wrote in the passage quoted earlier (p. 30 PI 389), 'one might come to regard the [mental] image as a super-likeness' or 'super-picture' (*Überbildnis*), since it 'must be more like its object' than any ordinary picture could conceivably be. But to postulate a picture with magical powers is not to put forward an explanation.

We must also remember that the case of trying to find the right expression is a rather special phenomenon. Most of the time we make no such effort, but simply say what we want to say. Similarly, the occurrence of relevant thoughts or images while (or before or after) we speak is rather unusual (though this may vary with different people). A person who is day-dreaming is more likely to have thoughts and images passing through his mind than one engaged in practical conversation.

It is a feature of the mental theory that meaning is conceived as something separate or separable from saying – something that is 'coupled to the words' but separable from them, in the way that speaking and having a mental image are separate. Now calling up an image (or saying the words of a sentence in one's mind) is something we can do at will. But can *meaning* be done at will? 'Make the following experiment: say "It's cold here" and *mean* "It's warm here". Can you do it? – And what are you doing as you do it?' (PI 510). I could, if I chose, call up an image of warmth (or say the words 'It's warm' in my mind), but this would not affect the meaning of my words when I say 'It's cold', or anything else; this meaning is not subject to my choice.

Wittgenstein returns again and again to the 'myth of mental processes' (Z 211) – the belief that meaning, understanding and so on require, or consist in, something that exists or existed in the mind of the person concerned. So tenacious is this belief that some commentators have found it impossible to take Wittgenstein's remarks at face value. According to Saul Kripke, Wittgenstein was really putting forward 'a new form of scepticism' about meaning;

namely, that 'there can be no such thing as meaning anything by any word' (*Wittgenstein on Rules and Private Language*, 60, 55). Now Kripke admits that Wittgenstein, does not describe himself as a sceptic, and does not actually make the denials attributed to him. Why then should it be thought that this is his position? Wittgenstein, says Kripke, holds that 'there was no fact about me that constituted my having meant [one thing rather than another]', and from this it follows that there is no such thing as meaning anything by a word or instruction.

Now as we have seen, Wittgenstein did deny that if the instructor meant '1000, 1002', then he must have been thinking of this step when he gave his order. But this is far from claiming that he did not *mean* this, or that there is 'no such thing' as meaning it. Kripke's 'sceptical' reading turns Wittgenstein's argument on its head. Wittgenstein's point is that my meaning something is *not* 'constituted by a fact about me' (other than, of course, the fact that I mean it). There is nothing (apart from that fact itself) in or about me, that 'constitutes' my meaning what I mean. Kripke's reading, by contrast, is that since there is no such (additional) fact there can be no meaning. He thus assumes the very point that Wittgenstein is concerned to deny – unable to believe, apparently, that the latter really meant what *he* said! The result is indeed a 'new form of scepticism', but not one to which Wittgenstein would subscribe.

Some care is needed in the use of such expressions as 'no such thing' (as in the quotation from Kripke). Wittgenstein may be said to have held that there is no such *thing* as meaning – no entity or process that has to be there in a person's mind (or elsewhere) in order for him to mean X or Y. But the view that there is *no meaning* ('no such thing as meaning' in *that* sense) is not one that can be attributed to Wittgenstein. His aim was to remove misconceptions about meaning, and not to deny its existence.[12]

II

Wittgenstein's attack against the mental theory also concerns such concepts as memory and recognition. It is often thought that memory, in particular, requires the use of images which are brought into play to enable us to remember or to recognise. There is a vivid statement of this view in the writings of Augustine (*Confessions*, Book X). He speaks with wonder of the 'vast cloisters' of the memory. It is, says Augustine, 'a storehouse for countless images of all kinds which are conveyed to it by the senses' (*Confessions*, 214). He describes how he asks his memory 'to produce whatever it is I wish to remember'. Men may 'gaze in astonishment at high mountains' and other wonders of nature; but, says Augustine, they would do better to marvel at the inner world of memory in which all these things are reproduced. 'I could not even speak of mountains or waves, rivers or stars. . . , unless I could see them in my mind's eye, in my memory. . . .' (Penguin edn, 1961, 216).

How are human beings able to remember? How do we remember, among other things, the meanings of words? In the *Blue Book* there is an example of someone being asked to 'choose a yellow ball out of this bag'. Must he refer to a mental image to enable him to obey these words? 'To see that this is not *necessary*', replies Wittgenstein,

> remember that I could have given him the order, 'Imagine a yellow patch'. Would you still be inclined to assume that he first imagines a yellow patch, just *understanding* my order, and then imagines a yellow patch to match the first? (BB 12).

If we must postulate an image to account for the original ability (to select a yellow ball), then we ought to do the same for the ability to call up a suitable image; and so forth. If on the other hand, the latter is not in need of explanation, then we may as well say the same about the former.

This is not to deny that sometimes, in cases of difficulty, we do call up an image, and this seems to help us to remember. (Some people are more inclined to do this than others.) 'Often, if asked, "Do you know what a robin is?", you may, in order to be certain that you know, call up a picture before your mind.' But how can such a picture bestow certainty? Is it not itself in need of certification? 'But now I ask, "Do you know what you are calling up?" Or will you call *anything* that comes to mind a robin?' (Rush Rhees, Notes of Wittgenstein's Lectures, 1936; *Philosophical Investigations*, 1984, p. 136; cf. PI 239, 386).

It may be thought (as in the case of language-learning, pp. 61–2) that our abilities in memory and recognition are to be explained by reference to the brain. It is true, of course, that they are causally dependent on the brain; and some of them have even been correlated with certain areas and processes of the brain. But this will not satisfy the demand for explanation that is at issue in Wittgenstein's discussions. The question 'What makes you certain this is a robin?' demands a logical and not a causal explanation. The person questioned is to tell us what evidence, if any, *he uses* in reaching his verdict. But brain-processes are not available to be used in this sense.

Failure to distinguish between causal and logical explanation is liable to lead to the production of pseudo-explanations. This is especially striking in attempts to explain animal behaviour. 'So it seems', writes a naturalist, 'that many migrating birds must carry in their brains a clock, a compass and the memory of a map. Certainly a human navigator would need all three. . . .' (David Attenborough, *The Living Planet*, 186–7).

It is true that a human navigator would need such equipment. He is not endowed by nature to undertake such journeys; and his ability to do so might be *explained* by reference to this equipment. But this explanation will only work if we can assume that he has (or had) these instruments available for inspection (in his hands, for example). It would be a different matter if they were said to be in his brain. Again, he must use the instruments in a rational way, so that he could explain (justify) his actions by reference to them. But this would not be so with 'instruments' located in his brain, or in the brain of the bird. Finally, a person can be *taught* how to use a compass and so on; and then his ability can be explained in the same terms in which it was taught to him. But this, again, is not so with the instruments in the brain. It is thought that by postulating such instruments in a bird's brain, its behaviour can be made intelligible in the same way as that of a human navigator. But this hope is an illusion. An entity in the brain, whether animal or human, cannot serve to yield this type of explanation.

From what we know of the brain, it is most unlikely that a clock or compass, in the literal sense, should be discovered there. But what if they were? A comparable case is that of the fluid in the inner ear which enables us to keep our balance. This might well be described as a 'spirit level', since it works in a similar way to ordinary spirit levels, as used by builders. It may be said that 'we use' an inner spirit level to keep our balance. But this 'use' is different from that of the builder. The builder's instrument is available for inspection, and he uses it accordingly. He can teach others how to use it, and he can explain (justify) what he does by reference to the instrument. But these ideas have no application to our 'use' of the inner spirit level – any more than to the processes of digestion or other happenings in the natural world. And the same is true of entities in the brain.

III

Again and again, with many different examples, Wittgenstein points out that mental processes are neither necessary nor sufficient for meaning, remembering, recognising and so on. Now a moment's reflection will show that the cases in which we are conscious of a relevant image or thought are in fact rather rare. And the idea that *all* of our speech is accompanied by a stream of corresponding imagery may strike us as quite implausible. Again, while there is a kind of 'remembrance of things past', in which (for some people at least) imagery plays a large role, this is not something of which we are conscious in other, more commonplace cases of remembering. It is strange, therefore, that belief in the mental theory should be as tenacious as it is; so much so, that many readers will cling to it in spite of Wittgenstein's remarks and reminders, perhaps resorting to the postulation of images in a realm beyond consciousness (the brain or 'the unconscious'). What is behind this conviction?

A common reaction to Wittgenstein's denials is to ask: But how *can* I remember or recognise without a mental image? How *can* a bird find its way without some kind of map in its mind or brain?[13] It may seem incredible that an ability which can be explained (in the human case) by the *presence* of an instrument or sample should also exist when these are *absent*. A similar difficulty arises in connection with abilities which, in some species, are learned from parents, and in others not. How, it is asked, can the young of some animals find and recognise their food without the parents being there to show them? And how is it that newly fledged cuckoos can make the flight 'back' to Africa, as they do, several weeks before their parents? (I once heard it suggested that perhaps their foster parents show them the way!) Such abilities are, no doubt, a suitable object of wonder. But we should not suppose that the question 'How?' does not arise in the case of species in which the parents *are* present. For in these cases we could ask, with equal justification: how does the young animal know whom, and which behaviour, it is to imitate? And where has it learned how *imitating* is done? (How can that which is *seen* be transformed into something that is *done*?) If these things must be taken for granted, then the same may be said about other abilities. Either way, 'explanations come to an end'.

A human being can often explain his ability to recognise or behave in certain ways by reference to a sample or other equipment. How do I know this is a robin? Because it looks like *this*, I explain, pointing to the picture in my bird-book. How do I know that is the way to go? Because, I reply, this is indicated by the map and compass which I have before me. But what if no such pictures or instruments are present? 'Nothing *makes* me call it red; that is, *no reason*. I just looked at it and said "It is red"' (BB 148). This may seem a very lame reply. It might be compared to that of a mechanic who, unable to find the cause of a breakdown, suggests that perhaps *nothing* caused it. But this is a misleading comparison. For in this case it may be said that there must be a cause, even if no-one has yet found it. But this is not so in the case of 'How do you know?' In this case we are enquiring about reasons that must be *available* to the person concerned, and not causes that may or may not be discovered. But if, in such a case, no reason is forthcoming, then we may be tempted to insist on the existence of something in the mind (or brain) which would account for the knowledge in question, in the same sort of way.

Wittgenstein sometimes made the point that the mind is especially suitable for this (supposed) role, because of the sense of mystery with which it is regarded.

> These . . . activities seem to take place in a queer kind of medium, the mind; and the mechanism of the mind, the nature of which, it seems, we don't quite understand, can bring about effects which no material mechanism could. (BB 3).

One of his ways of dealing with the mental theory was to suppose that the mental entity (such as an image) were replaced by a straightforward physical one.

> If the meaning of a sign [or word] . . . is an image built up in our minds when we see or hear the sign, then first let us [replace] this mental image by some outward object seen, e.g. a painted or modelled image. (BB 5).

Such an image would not do the trick, because its meaning could itself be questioned. But we may feel that the *mental* image would have special powers. 'The [mental] image must be more like its object than any picture. . . . Thus one might come to regard it as a super-likeness' (PI 389; a longer quotation was given on p. 30). This magical power would not belong to the physical image. 'It was', he says to his imaginary partner, 'just the occult character of the mental process which you needed for your purposes' (BB 5).

Contrary to what is sometimes alleged, it was far from Wittgenstein's intentions to deny or cast doubt on the existence of mental processes – mental images, words or melodies running through one's mind, the experience of trying to find the right expression. His aim was to clarify the role of these phenomena, and not to question their existence. Now it is clear that *thinking* is an important aspect of human life. We ask one another what we think about this or that, we think about absent friends, and we think things over before taking a decision. And some of this thinking is indeed done silently, 'in the mind'. But what is the importance of this kind of thinking? 'Imagine people who could only think aloud. (As there are people who can only read aloud.)' (PI 331).

Could there be a human society in which people can only think aloud? Imagine an anthropologist living with a remote tribe for some considerable time. He learns their language, makes a careful study of their customs, religion, beliefs about the world and so on partly by questioning and partly by observation. In short, he becomes thoroughly acquainted with their language and way of life. After some time it occurs to him that he has never heard anyone speak of an 'inner' life of thoughts and images. (He has never heard them use language which seems to need translating in these terms.) When he questions members of the tribe about the inner life he meets with incomprehension. Using his professional skill, he puts the matter in various ways, but still meets with a total lack of understanding. How can an image (like that one standing there?) be 'in the mind'? How can a thought be 'running' through a person's mind (or head)? (Running? What a strange word to use in this connection.)

This is not a supposition about thinking in the sense of *believing* (believing – thinking – that such and such is the case). Whether there can be a human society without *this* concept is an altogether different question. We may assume that our anthropologist has not had any difficulty about the existence of beliefs in that society, or about attributing beliefs to particular people in it. Similarly, we may assume that *imagining*, in the sense of supposing, has a place in that society. A person can be asked, for example, to suppose (imagine) that *p* were true – perhaps in order to consider what he would do if it were. But this kind of imagining, again, does not (if Wittgenstein is right) require the existence of mental images.

It appears that these mental processes, fascinating as they are, are not essential to the human condition, in the way that believing, supposing, meaning, and understanding are. In a society in which 'people can only think aloud', human life might go on in much the same way as elsewhere. But the existence of *silent* mental processes has had momentous consequences for the history of human thought, affecting our ideas of what we are and what is important to human life. One might almost think that a Cartesian demon had planted these processes in us, with the aim of deceiving us about these matters.

5

Language and the Privacy of Experience

A. THE 'PRIVATE LANGUAGE' ARGUMENT

The person who wrote '1004' in Wittgenstein's example represents a challenge to ways of going on that we regard as self-evident. But according to Wittgenstein, there is no way of justifying our procedure to a person for whom another way is self-evident. In the end we can only say *'that's how we do it'* (RFM 199); and the same is true of uses of language in general. It is a fact of human nature that we agree in using language in such and such ways, without question. This is part of the 'framework' of our language.

> Disputes do not break out (among mathematicians, say) over the question whether a rule has been obeyed or not. People don't come to blows over it, for example. That is part of the framework on which the working of our language is based (for example, in giving descriptions). (PI 240)

But, it may be asked, is there no right and wrong in this matter? Is our way of going on no more correct than that of the person who wrote '1004'? 'So are you saying that human agreement decides what is right and what is wrong?' (PI 241); cf. p. 226 and Z 428ff). Wittgenstein replies:

> It is what human beings *say* that is right or wrong; and they agree in the *language* they use. This is not agreement in opinions but in form of life. (PI 241).

If people say that the earth is flat, for example, then what they say is wrong, and we are right if we disagree with them. But if the word 'flat' is to have any meaning at all, then there must also be agreement, at a more fundamental level, in the use of this word in describing straightforward objects (such as tables or landscapes) as flat or not flat (and similarly with the words 'plus' and 'two'). Thus, 'if language is to be a means of communication there must be agreement not only in definitions but also (queer as this may sound) in judgements' (PI 242).

Wittgenstein's position has a negative and positive aspect. The negative aspect is that justifications 'come to an end'. Within the 'framework', we can justify a given assertion or denial; but not beyond that. The positive aspect is that there must *be* such a framework, such an agreement in judgements, if language is to do its work at all. Language is, therefore, essentially a communal activity.

Having reached this conclusion, Wittgenstein proceeds to test it by introducing the ideas of a 'private' language. Could there not be a language in which one communicates with oneself? If so, then the conclusion about public agreement will be false.

Wittgenstein's discussion proceeds at two levels. First he considers whether some of our actual language is private in the relevant sense. When a person speaks of his own sensations, for example pain, is not his meaning private? In this case it may seem that correct usage is not dependent on a consensus, but on an individual's recognition of his own sensation. But Wittgenstein claims that the meaning of 'pain' is connected with certain behaviour, so that correct usage of this word is not a private matter but subject to the check of others. Secondly, we are asked to consider a fictitious example, in which someone uses a private sign for 'a certain sensation', and writes this in a diary 'for every day on which [he has] the sensation' (PI 258). Wittgenstein brings out the difference between this procedure and what we normally regard as language.

The issue should also be seen in a wider context. In PI 244 Wittgenstein asks: 'How do words *refer* to sensations? . . . How is the connection between the name and the thing named set up?' Here he reminds us of the view of language that he had introduced in the opening section of his book. 'Every word has a meaning. This meaning is correlated with the word. It is the object for which the word stands' (PI 1). On this view, he continued, there does not seem to be 'any difference between kinds of words'. The rejection of this view is one of the main aims of the whole book, and indeed of Wittgenstein's later philosophy. He now denied that there was anything that 'is' the meaning of a word; and dwelt on the great diversity of kinds of words and language-games in which they are used. These points, as we shall see, are also central to the 'private language' argument.

If there were something that 'is' the meaning of the word 'pain' when I say 'I have a pain', then, it would seem, it could only be the pain itself. And in that case the meaning of the word would be personal to me and not communicable to others; and the correct use of the sentence would depend on my recognition of what I feel and not on any agreement with others. But even if the word-object theory is rejected, it may still be tempting to regard the meanings of sensation-words as private. This may come about through comparing them with words like 'red' or 'apple'. Other people can check my use of the word 'apple' by observing that the objects I call 'apples' are indeed apples; and in this way the meaning of the word is established by public agreement. But my use of 'I have a pain' cannot be checked in this way. It may seem, therefore, that its meaning, and correct use, must be private and personal matters. But, here as elsewhere, Wittgenstein rejects the assimilation of one use of words to another. The way in which sensation-language is used, and is subject to public control, is different from the case of apples; but this does not mean that there is no such control and that, therefore, the meaning is private.

We shall see that the points mentioned so far make up the three main strands of the private language argument. Wittgenstein shows, firstly, how the idea of a private sign (as mentioned above) diverges from what we normally mean by language; secondly, that in the language of sensations (as elsewhere) the meaning of a word is not an 'object for which the word stands'; and thirdly, that although the meanings of sensation-words are subject to public agreement, they are so in a way that is appropriate for them and not for others.

There is also a historical context for Wittgenstein's discussion. The conception of meaning that he rejects is an essential ingredient of empirical philosophy, such as that expounded by John Locke in the seventeenth century. Locke maintained not only that words have meaning by being correlated with an object but that this object is always a mental entity (an 'idea'), known only to the speaker (as quoted p. 78). Wittgenstein, it appears, did not read the works of Locke or Hume; but similar views have been held by many thinkers in the present century, including Russell and Schlick, with whom Wittgenstein was in close contact. This view of meaning is connected with the empiricist belief that all knowledge can be analysed into items of experience, described as 'sensations', 'sense-data', 'ideas' and the like. On this view, we have *sensations* of shapes and colours, tables and chairs no less than sensations of pain; and when we speak about the empirical world we are really speaking of our sensations, and in every case the meaning is private. This is similar to the view, widely held among ordinary people, that one person's 'green' cannot mean the same as another's, and that what we perceive is, necessarily, personal and private to each one of us.[1]

B. THE MEANING OF 'PRIVATE'

Having reached his conclusion, in PI 242, about 'agreement in judgements', Wittgenstein poses the question whether there could not be a language in which a person describes his inner experiences (such as feelings) 'for his private use' (PI 243). Now in one sense this is obviously something we can do in our existing language, in which we can keep private records, for example. Such records, however, *could* be understood by others, even if they are in fact kept private. Similarly, it would not be relevant to mention a private code such as that used by Samuel Pepys in his diary. Even if no-one knew what the code meant, it did mean something that *could* have been stated in the common language. This is not the sort of thing that has been meant in speaking of the privacy of meaning. What was meant was a meaning that could not con-ceivably be rendered into the common language (or subject to 'agreement in judgements'). This is the sort of privacy that Wittgenstein intends to discuss. 'The words of this language are to refer to what can only be known to the person speaking; to his immediate private sensations. So another person cannot understand the language' (PI 243).

Again, Wittgenstein's question is not about the conditions under which language might be acquired. In A. J. Ayer's 'Can there be a Private Language?' we are asked to 'imagine a Robinson Crusoe left alone on his island while still an infant, having not yet learned to speak' (p. 259). Is it not conceivable, asks Ayer, that such a person may 'invent a language', in which he is able to describe the objects and animals around him? Ayer thinks that if the answer is 'yes', then Wittgenstein must have been wrong in what he said about a private language. But Wittgenstein was not making claims about how language might or might not be acquired.[2] 'It is all one to us', Wittgenstein wrote in another discussion, 'whether someone . . . has learned the language, or was perhaps constituted from birth' to react to sentences of his native language as a normal person would (PI 495).[3] We might suppose that the infant Crusoe was similarly constituted, or that language comes to him suddenly, by way of a miracle. It is true that something would have to be said about his *use* of the language, to make the supposition coherent. Many of the normal uses of language would, of course, not exist in the absence of other people. (But the same may be said about the original Crusoe, in Defoe's novel.) Perhaps we may suppose that he uses a kind of language to make a note of the locations and times of ripening of various fruits on the island, and subseqently explains all this to his rescuers. If the explanation is intelligible to them, this would indicate that the *possibility* of public agreement had been there all along (as in the case of the original Crusoe, who continued to use language in his solitary condition).

No doubt further questions may be asked about the language of the infant Crusoe, but Wittgenstein was not concerned to rule out this kind of supposition. He himself puts a case to us, at the start of his discussion, which seems more difficult than that of the infant Crusoe. 'We could imagine', he claims, 'human beings who spoke only in monologue; who accompanied their activities by talking to themselves' (PI 243). But it is far from clear whether this supposition makes sense – whether, for example, such 'talking' could really be talking. But however that may be, Wittgenstein's point is that this is not, so far, a case of private language in the relevant sense; for

> an explorer who watched them and listened to their talk might succeed in translating their language into ours. (This would enable him to predict these people's actions correctly, for he also hears them making resolutions and decisions.)

As long as it is true that someone could, conceivably, translate the private language into ours, it is not private in the sense under discussion; it is no more a counter-example to Wittgenstein's thesis than any private diarist's code that has not so far been translated. The issue is about a kind of meaning that could not conceivably be rendered into the common language.

This is a very stringent requirement, and perhaps it will be thought that Wittgenstein would not have achieved very much in challenging such an idea. However, this is the sort of privacy to which Locke, Russell, Schlick and others have been committed, as we saw. It is also a view of meaning to which many ordinary people are attracted when they think in a philosophical way about these matters. On this view, meanings depend on personal experience, and since (to quote Locke) 'one man's mind could not pass into another man's body' (*Essay*, 2.32.15), we can never really know what another person means.

C. 'HOW DO WORDS *REFER* TO SENSATIONS?' (PI 244)

The words of the private language in Wittgenstein's question 'are to refer' to the speaker's 'immediate private sensations' (PI 243). But what is meant here by 'refer'? 'How do words *refer* to sensation?' (PI 244). He invites us to consider how the connection between words and sensations is made in the course of learning to speak. 'How does a human being learn the meaning of the names of sensations?' In the case of pain, he says, it can be done by connecting words with the natural, pre-verbal expressions of pain.

> Here is one possibility: . . . A child has hurt himself and he cries; and then adults talk to him and teach him exclamations and, later, sentences. They teach the child a new pain-behaviour. (PI 244)

This account of learning is brief and sketchy; but there is no need to say more. What is meant is just the ordinary talk and behaviour which everyone can observe – the natural pain-behaviour, and the natural reaction of adults who talk to the child and perhaps try to help. And out of this develops what Wittgenstein calls 'a new pain-behaviour' – the verbal expression of pain as opposed to 'the primitive, the natural' expression of it.

What the child learns in this situation is to replace one behaviour by another, and not to correlate a word with a private object. (In due course he also learns to speak of the pain of others, and this, again, is not done by correlating the word with a private object.) But if the word does not mean a private object (the pain *itself*, as we may be inclined to say), what does it mean? Is Wittgenstein saying that it means a certain kind of behaviour? 'So are you saying that the word "pain" really means crying?' Someone addicted to the word-object view of language may think that if the meaning is not a private object, then it must be another kind of object, in this case the pain-behaviour. Wittgenstein returns more than once to the charge that he is a behaviourist. 'Are you not really a behaviourist in disguise?', he has his interlocutor ask in PI 307; 'aren't you saying, at bottom, that everything except human behaviour is a fiction?' But Wittgenstein denies the charge. His aim, he says, is to reject 'the grammar which tries to force itself on us here' (PI 304), 'the model of "object and designation"' (PI 293). If we approach the language of sensations with this model fixed in our minds, then we may think that 'pain' is the name of a sensation in the same sort of way in which 'apple' is the name of a fruit. But the connection of pain with the word 'pain' is different. One cannot be taught this word, as one might be taught the word 'apple', by being shown examples; for pains cannot be shown in that sense – though they can be shown, in another sense, by pain-behaviour. What we must do, says Wittgenstein, is to 'make a radical break with the idea that language always functions in one way . . . ' (PI 304).

'But you will surely admit', exclaims the interlocutor, 'that there is a difference between pain-behaviour with pain and pain-behaviour without pain' (PI 304). 'Admit it?', replies Wittgenstein, 'What greater difference could there be?'

> 'And yet you again and again reach the conclusion that the sensation itself is a *nothing*.' – Not at all. It is not a *something*, but not a *nothing* either!

This remark has struck many readers as paradoxical. Of course the pain is not a nothing; it is a comfort, they may feel, that Wittgenstein admits at least this much! But in saying that it is not a something, is he not denying the obvious fact that we do feel pain? Moreover, is it not self-contradictory to say that it is neither a something nor a nothing? Wittgenstein's point, however, is to reject the dichotomy of something and nothing, with its implications that since pain is not a nothing, it must be a 'something' – a sort of object that we have learned to call 'pain', and which we recognise from time to time, in ourselves and in others, as we might recognise a fruit or a colour.[4]

The example of pain was one to which Wittgenstein returned again and again in his writings and lectures. He found here one of the most powerful counter-examples to the idea that 'language always functions in one way'. It is of some interest to see how the new insight first appeared in Wittgenstein's thought. When he returned to Cambridge in 1930, his class there became known as the 'toothache club', from his frequent use of that example. At that time he was still an adherent of the 'verification principle', according to which 'the meaning of a proposition is the method of its verification' (cf. p. 43). But in one of his lectures he questioned how this principle would work with first and third person uses of the word 'toothache', since 'what verifies or is a criterion for "I have toothache" is quite different from what verifies or is a criterion for "He has toothache" ' ('Wittgenstein's Lectures in 1930–33', in G. E. Moore, *Philosophical Papers* (Allen & Unwin, 1959), 307). This being so, he added, must not the meaning of 'toothache' be different in each case? But, he went on, in these cases even the meaning of 'verify' could not be the same; and on a later occasion he came to see that 'there is no such thing as verification for "I have", since the question "How do you know that you have toothache?" is nonsensical'. It was this fundamental difference between the function of statements like 'I have a toothache' and others that led Wittgenstein to question and finally reject the assumption that there is some single model or principle underlying all uses of language – whether the verification principle or the picture theory of the *Tractatus*.

D. 'IN WHAT SENSE ARE MY SENSATIONS *PRIVATE*?' (PI 246)

I

'The verbal expression', says Wittgenstein in PI 244, 'replaces' the primitive behaviour. It is not, therefore, an example of private meaning that 'another person cannot understand'; for if the adult was able to understand the primitive behaviour, then he will also understand the verbal expression that replaces it. But is there not some sense in which sensations are private? 'Only I can know whether I am really in pain; another person can only surmise it' (PI 246). In reply (as we saw in a previous chapter, p. 52), Wittgenstein points out that this is contrary to the normal use of the word 'know'. 'If we are using the word "know" as it is normally

used (and how else are we to use it!), then other people very often
know when I am in pain' (PI 246).

The discussion in these pages is sometimes described as being
about the sceptical problem of 'other minds'. Sceptics have argued
that one can never really be sure of the thoughts and feelings of
others – or, indeed, whether they have any – since they are not
amenable to direct observation. Our knowledge, it is claimed, is
confined to the behaviour that we observe, and anything beyond
that is mere speculation. Now in presenting this view it is
sometimes forgotten that in addition to observing the other's
behaviour, one can also make use of what he *says*. Thus, if I want
to find out whether so-and-so is in pain, I can do so simply by
asking him. This may provoke further sceptical argument, to do
with the possibility of lying. But however that may be, the private
meaning issue that Wittgenstein is concerned about is more
fundamental than these disputes. It is about what (if anything) it
means to ascribe pain to another person, rather than about the
sceptical problems.

From this point of view the statement in PI 246 ('Only I can
know . . . ') is something of a digression. If the statement were
correct, it would not support the view that meanings are private;
for if another person can *surmise* that I am in pain, while I myself
can know it, then we must be using this word with the same
meaning. If, conversely, the meaning of the word were private,
then it would mean something different to each one of us; and
then another person could not even surmise that which I know,
for it would be meaningless to him. The issue is not about greater
or lesser certainty, but about what, if anything, it *means* to ascribe
pain to others.

The objector returns to the attack with another way in which
sensations may be regarded as private. 'Another person can't have
my pains' (PI 253). But would this remark support the view that
meanings are private? We would not say, in general, that a person
must *have* an X, in order to know what the word 'X' means. It may
be true that another person can't have my apple or, to take a
different example, my nose; but it would not follow that he cannot
know what I mean by these words. In these cases, however, we
are dealing with objects that the other can inspect; and he would
be able to see that they are *the same* as others of their kind. And
this is not so in the case of sensations. Yet, as Wittgenstein points
out, the expression 'the same' is also applicable to sensations, in a

sense appropriate to them. 'In so far as it makes *sense* to say that my pain is the same as his, it is also possible for us both to have the same pain' (PI 253).

The fact is that we do speak of different people's feelings as being the same. One person says he gets a jabbing sensation after meals and another replies: 'I know what you mean; I get the same'. When a reporter, some years ago, asked Mrs Thatcher how she would feel fighting an election against Mr Wilson, she replied: 'I expect I shall feel the same as he will, fighting an election against me'. In these and other ways we speak of sensations and feelings as being the same or similar. It is true that the use of 'the same' is not the same here as elsewhere; but, Wittgenstein would ask, why should it be? 'Perhaps a logician will think: The same is the same – how sameness is established is a psychological question' (PI 377). But 'the same' is used in different ways, according to the context. It is one thing to speak of the same apple, another to speak of the same nose, yet another to speak of the same height, or the same number, and still another to speak of the same sensation.

But is there not some sense in which understanding depends on experience? 'Could someone understand the word 'pain', who had *never* felt pain?' (PI 315). Now if understanding means being able to use the word correctly, then there is no reason why such a person should not be able to understand it – at least as applied to others. He would apply the word correctly to them, under the same conditions as ordinary people. Similarly, someone who had never experienced malaria in himself would be able to ascribe that experience to others; and even a man born blind would be able (though only to some extent) to ascribe visual experiences to sighted people.

It is true that, in another sense, experience is an essential condition of understanding. Of someone who has never been in love, we might say 'He doesn't understand what love is', or even 'He doesn't know what the word "love" means'. But these statements should be kept distinct. The first is about 'knowing what it's like', in the sense of having had the experience, while the second is about competence in using the word. If someone uses such a word as 'love' correctly and sensitively in conversation, then he may be said to know what it means. And the same is true (returning to Wittgenstein's discussion) of the word 'pain'.

Again, it may be said that the experience of being in love is indescribable; so that someone who has experienced it cannot describe to others what it is like. Now it is true that such feelings are hard to describe, and there are limits to what is describable. (In this matter a poet may be able to go further than an ordinary user of language.) But this is not to say that a word like 'love' has a private meaning. For in so far as I cannot describe my feelings to others, I cannot describe them to myself either.

It may be thought that in speaking as I have done about indescribable aspects of experience, I am going against Wittgenstein's insistence on publicity. But Wittgenstein's arguments were directed against the idea of privacy of *meaning* – that the meanings of words, or certain words, are private; and not against the private or personal nature of experience. Indeed, once the correlation theory of meaning is rejected (as it was by the later Wittgenstein), there is *more* sense in speaking of indescribable aspects of experience than would otherwise be the case. For according to the correlation theory, my experience (like everything else in the world) would be describable, fully and definitively, by the corresponding names and sentences; but according to the later Wittgenstein's account, there are no such correspondences. This is true, not only of experiences, but of reality in general. Thus the facts of a given situation cannot be *reproduced* by a corresponding piece of language, as would be the case under the picture theory.

II

In his discussion of sensation in the private language argument, Wittgenstein uses pain as his main example. He probably considered that the attraction of the 'private object' view was especially powerful in this case. But the view is also attractive in the case of other feelings. 'But', exclaims the interlocutor in another discussion, ' "joy" surely designates an inner thing' (Z 487). 'No', replies Wittgenstein ' "joy" designates nothing at all. Neither an inner nor an outer thing'. Here again, the point is not, of course, that the word is meaningless, or that there is no such experience of joy, but that the word does not have meaning by standing for a corresponding 'thing'.

In this passage he goes on to distinguish between the 'object' and the 'cause' of a feeling. Such feelings as joy and fear are, he says, 'directed': 'Fear *of* something, joy *about* something' (Z 488).

Someone who says he is afraid or joyful has told us something that is, in a certain sense, incomplete. To understand what he is feeling we need to know the *object* of his fear or joy. (This may of course be evident from the circumstances.) But this is not so in the case of (physical) pain, which is not 'directed' in this sense. And while we may be interested to know the *cause* of a pain, this is not necessary in order to understand what someone is feeling. Again, a person should be able to say what he is afraid or joyful about, but he may very well be ignorant of the cause of his pain. Finally, a person cannot – logically – go on feeling afraid or joyful when he finds out that he was *mistaken* about the object (the danger does not exist, the good news was false); but there is no such logical constraint in the case of pain.

Some feelings, including some 'directed' ones, are attributable to animals, others are not. 'Why can a dog feel fear but not remorse? Would it be right to say "Because he can't talk"? Only someone who can reflect on the past can repent . . .' (Z 518–19). The logical environment of grief also has temporal implications. Thus, while it makes sense to suppose that 'for a second he felt violent pain', 'why does it sound queer to say: "For a second he felt deep grief"? Only because it so seldom happens?' (PI 174). Again, 'love is put to the test, pain not. One does not say: "That was not true pain, or it would not have gone off so quickly" ' (Z 504).

In these and similar passages Wittgenstein brings out the diversity of the logic of sensations and feelings. The private object view does not merely break down, but it breaks down in different ways, when applied to pain and other feelings; and that is because the concept of a feeling is itself multifarious, contrary to the essentialist view of language.

Wittgenstein did not discuss feelings in the *Tractatus*, but an earlier atomist and reductionist, David Hume, held just the kind of view that is here at issue: that feelings are all objects of the same type, existing independently of any 'outer' logical constraints. 'A passion', according to Hume, 'is an original existence. . . . When I am angry, I am actually possest with the passion, and in that emotion have no more a reference to any other object, than when I am thirsty, or sick, or more than five foot high. 'Tis impossible, therefore, that this passion can be opposed by, or be contradictory to truth and reason . . . ' (*A Treatise of Human Nature*, ed. Selby-Bigge (OUP, 1888), 415). (It is curious that Hume should regard *thirst* as having 'no reference to any other object' – as if that sensation did not imply a desire to *drink*.)

E. THE DOUBLE MEANING THEORY

The private language argument is mainly about sensations, but the view that meanings are private has been held about language in general. It results from a combination of the name-object assumption with the view (characteristic of empiricism) that the named objects must be private entities, known only to the person concerned. Thus Locke tells us that words 'can properly and immediately signify nothing but the *ideas* that are in the mind of the speaker' (*Essay*, 3.2.4). Russell (using 'acquainted' in a special sense) claimed that 'when one person uses a word, he does not mean by it the same thing as another person means by it', since 'different people are acquainted with different objects' (LK 195). And Schlick, using the word 'content' in a special way, tells us that when we observe some object, 'every observer fills in his own content'; 'each one has to consult his own experience, thereby giving [his words] a unique meaning' (*Philosophical Papers* p. 334).[5]

But if we are to take seriously the idea that meanings are private, then the fact that people communicate with one another will call for explanation. And indeed, what we find in the works of these and other philosophers is the view that meaning is twofold; so that alongside the private meaning, there is also a shared meaning (or a shared *use*, as distinct from the meaning), which comes into play when people talk to one another.[6] According to Russell, the inter-personal *use* of language would actually be 'impossible' unless people 'attached quite different meanings to their words'.[7] Schlick explains that though 'content' is 'ineffable', there is also something called 'form' or 'structure', possessed by both statements and facts, which is what people communicate to one another. Locke was less concerned about the problem, but the following passage shows that he too was committed to a double meaning view. It would not matter, says Locke,

> if the idea that a violet produced in one man's mind . . . were the same that a marigold produced in another man's . . . . For, since this could never be known, because one man's mind could not pass into another man's body, neither the ideas hereby, nor

the names, would be at all confounded, or any falsehood be in either. (*Essay* 2.32.15)

Such a man, says Locke, would use the words 'blue' and 'yellow' to describe violets and marigolds respectively, just as if 'the ideas in his mind, received from those two flowers, were exactly the same with the ideas in other men's minds'. Thus, although in one way the man's meaning, when he uses these words, would be different from other men's (the 'ideas' for which they stand being different), yet, in another way, it would be the same; there would be (as Wittgenstein put it) 'agreement in judgements', when it came to talking about violets and marigolds.

The double meaning theory may seem to offer a way of accommodating both a private and a shared, public meaning. But is it really possible to distinguish two such meanings? This question was raised in the *Blue Book*, where Wittgenstein considered 'that peculiar temptation to say "I never know what the other really means by 'brown.'"' We might, he suggested

> propose to one who says this to use two different words instead of the one word 'brown'; one word *for his particular impression*, the other word with that meaning which other people besides himself can understand as well.

'If', he continued, 'he thinks about this proposal, he will see that there is something wrong in his conception of the meaning, function, of the word "brown" and others'.[8]

It is indeed hard to see how this proposal could be carried out. Suppose we leave 'brown' as the word that is used for communication with others, and adopt 'X' to stand for my 'particular impression' of brown. It is hard to see how the meaning of 'X' could be anything distinct from that of 'brown'. Suppose that, whenever I describe anything as 'brown', I also mutter 'X' to myself, or write 'X' in a diary. What if someone asked me what 'X' means? I might tell him that it means a 'particular impression' that I have. But what would be particular about the impression? Why would I call it 'X' each time, rather than, say, 'X' alternating with 'Y'? The answer must be that X is the impression I have when observing *brown* things – things which, in ordinary language, I describe as 'brown'. But then 'X' will not be a word that others cannot understand; and to say that I had this impression will mean nothing more or less than that I saw (or thought I saw) something brown.

F. 'ONLY OF A LIVING HUMAN BEING . . .' (PI 281)

I

If we think of pain as a kind of 'private object', then we might try to overcome the difficulty about communication by supposing that each of us has *the same* kind of object before him when he has a pain. 'But if I suppose that someone has a pain, then I am simply supposing that he has the same as I have so often had' (PI 350). But, says Wittgenstein, 'that gets us no further'.

> It is as if I were to say: 'You surely know what "It is 5 o'clock here" means; so you also know what "It's 5 o'clock on the sun" means. It means simply that it is just the same time there as it is here when it is 5 o'clock.' – The explanation by means of *sameness* does not work here. (PI 350)

One might as well, says Wittgenstein, explain the meaning of 'the stove is in pain' by saying that 'the stove has the same experience as I' (PI 350). Thus we are left without any meaning for the ascription of pain to others, if the private object view is correct.

There is worse to follow, however. 'The explanation by means of sameness' does not work in the case of other people; but neither does it work in the case of myself. For how can I say that this – the sensation of which I am now conscious – is the same as that which I described as 'pain' yesterday? And if I cannot, what entitles me to use the same word, 'pain', yesterday, today and tomorrow? These questions must arise if the private object view is correct. According to Wittgenstein, however, we have here a distorted view of the use and meaning of the word 'pain' and a person who asked such questions would merely betray a misunderstanding of this concept. 'If someone said "I don't know if what I have got is a pain or something else", then we would think, perhaps, that he doesn't know what the English word "pain" means' (PI 288; cf. 271). Someone addicted to this kind of view is advised by Wittgenstein to 'get rid of the idea of the private object in this way:

assume that it constantly changes, but that you do not notice the change because your memory constantly deceives you' (PI 207).

Now according to the model that Wittgenstein rejects, 'pain' designates a private something, in the sense in which other words may be said to designate objects (qualities, processes) in the physical world. But if this were so, then there would be no logical restriction on the environment in which a pain might, conceivably, occur. Just as, say, an electric charge might conceivably be present in the most unlikely places, so it would be with pain. This conceptual model has led to widespread puzzles and confusions about the existence of feelings and thoughts in non-human beings. Descartes, for example, was fascinated by the 'conjecture' that animals of all kinds may have thoughts like ourselves. He was reluctant to admit that they do, but confessed that his only reply to the conjecture was that if they did, 'they would have an immortal soul like us' (*Philosophical Letters*, Blackwell, 1981, 208). This, he said, was 'unlikely', because if it were true of some animals it must be possible for others as well; and he could not bring himself to believe that 'oysters and sponges' can think and have an immortal soul. But if, as Descartes held, thought and the soul are entities 'attached' to organs of the body, then there is no reason a priori why they might not be attached to organs of the most unlikely creatures – or, for that matter, to inanimate objects like sticks and stones.

Wittgenstein's position, and its relation to behaviourism, are well expressed in PI 281:

> 'But doesn't what you say come to this: that there is no pain, for example, without *pain-behaviour*?' – It comes to this: only of a living human being and what resembles (behaves like) a living human being can one say: it has sensations; it sees; is blind; hears; is deaf; is conscious or unconscious.

One might say that Wittgenstein's answer to the first question is yes and no. No, because he is not saying, as a behaviourist would, that there is no more to pain, and other modes of consciousness, than certain kinds of behaviour; nor is he trying to minimise the distinction between pain and pain-behaviour. ('Admit it? What greater difference could there be?' (PI 304)) Yes, because he *is* saying that we can ascribe sensations only to beings that are *capable* of behaving in appropriate ways.

These beings are, in the first place, human beings. It is here that the complex language-games of sensation and consciousness have their full application. Here we have the kind of situation that enables us, and compels us, to speak of pain and other feelings, and to respond in certain ways – for example, with feelings of sympathy and a desire to express this in speech or deed. But these language-games cannot be played in the case of inanimate objects such as a chair or a stone (PI 361, 284). If the model of object and designation were correct, then we should be able to ascribe sensations and thoughts to such objects, at least in imagination. But there is no sense in ascribing sensation to objects that cannot behave like ourselves. 'One might as well', says Wittgenstein, 'ascribe it to a number' (PI 284). But 'now look at a wriggling fly and at once these difficulties vanish and pain seems to get a foothold here, where before everything was, so to speak, too *smooth* for it'.

The relevant resemblance to 'a living human being' is a matter of degree. In the case of a fly, the concept can get a 'foothold', but it would not be as extensive a foothold as in the case of, say, a dog, which can engage our feelings in a deeper and richer way than an insect. (The possession of something like a human face is important in this connection.[9]) But the case of the dog still falls far short of that of a fully developed human being. The latter can, for example, be accused of lying or pretence in regard to his feelings and other matters; but can we speak in this way about a dog? If not, is that because we don't know what is going on inside the dog? According to Wittgenstein it is the logical 'environment' that is lacking.

> Why can't a dog simulate pain? Is he too honest? Could one teach a dog to simulate pain? Perhaps it is possible to teach him to howl on particular occasions as if he were in pain, even when he is not. But the environment which is necessary for this behaviour to be real simulation is missing. (PI 250).

Again, 'are we perhaps over-hasty in our assumption that the smile of an unweaned infant is not a pretence?' (PI 249) 'Lying', replies Wittgenstein, 'is a language-game that needs to be learned like any other'.

Although we can (and need to) ascribe sensations to unweaned infants and other suitable creatures, the concepts of lying and pretence have no place here, as they have in the full language-game of sensation that is played among human adults. There are also limits to the kind of pain that might be ascribed. Could we say of a dog, for example, that it has a headache? What would this mean? Under what circumstances would we need to say it? Of a dog that has hurt its head we might (and would, given suitable behaviour) say that it feels pain in (or in that part of) its head. But this would not be the same as speaking of a headache. Perhaps the difficulty here is that we usually ascribe headache to a person because he *tells* us he has a headache, rather than on the basis of non-verbal conditions, such as might also exist in the case of a dog or other animal.

It is sometimes thought that there is a special mystery about animals because we cannot converse with them. Do animals feel pain? 'We can present a stimulus which would be painful to a human and observe the animal's response', write the authors of an introduction to psychology. (D. and J. McFarland, *An Introduction to the Study of Behaviour*, Blackwell, 1969, 21–2.) But can we be sure that the pain – the thing itself – is really there? According to the authors, 'we have no means of knowing whether it consciously experienced pain', because 'we cannot ask the animal'. But what if we could ask the animal? We would be no further forward, because, if the original 'animal's response' – the pain-behaviour – is discounted, then we would have no means of knowing whether the animal understands *the same* by the word 'pain' (and the expression 'consciously experienced') as we do. But on this view, we could not check the meanings of human individuals either. If, however, we reject the misleading model that lies behind these problems, then we can say that the grounds for attributing pain to an animal are of the same kind, and may be no less strong, than those for attributing it to a human being. It is true that a human being can, in addition, use language to express his pain; but this language can only function if the private object model is rejected, and due weight given to the role of pain-behaviour in determining the meaning of 'pain'.

This conclusion has implications for moral questions concerning our treatment of animals. It is sometimes thought that these must be answered on the basis of scientific knowledge about neural processes in the brains or bodies of animals, their DNA genetic material, and the like. Such findings are thought to make it more or less likely (perhaps highly likely – though the matter can never be proved) that animals feel pain, have consciousness and so on.

But these views rest on a misunderstanding of the language involved and, consequently, of our moral duties in this field. When a human being complains of pain and behaves accordingly, we have a duty to do what we can to help. But this duty does not depend on an *inference* (not even a highly probable one) that the person concerned is really in pain (or really conscious); nor is it contingent on the presence of certain neural processes or DNA material inside that person. There are cases in which we do *infer* that someone is in pain, for example if we observe him taking a tablet; and then the duty to help (if any) would be mediated through that inference. But in other cases we *see*, and do not infer, that someone is in pain. And then the moral duty comes directly from this perception and not from any inference. Similarly, we may see that an animal is in pain, and then our moral duty comes directly from what we perceive, and is not contingent on scientific findings (or, beyond these, metaphysical speculations about the animal's mind).

II

It is common nowadays to attribute rational processes to the brain. The brain, we are told, interprets and uses information, works out problems, issues instructions and so on. One may get the impression that the brain is (or contains) a kind of miniature person – or perhaps that it *is* the real person.[10] Another recent trend is to attribute moral qualities to *genes*, as in 'The Selfish Gene'.[11] But brains and genes cannot be said to 'resemble (behave like) a living human being', even to the extent of a fly. The activities in question take place in a logical environment of human motives and interests, such as are observed, discussed and evaluated among living human beings, but not among brains or genes. People behave in selfish ways in appropriate moral situations; they are criticised by others, make excuses and so on. To interpret information is to make it usable for some particular purpose; and similarly with issuing instructions. And these activities, again, are subject to evaluation and criticism in both a logical and a moral sense. An interpretation may be correct or incorrect, suitable or unsuitable for the purpose in hand; and someone may or may not have the right, or qualification, to issue instructions in a given case.

Hence the ascription of such activities and moral qualities to brains or genes must be understood, if at all, in some metaphorical sense. The brain is an organ in which all sorts of complicated processes take place, and some of them, no doubt, are *necessary conditions* of our ability to have and use information, behave in selfish ways, and so on. But to say that X and Y are necessary conditions of Z is not to say that Z is *done* by them; it is, on the contrary, to rule out that idea.

Can machines think? Can they feel pain? Do they have consciousness? Wittgenstein again replies by reference to 'a human being and what is like one' (PI 359–60). Nowadays it is quite usual to attribute thought and intelligence to computers. It is sometimes believed that what matters here is the complexity of the machine, or its performance in dealing with complex problems in playing chess, for example. Sometimes it is asked whether computers match, or can ever match, the complexity of the human brain. But if Wittgenstein is right, the issue does not depend on internal complexity, but on the extent to which the machine's behaviour resembles that of a human being, for example in engaging our sympathies. A machine standing in the corner may not satisfy this condition any more than a stone or a chair would – however great its complexity or powers of problem-solving may be. But we can conceive of artefacts of suitable appearance and behaviour (such as are described in science fiction) which *would* satisfy this condition – which, indeed, would be indistinguishable from our fellow human beings as far as behaviour is concerned. Such beings would (we may suppose) participate in the language-games of thought, sensation and consciousness (including, among others, the language-game of lying) just as we all do; and we would use, and need, this vocabulary in our dealings with them. Whether we would still call them 'machines' is another matter. We may suppose that if we did, they would express resentment – just as a human being would; and similarly if we questioned whether they really felt pain and so on. The ascription of thoughts and feelings to these beings would not depend on the existence of a special something ('consciousness') inside their minds or brains – any more than in the case of an ordinary human being, born of woman.

Another kind of speculation that has fascinated philosophers and others is about the existence of consciousness on other planets. It is conceivable, of course, that conscious beings, resembling ourselves in the relevant ways, exist in other parts of the universe.

(It would not matter if they were little green men, with various exotic features, provided they resembled us, in the relevant ways, to a sufficient extent.) These speculations are intelligible enough, and present no special difficulty as far as philosophy is concerned. It has also been claimed, however, that in other parts of the universe 'conscious experience' may 'occur in countless forms totally unimaginable to us', and 'not describable even in the most general experiential terms available to us' (Nagel, 'What is it like to be a bat?' in *Mortal Questions*, Cambridge University Press, 1979, 166, 170).

Now this might seem reasonable if we thought of 'conscious experience' as some kind of inner object, of which each of us has a private sample. (But in that case, the consciousness of other human beings on *this* planet would also be 'totally unimaginable' to us – each one of us – and there would be no need to talk about other planets.) But consciousness and experience are not inner objects; and when we talk about beings having such and such feelings or experiences, we are talking about something that is manifested in ways we can all recognise. And if these are ruled out, then it makes no more sense to speculate about consciousness on other planets than to attribute it to a chair or a stone.

G. INVENTING A NAME FOR A SENSATION

The word 'pain', if Wittgenstein is right, is not one that only I can understand, because it is connected with the natural expression of that sensation. There are, however, various sensations which do not have a natural expression in the way that pain does. 'Pins and needles', for example, is not identified by a natural, pre-verbal behaviour. It hardly makes sense to ascribe this sensation to a pre-verbal infant. Still, 'pins and needles' is, by whatever means, part of the common language that we all understand. In PI 258, however, Wittgenstein introduces a sign that is not part of that language. 'I want to keep a diary about the recurrence of a certain sensation. To this end I associate it with the sign 'S', and write this sign in a calendar for every day on which I have the sensation'.

We seem to have here a kind of 'private' or 'inner' ostensive definition, which one gives to oneself. 'I concentrate my attention on the sensation – and so, as it were, point to it inwardly' (PI 258). Having given myself this 'private definition' (PI 262, 268), I go on to use the word in accordance with it, in keeping my diary. But can such a definition really work? At first sight it may, indeed, seem to have an advantage over the kind that are given by one person to another. The latter, as Wittgenstein pointed out (see Chapter 4), only work if a suitable know-how on the part of the learner can be assumed, failing which they would be liable to all sorts of misunderstandings. But in the case of the private definition, it seems, the thing I concentrate my attention on is the very thing I mean by the corresponding word; and I could hardly be supposed to misunderstand a definition that I give to myself!

It is easy enough to imagine oneself having a sensation for which there seems to be no suitable name,[12] thinking to oneself 'I'll call it "S" ', and resolving to keep a diary as described in the example. Wittgenstein's question, however, is not whether this can happen, but whether it amounts to a case of naming and a use of language. An act of naming, he argues, does not consist merely in what is done at the time, but also in the consequences. If one person hands money to another, then in suitable circumstances, he will have made a gift. But can my right hand give money to my left hand? The 'further practical consequences', says Wittgenstein, 'would not be those of a gift'; and similarly in the case of the private definition (PI 268). Now one of the consequences of giving a definition is the possibility of a new set of true or false statements. If, for example, I define the word 'sepia' by reference to a colour sample, then it can be used, thereafter, to make true or false statements about objects, depending on whether they conform (to a sufficient extent) to the sample. But does the introduction of the sign 'S' have similar consequences? Wittgenstein objects that when I try in the future to remember what I meant by 'S', there will be 'no criterion of correctness'. 'One would like to say: whatever is going to seem right to me is right. And that only means that here we can't talk about "right" ' (PI 258). Someone who describes an object as sepia may be right or wrong; and to say that he is right would not mean merely that it seems to him to be so. In this case there would be a criterion of correctness – the colour sample – against which his statement could be checked. But this is not so in the case of 'S'.

But is there no right and wrong in the case of 'S'? It might be thought that the answer is simple: the entry 'S', it may be said, will be right if one had in fact experienced S, and wrong if one hadn't. But this answer is useless unless the meaning of 'S' is already established. Without that, what can it mean to say that one had in fact experienced S? To describe *this* statement as right (or true) one would, again, need the distinction between being and seeming which is precisely what is missing from the example, as Wittgenstein points out.

In a further section, we are asked to consider the idea of checking the use of 'S' against a memory image. 'For example, I don't know if I have remembered the departure time of a train correctly, and to check this I call to mind an image of that page of the timetable' (PI 265). Could one not, similarly, call up an imaginary table or dictionary to check one's use of 'S'? No, says Wittgenstein; for 'justification consists in appealing to something independent . . . . If the mental image of the timetable could not itself be *tested* for correctness, how could it confirm the correctness of the first memory?' In the case of imagining a timetable, there exists something independent of the image, in virtue of which the latter can be described as correct (or incorrect). But what would it mean 'to call up the *right* memory'[13] in the case of S?

This section has given rise to a misunderstanding of Wittgenstein's position. It has been thought that his argument is that of a sceptic – as if what is wrong with 'S' is that one's memory might always be mistaken. Against this it is pointed out that sceptical doubts can be raised just as easily about any use of language. For example, the 'test for correctness' of which Wittgenstein speaks in regard to the timetable could itself be subjected to sceptical doubt; and in general, if we ask for the grounds for any assertion, these can in turn be questioned, and so on *ad infinitum*. However, 'we know how Wittgenstein replies to sceptical challenges of this kind: he simply points out that in certain cases we *do not doubt* and our language games go forward on that basis'. Why then should not the same attitude be taken in the case of S?[14]

But Wittgenstein is not, in these pages, arguing about scepticism. He is not saying, for example, that whereas the use of words like 'red' or 'pain' is proof against scepticism, that of 'S' is not. The point is, rather, that whereas the introduction of 'red' and 'pain' into the language has 'practical consequences', that of 'S' has none. Given the shared usage of 'red' among speakers of the language, we can use this word in buying apples, describing sunsets and controlling traffic. But there are no such language-games in the case of 'S'. This point also applies to the language-game of keeping a private diary. Thus I might inform myself, from private notes, that I saw a red sunset six months ago or had stomach-ache last

Tuesday; but I cannot similarly inform myself that I experienced S, because no meaning has been fixed for 'S', and no distinction can be made between a sensation that is, and one that merely seems to be, S.

That the issue is not about the trustworthiness of memory is also brought out by Wittgenstein's remarks, in other sections, about 'pain'. The appeal to memory is, indeed, of no more use in the case of this word than in the case of 'S'; and as far as this is concerned, they stand or fall together. But, as Wittgenstein points out, using the word 'pain' correctly is not a matter of having a reliable memory; it depends on other conditions.

> 'Imagine a person whose memory could not retain *what* the word "pain" meant – so that he constantly called different things by that name – but nevertheless used the word in accordance with the usual symptoms and presuppositions of pain' – in short, he uses it as we all do. Here I should like to say: a wheel that can be turned though nothing else moves with it is not part of the machine. (PI 271; cf. 289 and p. 207)

Is my use of the word 'pain' subject to 'criteria of correctness'? Not if this means remembering correctly what it was that I called 'pain' in the past. 'Correct' in this case means that I use the word 'in accordance with usual symptoms and presuppositions' – for example, when an infant has hurt himself and cries, or when I have hurt myself and show the symptoms of pain in my face or in my behaviour. (This is not to say that these conditions must be present every time.) But these criteria of correctness are not available in the case of 'S'. If they were, then 'S' would not be private; it would be a word that others could learn.

There is, of course, a difference between correctness in the case of 'pain' and correctness in the case of words like 'red' or 'apple'. My use of these words can be checked by noting whether I call apples 'apples', red things 'red', and so on; and this is not so in the case of pain. The conditions ('symptoms and presuppositions') to which Wittgenstein draws attention are other than the pain itself. An object cannot be red without being red, but a person can be in pain without satsifying the conditions mentioned by Wittgenstein, and he can satisfy those conditions without being in pain. However, this does not mean that we cannot (as in the case of 'S') 'talk about "right"'; it only means that 'right' functions differently in the case of different words.

That the issue is not about memory is also apparent if we consider Wittgenstein's treatment of another topic, dreaming.

> Must I make some assumption about whether people are deceived by their memories or not; whether they really had these images while they slept, or whether it merely seemed so to them on waking? . . . Do we ever ask ourselves this when someone is telling us his dream? And if not – is it because we are sure his memory won't have deceived him? (And suppose it were a man with a quite specially bad memory?) (PI p. 184; also see p. 222)

These 'sceptical challenges' do not prevent the existence of dreaming as a genuine language-game. The words used in descriptions of dreams *already have* an established meaning, and this is enough to make them usable in that (rather peculiar) context. The dreamer's memory cannot be verified, but this does not put the meaning of his words in doubt.

H. IMAGINING A USE FOR THE SIGN 'S'

As we saw at the start of this chapter, the supposition of a private language is introduced to test the conclusion previously arrived at, about agreement in judgements. After showing that actual sensation-words like 'pain' are not private in the relevant sense, Wittgenstein turns to the imaginary example of 'S', which is private in a stronger sense. But are we to conclude that the entering of 'S' was no use of language at all? It is sometimes thought that Wittgenstein was here drawing a sharp boundary between language and not language. Some commentators have even claimed that the very supposition of the private diary example is unintelligible.[15] But Wittgenstein's concern, here as elsewhere, is to investigate rather than to eliminate. His aim is to show how this (alleged) use of language differs from normal ones, rather than to draw a sharp boundary. We should hardly expect him to do so, in view of what he says about 'family resemblance' and 'overlapping similiarities', and against the idea of an 'essence of language' (Chapter 4 Section B). As he wrote in an unpublished manuscript, 'Languages: these are, first of all, the languages that are spoken by the nations of the earth; and then we also describe as language phenomena which have similiarities with these' (MS 165, p. 106).

(In a deleted passage he wrote of 'a language that each person speaks only to himself' as such a phenomenon.)

A nice example of Wittgenstein's 'investigative' method is to be found in PI 342, in which he recounts the story of a deaf-mute, who claimed to have thought about such questions as 'How came the world into being?' before he had learned to speak. (The case had been cited by William James, in order to show that 'thought is possible without speech' (PI 342).) Initial reactions to this story will probably differ sharply. Some would regard it as sheer nonsense, while others would accept it as entirely possible. It might be thought that, given the general trend of his argument, Wittgenstein would adopt the first position. But this is not so. His reaction is to draw attention to the difficulties of the example, to the strange questions that would arise here, in contrast to normal cases of memory. (The difficulties are conceptual and not merely probabilistic.) 'Do I want to say that the writer's memory deceives him? – I don't even know if I should say *that*.' The example is far removed from normal uses of the concepts in question, and therefore (concludes Wittgenstein) 'I do not know what conclusions one can draw from them about the past of the man who recounts them'.

Wittgenstein would not, of course, say that the use of 'S' as described in the example above, *is* a use of language; but he does, in a further section, show how easily it can be moved a step nearer in that direction. The relation between these examples and normal uses of language is one of continuity rather than abrupt cut-off. 'Let us', he proposes, 'imagine a use for the entry of the sign "S" ' (PI 270).

> I discover that whenever I have a particular sensation a manometer shows that my blood-pressure rises. So I shall be able to state increases in my blood-pressure without the aid of any apparatus. This is a useful result.

We can easily imagine how, in these circumstance, a diary showing 'S' for some days and not others might be useful to a doctor. And, given Wittgenstein's identification of meaning with use, this would seem to entail that 'S' now has a meaning.

How sharp is the difference between this case and that of the original 'S'? It might be thought that in the new case 'S' only has meaning in so far as it is connected with the condition about blood-pressure; leaving the original 'S' altogether without meaning. 'Here', writes Kenny, ' "S" has a genuine use, but not as part of a private language: it is tantamount to "sensation which means my blood-pressure is rising".'[16] But if this were so, then, instead of 'S', I might as well have recorded 'sensation which means my blood-pressure is rising'. But how, in that case, could it have been (as Wittgenstein supposes in PI 270) a *discovery* that 'whenever I have a particular sensation . . . my blood-pressure rises'? It can only have been a discovery if 'S' did *not* mean merely that.

The relation between the situations described in PI 258 and 270 is one of continuity; there is no abrupt leap from meaningless to meaningful. This can also be seen if we imagine the sequence in reverse. Suppose that one day the correlation described in PI 270 begins to go wrong. I discover that, on a few occasions, I have (or seem to have) sensation 'S' when there is no rise in blood-pressure; and gradually the correlation fades away altogether. Does the sign now become meaningless? At what point did it become meaningless? What if I spoke of 'S' (in accordance with Kenny's account) as being a sensation that *used to mean* that my blood-pressure is rising? (Would that make all the difference?)

Perhaps it will be thought that what makes all the difference is that in PI 270 we have 'a useful result'; that this is what enables us to speak of a use, and hence a meaning, for the sign 'S'. There is, of course, no such useful result in the original example of PI 258. However, 'use', in the sense that is relevant to the meaning of language, should not be confused with usefulness. Among the various uses of language, there are many that could be described as useless. We ask useless questions, exchange useless information, make useless comments, and so on. The uselessness of entering 'S' in the original example is not a reason for denying that 'S' has (in the relevant sense) a use.

Is there, in contrast to the original example, a distinction between right and wrong in the new adaptation? As far as the 'useful result' is concerned,

> it seems quite indifferent whether I have recognised the sensation *right* or not. If we suppose that I regularly identify it wrong, it does not matter in the least. And that just shows that the supposition of a mistake is a mere illusion. (PI 270).

But in that case, is there any need to speak of 'a particular sensation' at all? According to R. J. Fogelin, the correlation that matters is not 'between the occurrence of a private sensation and the rising of my blood-pressure'; it is 'between my inclination to write down the letter 'S' and the rising of my blood-pressure'. He concludes that (according to Wittgenstein) the sign 'S' 'loses all essential connection with a private sensation'.[17] Presumably this would, again, leave the original 'S' altogether meaningless.

But if this were so, then what I ought really to report is not 'a particular sensation', but an inclination to write down the letter 'S'. Yet this case is far less intelligible than that presented in the text. If there is no 'essential connection with a private sensation', then why should I have such an inclination? Is it some kind of neurosis? If *I* were asked why I have that inclination, I would answer, of course, that it *is* connected with a particular sensation; my entries of 'S' being a record of that sensation. It is true that we need to be careful in our understanding of words like 'particular' and 'name' in such a case.

> What is our reason for calling 'S' the name of a sensation here? Perhaps the kind of way this sign is employed in this language-game. – And why a 'particular sensation', that is, the same one every time? Well, aren't we supposing that we wrote 'S' every time? (PI 270)

Thus Wittgenstein draws attention to the limitations of these words in this context. He does not, however, deny that they have any place there.

In certain ways the entering of 'S' – even in the original example – is akin to a use of language. This is not to say, however, that it is a counter-example to Wittgenstein's claim about agreement in judgements, with which the argument began. The claim was that such agreement is necessary 'if language is to be a means of communication'. And the entering of 'S' is not a means of communication – even for the diarist himself.[18]

I. THE NON-PRIVATE CONTEXT

The example of the sign 'S' occurs in a discussion of whether there can be a private language, which no other person could understand (PI 243). But there must be more to a language than just one sign. The point is not merely that a language has many signs (or words), but also that they are interrelated in various ways. A word does not have meaning in isolation. If someone wrote an ordinary English word, say the word 'big', in his diary, we would not know what, if anything, this means. Some grammatical setting is required. Now in the case of the sign 'S', there is such a setting, for we have been told that it is to be the name of a sensation which recurs from time to time. But could this setting itself be stated in the words of a private language? If not, then the meaning of 'S' will be private only in the context of a language that is not private.

> For 'sensation' is a word of our common language, not of one intelligible to me alone . . . . And it would not help either to say that it need not be a *sensation*, that when he writes 'S' he has *something* – and that is all that can be said. 'Has' and 'something' also belong to our common language. – So in the end when one is doing philosophy one gets to the point where one would just like to emit an inarticulate sound. (PI 261)

This is an important section, which puts the whole discussion into perspective. A word, unlike an inarticulate sound, has a certain position in the conceptual system; and this position has to be understood when we define a word or use it as a name. The idea of a private language (or that the language we actually have is private) may seem straightforward if we think in terms of names for particular sensations, colour and the like, and forget about their grammatical settings in the common language. Taking for granted the non-private word 'sensation' (and the wider context in which *this* word has its setting), we can think of fitting a new, 'private' sensation alongside those already in place. A person who is competent in using the word 'sensation', and the names of ordinary sensations, may tell us of a sensation for which there is no ordinary name or description. But the idea of a private *language* is a much more difficult matter. How could such a thing even be discussed? The example of the sign 'S' would not serve as a model, for while that example makes (as I have argued) some sense, it does not show us how the same kind of thing could be done for language in general. We can imagine a private counterpart of the ordinary sensations for which we have names in the common language, which can take its place alongside them; but we cannot, likewise, imagine a private counterpart of *sensation*, which can take its place alongside sensation. And the idea of private counterparts in the case of 'has' and 'something' is, if anything, even more obscure. (By 'private counterparts' I do not mean private entities corresponding to these words, but – even more obscurely! – private entities which stand to what is meant by such a word, in the way in which sensation 'S' is supposed to stand to what is meant by 'pain'.) If these ideas make any sense, it is not one that can be gathered from the example of the sign 'S'. It is, indeed, misleading to regard Wittgenstein's discussion of that example as being about a private *language*.

As we saw earlier (p. 100), the view that language – the language we actually have – is private, has been widely held and had its classic expression in Locke's *Essay*. On this view, words have meaning by standing for entities ('ideas' and the like) in the mind of each speaker. We saw how Locke addressed the problem of whether one man's 'blue' might not mean the same as another man's 'yellow', given that these words stand for ideas imprinted on the mind of each individual in the course of perception. But there is also a passage in which he considered how we get the idea of perception itself. 'What perception is', he wrote,

> everyone will know better by reflecting on what he does himself when he sees, hears, feels, etc., or thinks, than by any discourse of mine. Whoever reflects on what passes in his own mind cannot miss it. And if he does not reflect, all the words in the world cannot make him have any notion of it.[19]

A question that arises here is about the word 'reflection', as used in the quoted passage: are we to reflect on reflection in order to know what *this* word means? And how could we distinguish these mental items, unless we already had the concepts in question? But a more fundamental difficulty is that 'the difference between kinds of words' (PI 1) is left out of account. If one reflection (or introspection) teaches me what perception is, another what pain is, and a third what sensation is, how do I learn the difference in type between these concepts, and their grammatical relation to one another? The private naming procedure would leave us with a kind of grammatical anarchy. There is more to the private meaning issue than is appreciated by those who speculate whether one person's 'blue' might not be another person's 'yellow'. For, as Wittgenstein pointed out in his 'Notes for a Lecture', the speculations would have to be pressed much further. Thus, 'isn't it just as uncertain that I mean by "colour" what they mean as that I mean by "red" what they mean? And the same applies of course to "seeing" . . . ' (in *The Private Language Argument*, ed. O. R. Jones, (pp. 245–6)).

If we are to take seriously the idea of a language that 'another person cannot understand', then we must try to imagine away the grammatical setting which 'indicates the post at which [a] word is stationed' (PI 257, 29), and which manifests itself in the inter-personal language-game. We cannot simply take this for granted in formulating our examples of private meaning. But then it is not clear how such examples could even be offered. One private language philosopher who tried to face up to this difficulty was Schlick. About the private 'content' which was to give 'a unique meaning' to the words of each person (p. 100 above) he wrote:

> there is no sense in asking any questions about it. There is no proposition about content, there cannot be any. In other words: it would be best not to use the word 'content' at all. (pp. 306–7)[20]

But (as Schlick saw to some extent) this is a self-refuting recommendation; for if there cannot be any proposition about content, how can we even understand what is being said here? 'So [to quote Wittgenstein again] in the end when one is doing philosophy one gets to the point where one would just like to emit an inarticulate sound.'[21]

J. CRITERIA AND THE PROBLEM OF 'OTHER MINDS'

I

In the case of the sign 'S', there was, said Wittgenstein, 'no criterion of correctness', and therefore no distinction could be made between right and wrong in the use of this sign. It is sometimes thought that the term 'criterion' plays a crucial role in the private language argument, and the remark 'An "inner process" requires outer criteria' (PI 580) is quoted in this connection. But this remark occurs in an altogether different part of the book, where it is made in connection with feelings of expectation and the like (and not pain). Nothing like it occurs in the private language argument, where, indeed, the word 'criterion' appears only rarely.

Wittgenstein did speak of 'the usual symptoms and presuppositions' which are part of our concept of pain (PI 271). We can tell whether someone uses the word 'pain' correctly, not by observing (*per impossibile*) his 'inner state', but by noting whether he uses it in accordance with these 'outer' conditions. Now Wittgenstein does not (in the *Investigations*) refer to these conditions as 'criteria', and it would not be normal usage to do so. But in any case, what is true of pain is not true of other sensations; nor did Wittgenstein put forward any general claim to this effect. (The short remark quoted above can hardly be taken as such a claim.) In the case of pain the connection with outer conditions is particularly strong and characteristic; but it is not so with other sensations. Such sensations as tingling and 'pins and needles' are only vaguely connected with outer conditions; and such conditions as there are would hardly enable us to determine whether a person is using these words correctly. It has been claimed that we 'recognise that a man has pins and needles when he gets up and shakes a hand or foot'.[22] We may add to this certain causal conditions, say that the hand or foot has been under pressure for some time. It is true that in these circumstances we might guess that the man has pins and needles; but it would be no more than a (reasonable) guess. By contrast, when 'a child has hurt himself and he cries' (PI 244), we are not *guessing* that he is in pain. In the case of such sensations as pins and needles, the main criterion for attributing the sensation to a person is that he *says* he has it. (Accordingly, it hardly makes sense to attribute such sensations to a pre-verbal infant.)

Can we talk about right and wrong in such cases? What would it mean to say that a person is using such an expression wrongly? Well, it could mean that he has not even realised that it is the name of a sensation (if he thought, for example, that 'tingling' is the name of a digestive process). Again, we would say that he is using it wrongly if he used it in place of a word for which there *are* clear outer conditions – such as the word 'pain'. But assuming that this is not so, what foothold will there be for talk about right and wrong on the basis of outer conditions? Suppose that someone uses 'pins and needles' in describing his sensations, but without correlation with causal conditions and behaviour (perhaps he is not inclined to make any particular movements): must we say that he cannot be using these words correctly? It is not clear that we must; nor is there any particular behaviour that would count *against* his having that sensation, as there is in the case of pain. On the other hand, it is true that someone who uses the expression 'pins and needles' would be expected to have some general knowledge of causal and behavioural correlations.

Again, consider the vocabulary that is used for describing a pain (as distinct from saying that we have one). There are jabbing pains, grinding pains, splitting headaches, sharp pains, dull pains and so on. These descriptions are not correlated with distinct causes, or kinds of behaviour. According to Gilbert Ryle, when someone 'describes his pain as a stabbing, a grinding or a burning pain, though he does not necessarily think that his pain is given to him by a stiletto, a drill or an ember, still he says what sort of pain it is by likening it to the sort of pain that would be given to anyone by such an instrument'.[23] But while most people would understand what is meant by a 'stabbing pain', say in the stomach, few would have any idea of what it would be like to be stabbed there by a stiletto or any similar instrument. (In any case, the result would probably not be a stabbing pain.) Nor do we learn this vocabulary in any such way. A child does not learn to describe certain pains as sharp or dull because they have been caused by a sharp or blunt instrument (nor does he cry in a special way, according to the kind of pain). Again, when David Pears speaks of 'pins and needles' as an 'analogical description',[24] he seems to think that we could link the meaning of this description to some action done with pins and needles. But it is not at all clear what this action could be, or how it could produce this sensation. Someone who thought that pins and needles is a sensation produced by pins and needles would, indeed, be confused about the meaning of this expression. (The same would be true of the German 'Ameisenlaufen' – 'ants running'.)

The logical diversity of feelings may be further illustrated by Wittgenstein's discussion, in the *Remarks on the Philosophy of Psychology*, of a 'feeling of unreality'. He tells us how he once had such a feeling. 'Everything seems somehow not *real*; but not as if one *saw* things unclear or blurred; everything looks quite as usual'. But how, in that case, could the word 'unreality' serve to describe his feeling?

> Surely not because of its sound. (A word of very like sound but different meaning would not do.) I choose it because of its meaning. But I surely did not learn to use the word to mean: a *feeling*. No; but I learned to use it with a particular meaning and

now I use it spontaneously like *this*. One might say – though it may mislead – : When I have learnt the word in its ordinary meaning, then I choose *that* meaning as a simile for my feeling. But of course what is in question here is not a simile, not a comparison of the feeling with something else (RPP I/125).

A variety of other examples, from Wittgenstein's writings and elsewhere, might be given, but I hope enough has been said to show that the connection that exists between pain and its outer conditions ('criteria') cannot be generalised to other feelings.[25]

II

Wittgenstein's use of the term 'criterion' has aroused a great deal of critical attention, and some have attributed to him a general theory of meaning based on this term. Thus a recent writer tells us that 'according to Wittgenstein's criterial account of meaning, [a] sentence . . . only has meaning . . . , in so far as it has criteria'.[26] But this 'account of meaning' is not to be found in Wittgenstein's writings, and he would not have subscribed to a claim of such generality.[27]

Another commonly held idea has been that the term 'criterion' was an essential tool in Wittgenstein's treatment of the sceptical problem of 'other minds' – whether one can really know that other people have the thoughts and feelings (for example pain) that one attributes to them. According to a recent commentator, the remark 'An "inner process" requires outer criteria' (PI 580) expresses Wittgenstein's 'sceptical solution' of the sceptical problem.[28] An extensive literature has been generated in trying to establish what he meant by 'criterion', and whether his 'solution' really works. In a recent introduction to metaphysics, we are told of 'the decline of the Wittgensteinian Criterial Argument'. Philosophers, it is said, are again resorting to 'the good old inductive argument' in dealing with the problem of other minds.[29]

What is the Wittgensteinian argument, and what is wrong with it? Is the Wittgensteinian argument also Wittgenstein's argument? The former may be introduced as follows. Faced with scepticism about other minds, we have to consider whether our knowledge-claims can be justified by deduction or by induction. If deduction is the answer, then we cannot go beyond the person's behaviour, since there is no deductive entailment from this to his inner state. (Hence we may have to accept behaviourism.) The inductive answer is the so-called 'argument from analogy', a statement of which was given by Wittgenstein: 'You say you attend to a man who groans because experience has taught you that you yourself groan when you feel such-and-such' (Z 537; cf. 542). He rejected this because 'you don't in fact make any such inference'. Others have rejected it because the inference would be too weak to yield the desired knowledge. The 'good old inductive argument' has never seemed good enough to sceptics.

The 'Wittgensteinian' argument, however, is supposed to provide a *via media* between these bleak alternatives. According to it, the relation between (for example) pain-behaviour and pain is one of 'criteria'. Because of their internal relation to the concept, criteria can constitute evidence that is stronger than mere induction, in such a way as to withstand the sceptic's attack. On the other hand, this evidence is not strict in the manner of deductive entailment, so that the advocate of this view can freely admit – what it would be absurd to deny – that there may be pain-behaviour without pain.

It is thought that Wittgenstein's treatment of the problem is tied up with a special, technical notion of criteria, and that this is of importance for his philosophy of language in general. There has been much argument about what exactly Wittgenstein meant by the term, and it is sometimes held that, according to him, criteria owe their status to rules or conventions. This is thought to put them beyond the reach of sceptical attack, since one cannot doubt the truth of a rule or convention, or of the relevant 'language-game'.

Such, in brief, is the Wittgensteinian argument, which, as we are told, has declined in popularity in recent times. It is safe to say that in some quarters it never was very popular. How, a critic may ask, can the age-old sceptical problems be dissolved by reference to a convention? Of course we can, if we feel like it, agree to say certain words in accordance with rules that we have laid down; this could indeed be some sort of game. But how can this put an end to sceptical doubt? If we tell the sceptic that in this game such doubts are not raised, he may reply that this game is not his game. Again, if we draw his attention to the claim that the criterial relation is neither inductive nor deductive, he will seize on the latter point;

this, he will say, is all he needs in order to press his sceptical doubt.

Now someone who read the *Investigations* for the first time after hearing the 'Wittgensteinian' argument may well be puzzled.[30] Where, he may ask, does the author state the other minds problem, and where does he give the criterial solution? Where does he even say that pain-behaviour is a criterion of pain? I believe that Wittgenstein's position in the *Investigations* bears little resemblance to the 'Wittgensteinian argument'; that his usage of 'criterion' was not a technical one; that he did not use this term to deal with the problem of other minds, and would have been wrong to do so.

It is true that in the *Blue Book* (p. 24) Wittgenstein briefly claimed, or implied, that holding one's cheek is a criterion of toothache. He also, on the same page, raised the question 'How do you know he has toothache?', and contrasted criteria with 'symptoms' – but by reference to a very different example. (The whole passage is rather confused, with several points telescoped.) But this line of thought is not present in the *Investigations*. Wittgenstein's use of 'criterion' in that work is not about pain, nor is it used to deal with sceptical problems.

Did Wittgenstein use 'criterion' in a special sense? The term has been described as a 'Wittgensteinian term of art'.[31] Now Wittgenstein did sometimes introduce words explicitly with a special meaning. This is so with his introduction of 'language-game' in the *Investigations* (7) and the *Blue Book* (p. 17). His introduction of 'criteria' in the *Blue Book* (pp. 24–5) is also of this nature. 'Let us introduce two antithetical terms', he writes. 'To the question. "How do you know that so-and-so is the case?", we sometimes answer by giving *"criteria"* and sometimes by giving *"symptoms"*.' There is, however, no such introduction of 'criteria' in the *Investigations*. The word first appears in section 51, where it is used, *en passant*, in considering what would count as a mistake in following an instruction. ('What is the criterion by which this was a *mistake*?') A few sections later (56) he asks himself: 'What do we regard as the criterion for remembering [a certain colour] correctly?' And in section 185 he speaks of 'the usual criteria' (or 'ordinary criteria') for judging that someone has mastered a series of numbers.

It seems clear that Wittgenstein did not think of himself, in these sections, as introducing a special terminology. It also seems likely that if a reader who was not familiar with the word 'criterion' looked it up in a dictionary, he would have no difficulty in understanding Wittgenstein's meaning (or if he did, it would not be due to the use of this word). The same is true, I believe, of most if not all occurrences of the word in the *Investigations*.

The fact that Wittgenstein does not introduce 'criterion' as a term of art does not, of course, prove that he did not use it so. But how is this to be proved? It is safe to say that his use of it is not grossly or obviously at odds with the normal one. It is sometimes said that he used the word in more than one way, for different kinds of things and with different meanings. But this would not be enough to show that his usage was technical; for such variations may well be part of the normal usage. What is true of other words is true also of this one: the word 'criterion' is not used according to strict criteria.

Is the concept of a criterion one that Wittgenstein *might* have found useful in dealing with sceptical problems? Let us consider its logical features. The concept is frequently introduced by contrast with inductive evidence on the one hand and deductive entailment on the other. 'Clearly a criterial relation is neither factual (in which one thing is *evidence* for another), nor logical (in which one term *entails* another).'[32] But this is not correct. A criterion, or set of criteria, may be adopted for the very purpose of creating such entailment. Thus X, Y and Z may be laid down as criteria for admission to the police force, in the sense that satisfaction of them will *entail* that the candidate is qualified for admission. Again, if, as is supposed in the *Blue Book* (p. 25), a certain condition is accepted by medical science as the criterion of disease D, then whoever satisfies this condition must be said to have disease D.

On the other hand, the word may also be used without this intention. Sometimes we put forward 'a' criterion – meaning that this is one relevant condition; or we may speak of 'the main' criterion or criteria. And if X, Y and Z are laid down as criteria for admission, this *could* mean that though these conditions must be taken into account, their role is to incline rather than to necessitate. It would not be exceptional, therefore, if the 'criteria' for pain turn out to be non-deductive.

But if they do, is this not likely to encourage the sceptic rather than otherwise? It is indeed hard to see why he should be deterred by reference to a non-deductive category of inference. The relevant distinction as far as he is concerned will not be between criteria and mere evidence ('symptoms'), but between those criteria which *are* deductive and those which are not.

It has been thought that the peculiar anti-sceptical power of criteria springs from their characteristic of being 'internal' to a concept. The criteria for pain are, it is said, part of the very meaning of the term; one could not have this concept without being aware of their relevance. They are not like conditions whose connection with pain is merely a matter of empirical fact.

But what is the value of this point in anti-sceptical argument? If we made this point to a pre-Wittgensteinian sceptic, what would be its effect? The sceptic was surely aware that pain-behaviour is part of the normal understanding of the concept.

It has been said that criterial justification is underwritten by 'rules of grammar'.[33] Thus the rules

> 'If somebody moans and holds his injured foot, then he is in pain', or 'People who act like *that* are in pain' can be used to justify the assertion that a particular person is in pain . . . .

But it is a mistake to think that such 'rules' can provide justification for the assertion in question. To try to cast them for this role is already to put a foot on the sceptic's slippery slope. In what circumstances could these rules be used for such a role? Suppose that A and B come across C, who is moaning and holding his foot. A remarks that C is in pain. What if B asked A to justify his assertion? It would be futile for A to cite the quoted rule. If A and B are playing the *normal* language-game, then (unless other factors are present) no further justification can be demanded. If B were to make such a demand, A would be puzzled; perhaps he would respond, in the words of the *Brown Book* (p. 131), 'Don't you see?' But this would be a questioning of the question, rather than an answer to it. A's justification consists in what is there to be seen; and to interpose a 'rule of grammar' between this and his assertion is to distort the language-game. If, on the other hand, A and B are playing a *sceptical* language-game, then citing the rule would be futile in another sense. In that case the sceptic would make his usual, if tedious, claim that nothing short of strict entailment will suffice for knowledge, and that since, as Baker and Hacker readily concede, 'criterial support is defeasible' (p. 110), it is not proof against sceptical challenge. It makes no difference (he will add) if the relation between pain and pain-behaviour is attributed to a 'rule of grammar'.

It is sometimes thought that Wittgenstein's solution, or attempted solution, of the other minds problem, is one of his main contributions to philosophy. Yet it would be difficult to point even to a statement of the problem in his main work, let alone a 'solution' of it by means of criteria.[34] In the private language argument, as elsewhere in the *Investigations*, his main concern is about meaning rather than knowledge; the argument is an investigation into the limits of language. His question, in the Kantian spirit, is 'How is language possible?', rather than the empiricist's 'What can we know?' The answer to his question is in terms of an agreement existing among human beings in their behaviour and speech. This answer will not produce a refutation of the sceptical case; and in the *Investigations* Wittgenstein attempts no such refutation. In the course of his lengthy investigation of meaning, he disposes of the sceptical problem in what may fairly be called a throw-away remark. 'If we are using the word "know" as it is normally used (and how else are we to use it!), then other people very often know when I am in pain' (PI 246). Here we have 'a whole cloud of philosophy condensed into a drop of grammar' (PI p. 222).[35] Wittgenstein's approach to the other minds problem, in terms of criteria, in the early pages of the *Blue Book*, was a false start. His position is more properly reflected in the dismissive treatment of PI 246.

The reader who has taken in Wittgenstein's remarks about meaning and use will hardly expect him to supply a refutation of the sceptic's claim. If, as Wittgenstein argues at length, there is no more to the meaning of a word than its use, what is left of the sceptical problem? In what sense is it a *problem*? If we are using the word 'know' as it is normally used – if *this* is what we mean by 'know' – then one often knows that another person is in pain. Of course a sceptic may say that in *his* usage of 'know' we do *not* know it; and this is perfectly true. What he cannot do, if Wittgenstein is right, is to claim that his is the *real* meaning of the word, for this would imply that there is, contrary to Wittgenstein's thesis, a standard of meaning other than, and superior to, the normal use.[36]

6

Language-games and Objectivity

A. REALISM AND ITS ALTERNATIVES

As we saw in Chapter 5, Wittgenstein holds that language depends on 'agreement in judgements', to provide the standard of right and wrong. We are not to think that there is a standard beyond that, a physical or mental reality with which our concepts can be compared and their validity established. This is also true of mathematics. The person who wrote '1004' instead of '1002' (Chapter 4) cannot be made to change his mind by being confronted with something outside language, about the meaning of which no dispute could conceivably arise. The final court of appeal is just the fact that any normal person would interpret the formula '+2' by writing '1002'. And similarly, the final court of appeal for a correct use of the word 'pain' and others is just the fact that they are normally used in such and such ways.

It is important not to confuse this claim, which is about meaning, with a rejection of objective truth. As we saw in the last chapter (5.A), Wittgenstein's imaginary objector poses the question whether, on his view, 'human agreement decides what is true and what is false' (PI 241). (Wittgenstein's reply is quoted on p. 88.) Consider again the example of the earth being flat. If everyone agreed that it is flat, would it follow, according to Wittgenstein, that it *is* flat? Would he also hold that this *was* true at one time (when everyone said so) and only became false later? Did the shape of the earth change, just because the agreed description of it changed? These incredible views would hardly be in accordance with the normal uses of 'true' and 'false'. They may, however, be rejected without affecting the point about agreement in judgements. This point may be put as follows. If we disagree with our forebears about the shape of the earth, this presupposes that we *mean the same* by the relevant words, for example the word 'flat'. And this sameness of meaning *is* established by a general agreement

127

in use – in spite of differences on particular questions. For example, if someone applied the word 'flat' to trees but not to pancakes, then we might conclude that he doesn't mean *flat* when he utters this word. But we may be sure that those who believed the earth to be flat did use the word in our sense, from the way they used it in other contexts. Without this fundamental agreement in use (and hence meaning), it would make no sense to speak of *dis*agreement as to particular matters of fact.

Such an agreement must also exist among the users of a word at a given time. 'What would it be like', asks Wittgenstein, if people did not 'generally agree in their judgements of colour?' (PI p. 226). 'One man would say that a flower was red which another called blue, and so on.' But this, he points out, would throw into doubt the question whether they *have* colour-words at all, thereby defeating the original supposition.

But, it may be asked, is there no reality behind the logic of our colour concepts, and others? Again, if we say that two plus two equals four, isn't that because two plus two really do equal four – and likewise with other mathematical propositions? 'Do these systems', asks Wittgenstein, 'reside in *our* nature or in the nature of things? How are we to put it? – *Not* in the nature of numbers or colours' (Z 357). Someone who (contrary to Wittgenstein) answers 'yes' to the second alternative may be described as a 'realist', and I shall use the term in this sense. It is clear from Wittgenstein's answer that he was not, in this sense, a realist. Nor, however, did he opt for the first alternative ('in *our* nature').

The rejection of realism opens the way for certain alternative conceptions of logic and mathematics, which may be ascribed, correctly or otherwise, to Wittgenstein. One of these is *pluralism* – the possibility of divergent systems in other cultures. The example of the person who wrote '1004' could indeed be generalised as being about the practice of a whole society. And, as we shall see, Wittgenstein gives a number of other examples, in which the practice of a whole society is imagined to diverge from ours in all sorts of surprising ways. Now if realism were true, then there would be an extra-linguistic standard by which the other systems – or ours, perhaps – could be proved *incorrect*. But according to Wittgenstein, there is no such standard, and pluralism cannot be eliminated in such a way. There are, however, limits to Wittgenstein's pluralism, as we shall see.

Then there is *conventionalism* – the view that our linguistic systems, not being imposed by an outside reality, are created by ourselves, in the manner of a convention or institution. This view entails pluralism, since it must be possible for different societies to differ in their conventions and institutions. Wittgenstein sometimes spoke of linguistic practices (including mathematics) as being 'conventional', 'arbitrary' and the like. His assimilation of them to games ('language-games') also seems to imply that they are created by us, and 'played' according to rules of our devising. I shall argue that this view is wrong, and its ascription to Wittgenstein doubtful.

Finally, there is *linguistic idealism*. According to this, the order of priority between language and reality is the reverse of that of realism. Instead of our systems being determined by reality ('the nature of things'), it is reality that is determined by our systems; and it makes no sense to speak of a reality that is independent of language. This view is called 'idealism' by analogy with the *mental* idealism of Berkeley in the eighteenth century, whereby it makes no sense to speak of a reality outside the mind.[1]

All of these views are contrary to realism; and the latter must certainly be false if one of them is true. This does not mean, however, that, having rejected realism, we – or Wittgenstein – must opt for one of these alternatives.

B. PLURALISM

That our ways of using language are not the only conceivable ones will be obvious to anyone who has read a little about societies remote from our own. Some of these differences can be readily explained by reference to the environment. The fact that Eskimos, for example, have several different words corresponding to our 'white' and 'snow' can obviously be explained in such a way; and so can the Tahitians' use of several different names for the coconut, depending on what can be done with it at different stages of its growth. In the *Brown Book* we are asked to imagine a society in which there is one word for red and green, and another for blue and yellow; this society being divided into two castes, one wearing red and green, and the other blue and yellow.

But these examples may give a wrong impression of Wittgenstein's position. He was not, or not merely, putting forward the view that different linguistic practices are to be explained by circumstances existing in different societies. Nor are we meant to conclude that the concepts in *our* society, or those that we share with mankind in general, are to be explained in that way (or any other). Wittgenstein's position is better illustrated by his question 'What do light blue and dark blue have in common?' (BB 134). He points out that there may not be any explanation. 'If you were asked "Why do you call this 'blue' also?", you would say "Because this *is* blue, too"' (BB 133–4). He imagines another society in which light blue and dark blue are called 'Cambridge' and 'Oxford', but 'if you asked a man of this tribe what Cambridge and Oxford have in common, he'd be inclined to say "Nothing"' (BB 134–5).

The examples in which explanations are available (or readily suggest themselves) may divert attention from Wittgenstein's primary concern, which is about language rather than languages – about the relation between language and reality, rather than between different languages. He rejects the view that language is shaped by an underlying reality ('the substance of the world'), independently of human needs and practices. But this view can be maintained in spite of differences of the kind described above. These can indeed be sorted out by reference to what is 'really there'. Suppose we put it to a member of the two-caste society that red and green are distinct colours: can he not see this? Perhaps he would reply 'Yes, of course; but for us the difference happens to be unimportant'. Again, it is hardly likely that the Tahitians would disagree with us about the ontology of coconuts; they would explain their terminology – as we might – by reference to economic circumstances. (The use of 'wood' and 'timber' in English shows how superficial such differences can be.) But the 'Oxford' and 'Cambridge' example is different. In this case, while agreeing that the two samples are distinct (light blue and dark blue), we perceive them as shades of one colour, while the other people do not. What is 'really there' for us is not really there for them. To be sure, there might be a 'social' explanation in this case too, and we might be able to agree on what is really there, as distinct from differences of terminology due to local conditions. But this is not so in the example as given; here there is no explanation and no perception that 'Cambridge' and 'Oxford' are really two shades of one colour. And neither, of course, is there an explanation from our side: the question 'What do light blue and dark blue have in common?' remains unanswered.

Some of Wittgenstein's most striking examples of pluralism are given in the *Remarks on the Foundations of Mathematics*. Here we find imaginary societies in which calculating, counting, inferring and so on are done in ways that would seem illogical and absurd to us. There are the people who buy and sell firewood.[2] They pile the wood 'in heaps of arbitrary, varying height' and sell it 'at a price proportionate to the area covered by the piles'. Perhaps they even justify this with words 'Of course, if you buy more timber, you must pay more' (RFM 94). It may seem as if such a case could not conceivably survive a confrontation with reality – in this case the reality of logic and mathematics. Yet 'how could I show them that – as I should say – you don't really buy more wood if you buy a pile covering a bigger area?'

> I should, for instance, take a pile which was small by their ideas and, by laying the logs in a different way, change it into a 'big' one. This *might* convince them – but perhaps they would say: 'Yes, now it's a *lot* of wood and costs more'. (RFM 94)

In another example he supposes that our measuring rods were elastic and not rigid. 'How should we get into conflict with truth, if our footrules were made of very soft rubber instead of wood and steel?' (RFM 38).

> 'Well, we shouldn't get to know the correct measurement of the table.' – You mean: we should not get, or could not be sure of getting, *that* measurement which we get with our rigid rulers. So someone who measured the table with an elastic ruler would be wrong if he said it measured five feet according to our usual way of measuring; but if he said it measured five feet according to his, this would be correct. – 'But surely that isn't measuring at all!' – It is similar to our measuring and capable, in certain circumstances, of fulfilling 'practical purposes'. (RFM 38)

Are these and similar examples really conceivable? A complaint sometimes made against Wittgenstein is that his examples are not sufficiently worked out. One critic has described them as 'thin and unconvincing'.[3] Their 'intelligibility and strength', writes another, 'derive from their being severely isolated and restricted. . . . The wider-reaching consequences of counting, calculating, and so forth, in these deviant ways are not brought out explicitly'.[4] And a number of writers have shown, by means of more or less elaborate scenarios, that if the 'deviant' ways of going on were generalised to other contexts, this would lead to difficulties far beyond those envisaged in the original example.[5]

The short answer to these objections is that there may not *be* any 'wider-reaching consequences'; that is, we may suppose that the deviant method takes place only in the kind of situation described in the example. Thus the people who calculate the price of wood according to the ground area may, in other situations, use methods that would be perfectly rational according to our ideas. It is indeed a striking fact about existing 'primitive' societies that their apparently irrational beliefs and practices in some spheres exist side by side with a strong sense of reality (as we see it) in others. This point was made by Wittgenstein in his comments on a well-known work of anthropology, J. G. Frazer's *The Golden Bough*. 'The same savage', wrote Wittgenstein, 'who, apparently in order to kill his enemy, sticks his knife through a picture of him, really does build his hut of wood and cuts his arrow with skill and not in effigy'.[6]

It may be thought that there is nevertheless a standard, acknowledged by all, by which we can adjudicate between alternative practices – namely, that of success. And this may seem to be confirmed by the history of interaction between Western and other cultures, in which the latter have, to a large extent, come to accept the superiority of Western practices. Yet this may be due to conquest and imposition, rather than to the force of logic. There is an example in which Wittgenstein illustrates the limitations of logic for such a purpose. We are asked to imagine a tribe in which there is oral calculation but no knowledge of writing. Moreover, 'among them mistakes in counting are very frequent, digits get repeated or left out. . .'. One day a traveller teaches them writing and proves, by means of a gramophone (or let us say, tape recorder), that they are making these mistakes in their calculation.

> Would these people now have to admit that they had not really calculated before? That they had merely been groping about, whereas now they walk? Might they not perhaps even say: our affairs went better before, our intuition was not burdened with the dead stuff of writing? You cannot lay hold of the spirit with a machine. They say perhaps: 'If we repeated a digit then, as your machine asserts – well, that will have been right'. (RFM 212)[7]

C. THE LIMITS OF PLURALISM

Wittgenstein's discussions of alternative practices follow a characteristic course. We are asked to imagine a society in which people use language or calculate in some strange way. There follows the objection that this would be an incorrect way of going on, an objection that Wittgenstein proceeds to question. But then he often raises what may be called the 'Transcendental Question' – whether a very strange way of doing X should be described as a way of doing X at all. Thus in the last example the question was raised whether 'they had not really calculated before'; and in the case of the elastic rulers the objector exclaimed 'But surely that isn't measuring at all!'

What is the answer to the Transcendental Question? If the answer is 'no' – if the case is not, say, one of measuring at all – then it cannot be regarded as a *different* way of measuring, one that would support a pluralist view of this concept. However, the answer to such questions may not be clear-cut. Take, for example, the game of chess, which is defined by a set of rules. If some of these were altered, would it still be chess? Would it be a different game, or the same game but played in a different way? If enough of the game is retained, then we may be inclined to give the second answer. Similarly, we may be able to say of the strange way of measuring that 'it is similar to our measuring', and to regard it still as a case of *measuring*, albeit an unfamiliar one.

But Wittgenstein also considers cases in which the Transcendental Question would receive a negative answer. In one passage he has his objector complain 'Then according to you everybody could continue the series as he likes; and so also make inferences in *any* way' (RFM 80). He replies: 'In that case we shan't call it "continuing the series" and also, presumably, not "inference"'. And in an extreme case the very existence of *language* would be thrown into doubt.

> '*This* follows inexorably from *that*.' . . . If someone doesn't acknowledge this, doesn't follow it as a demonstration, then he has parted company with us even before it comes to language. (RFM 60)

These cases seem to be about individuals rather than societies, but the point can also be made about societies. In an important passage in the *Investigations*, the limits of pluralism are drawn by reference to an explorer 'in an unknown country', who finds it impossible to learn the language of the inhabitants.

> Let us imagine that the people in that country carried on the usual human activities and in the course of them employed, apparently, an articulate language. If we watch their behaviour we find it intelligible, it seems 'logical'. But when we try to learn their language we find it impossible to do so. For there is no regular connexion between what they say, the sounds they make, and their actions; but still these sounds are not superfluous, for if we gag one of the people, it has the same consequences as with us; without the sounds their actions fall into confusion – as I feel like putting it.
>
> Are we to say that these people have a language: orders, reports, and the rest?
>
> There is not enough regularity for us to call it 'language'. (PI 206–7; cf. RFM 196, Z 390)

In such a case there would, no doubt, be a strong presumption that these people have a language, even if the translation had eluded us so far. But Wittgenstein's point is that *if* we held translation to be impossible, then we could not describe the sounds they make as language. In that case we would merely have an unintelligible correlation between the making of language-like sounds and what happens (or seems to happen) when we 'gag one of the people'.

One may now be tempted to accuse Wittgenstein of a kind of linguistic imperialism, for he seems to be saying that whether a sequence of sounds is to count as a language depends on its being translatable into *our* language. But Wittgenstein is not arguing: we cannot translate it, therefore it is not language. His point is that it is not possible 'for us to call it "language"', because in order to do that we would need a conception of language going beyond what we know as language. We would need, in the words of the *Tractatus*, to 'station ourselves . . . somewhere outside logic' (T 4.12), taking up a position from which we could contemplate our language as well as alternatives. But if Wittgenstein is right (in his early as well as in his later thought), there is no such perspective. In his early thought, as we saw, the 'limit of language' is set by a certain framework of names and objects, propositions and facts; but now it is 'the common behaviour of mankind [that] is the system of reference by means of which we interpret an unknown language' (PI 206).[8]

There is a sense in which there is only one language. Leaving aside subtle nuances, technical terms, religious language and the like, different languages are all translatable into one another. This is not affected by the grammatical, syntactical and categorial differences existing among them. Chinese, for example, has a very different structure from English, but this does not prevent us from carrying on trade negotiations with the Chinese, or reading the thoughts of Chairman Mao in English. And the same would be true of languages, real or imaginary, that we read about in works of anthropology or in Wittgenstein's examples. It is only against the background of a common language, tied to 'the common behaviour of mankind', that we can speak of *variations* among languages.

Wittgenstein's position may be contrasted with that of another opponent of realism, W. V. Quine. According to Quine, there *cannot be* a determinate translation of one language into another. The 'manuals for translating' a given language 'can be set up in divergent ways, all incompatible . . . with one another' (*Word and Object*, 27). Quine introduced his 'principle of indeterminacy of translation' by means of an example of some natives saying 'Gavagai' when a rabbit comes by. Like Wittgenstein in his discussion of ostensive definition, he pointed out that there is no one-to-one correspondence between word and object, so that the explorer could not tell from the given evidence whether 'Gavagai' should be translated 'animal', 'white' or 'rabbit' (29). Quine supposed that the explorer will ask 'Gavagai?' in 'various stimulatory situations', 'noting each time whether the native assents, dissents, or neither' (29). He then observed that assent and dissent are expressed differently in different languages; the Turks, he says, use gestures which 'are nearly the reverse of our own' (29). The explorer will attempt, therefore, to establish by trial and error which are the natives' words for 'yes' and 'no'; and armed with this information, he will proceed with the business of accumulating evidence for the translation of 'Gavagai' (30).

Now Quine's conclusion (unlike Wittgenstein's) is negative; he holds that there is no way of attaining 'determinacy of translation'. Yet in the very setting up of his example, he must take for granted that certain concepts are shared between the natives and the explorer. Among these are the concepts of question and answer: these are presupposed in the description of the example, as when the explorer says 'Gavagai?' and his listeners understand this as a *question*. Again, in posing questions about the natives' expressions for 'yes' and 'no', it is assumed that they have the *concepts* of yes and no, assent and dissent; these essential ingredients are assumed to be present in their language, awaiting identification.

But to achieve this identification, the explorer would not be confined merely to what the natives say 'in the conspicuous presence of rabbits and like' (as Quine puts it, 29); he would also be able to draw (as Wittgenstein says) on 'the common behaviour of mankind'. For assent and dissent do not merely take the form of saying 'yes' or 'no' (or equivalent words) when asked suitable questions; they also consist in certain ways of behaving – as when a hungry person is offered food and accepts it, or another is threatened with something unpleasant and rejects it. And while it is true (as Quine points out) that the gestures for 'yes' and 'no' in another society may be very different from our own, this cannot be said about yes and no *behaviour*, of the kind just mentioned. Here is part of that 'common behaviour of mankind . . . by means of which we interpret an unknown language'. Hence, *if* the concepts exist in the other language, then we can identify them by reference to this behaviour, and proceed with our translation. But if they do not, then we cannot suppose that we are dealing with a language at all.

There is also another sense in which language is one; and in this respect Wittgenstein's comparison of language with games can be misleading. The point is that the uses of language, various though they are, form a single interrelated system; and this is not so in the case of games. Consider the examples given in PI 23, in which we are invited to 'review the multiplicity of language-games'. They include giving and obeying orders, describing, reporting, speculating, story-telling, singing, joking, translating, asking, thanking and cursing. Now these activities are interrelated in all sorts of logical ways. Thus we may order someone to give a report, or report that he gave (or obeyed) an order. We may speculate whether he will make a joke, and thank or curse him for doing so. The language-game of asking is related to (or includes, we might say) that of answering; and answering might take the form of describing or translating. Story-telling is related in certain ways to reporting what really happened; and so on and so forth.

But this is not so in the case of games: what we do in chess is not related in any such way to what we do in football.

Having reviewed various examples of games in PI 66, Wittgenstein concludes that we see here 'a complicated network of similarities overlapping and criss-crossing'. Now in the case of language there is also a complicated network, with overlapping and criss-crossing. But it is a network of interrelations between the activities of language, and not merely one of similarities between them. That is why we can speak of the whole system of language as *language*; but there is no such system in the case of games.[9]

D. CONVENTION, INVENTION AND DISCOVERY

There is a well-known distinction between empirical propositions, whose truth depends on empirical facts, and others where this is not so. Mathematical propositions are usually held to belong to the second kind, and not to be liable to falsification by experience. Thus, 'if there are 3 apples there after I have put down two and again two, I don't say: "So after all 2 + 2 are not always 4"; but "Somehow one must have gone"' (RFM 96–7). but what makes such propositions true, if not empirical fact? It may be thought that just as there is an empirical reality corresponding to empirical propositions, so there must be a mathematical reality corresponding to propositions of that kind. Thus, in the case of the instruction (Chapter 4) 'add 2', we may be inclined to think that 'the steps are all already taken and he is just writing them down' (RFM 46). But is this right? Are we to suppose that the world contains numbers, square roots and Euclidean triangles, in addition to sticks and stones, apples and printed triangles? Does it also contain negative and irrational numbers, corresponding to mathematical propositions about them?

It may be thought that what makes these non-empirical propositions true is that we have, so to speak, put the truth into them ourselves. This is obviously so in the case of some non-empirical propositions. For example, the fact there are a hundred pence to one pound Sterling (that this proposition is true) is due entirely to a human decision. But can we say the same about truths of mathematics? The fact that two plus two equals four was not brought about by human decision.

What was Wittgenstein's position on this issue? There is a strain of thought running through his lectures and writings which may be called 'conventionalism' or 'voluntarism'. It is expressed in such terms as 'arbitrary', 'convention', 'decision', 'invention', 'game' and 'rule'. According to it, mathematical and other non-empirical truths are in some sense a matter of human choice. This view seems to me mistaken, and the attribution of it to Wittgenstein doubtful. He certainly had a tendency to such views, but his expression of them is usually hesitant and qualified – a fact that is sometimes overlooked by commentators, both friendly and hostile. Moreover, the tendency appears in his less finished writings, and notes taken of his lectures, rather than in his most authoritative work (in the *Investigations*).

In the *Lectures on the Foundations of Mathematics*, Wittgenstein is reported to have said that recognition of mathematical truths amounts to the 'acceptance of a convention' (LFM 63). 'We might', he said, 'have adopted 2 + 2 = 4', following an empirical observation; and when we do this, 'we make a *rule* of it', rendering it 'aloof from experiments' (LFM 98). In the *Remarks on the Foundations of Mathematics* the claim that 'the mathematician is an inventor, not a discoverer' occurs more than once (RFM 99, 111). He also claimed that 'the further expansion of an irrational number is a further expansion of mathematics'; something that 'has yet to be invented' (RFM 276).

In the *Investigations*, discussing experiences of 'suddenly understanding', he asked: 'what criterion *do we fix* for the identity of such an occurrence?' (PI 322; italics in original). And in a passage in the *Blue Book* he seemed to hold that our ability to know that another person is in pain is due to a convention, and that a philosopher who denied this knowledge would be 'objecting to a convention' (BB 24, 57).

The word 'convention' also occurs in the English version of PI 355, where we are told that a certain use of language is, 'like any other, founded on convention'. However, the German *Übereinkunft* might equally well be translated as 'agreement', and this word can be taken in a passive rather than an active sense – agreement *in* doing something rather than agreeing *to* do it. Thus we might say that we agree *in* our use of such and such words, without implying that we *made* an agreement to that effect. Wittgenstein did, however, speak sometimes of agreement in the active sense. The German *Abmachung*, translated as 'convention' in RFM 41, has the active sense of setting up an agreement.

As we have seen, the following ideas are to be found in Wittgenstein's lectures and writings in one form or another:

1) Mathematical propositions are rules.
2) The mathematician is an inventor and not a discoverer.
3) The usage of words is governed by convention.
4) The criteria for identifying mental occurrences are 'fixed' by us.

These claims can hardly be said to conform to Wittgenstein's dictum: 'Philosophy may in no way interfere with the actual use of language; it can in the end only describe it' (PI 124). To describe '2 + 2 = 4' as a rule is not a normal use of the word 'rule'. Rules do not have truth-values, but it is perfectly normal to describe a mathematical proposition as true or false. Again, if the criteria (or conventions or rules) for counting something as (say) an experience of understanding are fixed by us, this seems to deprive statements about these matters of their objectivity – as if facts depended on our choice of criteria, rather than being there independently of what anyone may say.

Is it normal to speak of mathematics as invention rather than discovery? In some cases it is; as when we speak of the invention of logarithms or the differential calculus. But in other cases it is not. We discover, and do not invent, the answer to 99 × 99 – or, to take an example used by Wittgenstein, that the sequence '7777' occurs in the expansion of pi. Does this mean that the sequence is 'already there', awaiting discovery? Is there, after all, a non-physical, mathematical realm of entities, which contains – or as the case may be, does not contain – this sequence in the expansion of pi? Wittgenstein considered this example in a number of passages.

'In the decimal expansion of pi either the group "7777" occurs, or it does not – there is no third possibility.' That is to say: 'God sees – but we don't know.' But what does that mean? . . . (PI 352).

Suppose that people go on and on calculating the expansion of pi. So God, who knows everything, knows whether they will have reached '777' by the end of the world. But can his *omniscience* decide whether they *would* have reached it after the end of the world? It cannot. (RFM 185).

(It is worth noting that of the two treatments, that in the *Investigations* is the more cautious.)

These remarks bring out the peculiarity of existential statements about numbers. But this peculiarity may be recognised without denying that there is discovery in mathematics. And it would be perfectly normal to speak of *discovering*, for example, that such and such a sequence occurs in the expansion of pi.

Again, while it may be correct to describe logarithms as an invention, that is not the end of the matter. For what we do with the system, once invented, may lead us to results that are not of our making. 'We make, and we do not make mathematics. The creation is stronger than the creator' (F. Waismann, *Lectures on the Philosophy of Mathematics*, 33). A mathematical demonstration may *surprise* us, and this implies that we are dealing with discovery rather than invention. 'If you are surprised', wrote Wittgenstein in reply to this objection, 'then you have not understood it yet. For surprise is not legitimate here, as it is with the issue of an experiment' (RFM 111). Now it is true that when we have thoroughly understood a demonstration, we may no longer be surprised at the result. We may also admit that our surprise was due to 'failure to command a clear view' (RFM 112, 113), and that we ought not to have been surprised. But it does not follow from this that there is no surprise and no discovery. A striking example of this are the conundrums in children's puzzle books, in which the 'obvious' answer turns out, to our amazement, to be the wrong one. (It should be noted that Wittgenstein himself goes on to speak of the surprise of 'mathematical puzzles', showing that his position is more tentative than that often ascribed to him. This will be further argued in my next section.)

Wittgenstein's talk of 'convention' is also out of step with actual usage. To describe a use of language as conventional is to imply that it does not have the full commitment of normal language. It is, we may say, 'merely' conventional. Of this kind are the use of 'cheers' when having a drink, and the German practice of calling out 'Gesundheit' when someone sneezes. By contrast, the fact that $99 \times 99 = 9801$ would not be described as conventional; and neither would the knowledge, or the claim to know, that another person is in pain. We can imagine a society in which there *is* a convention that when a person holds his cheek and moans (cf. BB 24), those near him say certain words (they might be 'He has toothache' or some other expression – say 'abracadabra'). But when *we* say that someone has toothache, we are not making a merely conventional pronouncement.

In the *Brown Book*, Wittgenstein wrote that 'we introduce into our language games the endless series of numerals' (BB 91), and he compared this 'introduction' with the way in which we might choose to play cards in an 'unbounded' manner – the players being allowed to use as many cards as they like. Now the latter would indeed be a matter of introduction and choice – we could choose whether to play this game or some other, or none at all. But is the same true of the 'game' of mathematics? The passage from the *Brown Book* was cited by Wittgenstein's former collaborator, Waismann, who pointed out that the mathematical case, unlike the cards example, might properly be described in terms of insight and discovery. A child may begin by learning numbers in a mechanical way,

> but then a point will come when he comprehends that he can go on forever, that there is no such thing as the last term: the idea may suddenly flash upon him. . . . He has then discovered the *potential infinity* of the series. . . . Now this is not getting accustomed to playing a game with marks on paper, or learning arbitrary rules: it is essentially an *insight*. . . . (*Lectures on the Philosophy of Mathematics*, 119)

In this matter, actual usage is on Waismann's side.

It may be that Wittgenstein's reluctance to recognise mathematical propositions as propositions, and his claim that 'surprise is not legitimate here', are a hangover from his view in the *Tractatus* that tautologies 'say nothing', and that 'the propositions of mathematics are equations, and therefore pseudo-propositions' (T 6.2). In Chapter 2 (p. 27) I argued that this view fails to distinguish between propositions of logic or mathematics which may be described as 'saying nothing' because their truth must be evident to anyone who speaks the language, and other, more complicated ones, where this is not so. To treat them all as being on the same level is to fail to mark a distinction that is apparent from their use in practice.

E. CONVENTIONALISM AND 'THE GIVEN'

To some extent, as we saw in sections B and C, Wittgenstein was a pluralist, defending the autonomy of different ways of measuring, calculating and reasoning. There was, he held, no standard outside human practices by reference to which they could be justified or refuted. Conventionalism too is opposed to the idea of such a standard, for according to it logic and mathematics are man-made and not determined by an outside standard or pre-existing reality. Wittgenstein, as we have seen, had a tendency towards conventionalism; but to what extent was he committed to it? A recent commentator quotes at length eight passages from RFM to prove 'the overwhelming case for interpreting Wittgenstein as a conventionalist' (Crispin Wright, *Wittgenstein on the Foundation of Mathematics* (Duckworth), 1980, 39–40, xii). He does not notice that most of these remarks are expressed in such terms as 'I could say . . .', 'I want to say . . .' and 'Why should I not say . . . ?'. These phrases are not merely ornamental; Wittgenstein was quite capable of expressing himself in more definite terms when that was his intention.

One of the pitfalls of reading Wittgenstein is the failure to distinguish between passages in which his aim is to arrive at a definite conclusion (one that may be crucial to his overall position) and others in which he is concerned to 'investigate' – to probe, ask questions, look at things from different points of view and so on. Again, in reading his numerous questions it is necessary to distinguish those that are clearly rhetorical, having an 'obvious' answer, from others that are really meant as *questions*. 'In philosophy', he once wrote, 'it is always good to put a *question* instead of an answer to a question' (RFM 147). (He went on, however, to question whether he should follow this maxim in that particular discussion!) Many commentators, not content to leave matters there, have insisted that Wittgenstein must have meant such and such an answer, even if he did not say so; or have blamed him for not coming out with a clear-cut answer. But there is no reason to suppose that such answers must always be available. Wittgenstein, at any rate, did not think so. To a student who wanted to dissuade him from destroying some of his notes, he replied 'I do not wish to allow my questions to be used as answers'.[10]

The conventionalist position cannot be attributed to Wittgenstein without considerable qualifications. It is hardly present in his most finished work, the *Investigations*. There is more of it in RFM, and still more (sometimes to the point of crudeness) in the volume of lectures (LFM) compiled from students' notes.[11] But even in these writings we also find expressions of an opposite tendency. 'Come', he had an imaginary objector say in one of the lectures, 'a child when he calculates 25 × 25 and gets 625 doesn't *invent* this. He finds it out.' His reply was:

> Of course he doesn't invent the mathematical fact – it would be absurd to say that. And there is nothing wrong in saying that he found it out. (LFM 92; cf. 101).

Sometimes he made the point that it is useful to look at things from a conventionalist point of view in order to counteract the opposite, realist tendency, which he regarded as the more dangerous. There is a passage in *Zettel* in which he spoke of the temptation 'to justify the rules of grammar by statements like "But there really are four primary colours"' (Z 331). It was, he remarked, against this temptation that 'the saying that the rules of grammar are arbitrary is directed'. And in one of his lectures he said: 'It is sometimes useful to compare mathematics to a game and sometimes misleading' (LFM 142). 'The thing to do', he concluded, 'is not to take sides, but to investigate'. Again, having answered a firm 'no' to the question (in Zettel) whether our systems of numbers and of colours lie 'in the nature of things' (quoted p. 128), he went on: 'Then is there something arbitrary about this system? Yes and no. It is akin both to what is arbitrary and to what is non-arbitrary' (Z 357–8).

So much for Wittgenstein's reservations about conventionalism. There are also more fundamental reasons for not attributing this position to him. To speak of mathematics and 'grammar' as matters of invention and choice is to imply that we have a perspective *outside* this invention or choice; as if we could – or did, prior to the choice – 'station ourselves . . . somewhere outside logic' (T 4.12). And this idea was rejected by Wittgenstein both in the *Tractatus* and in his later philosophy. Given that we *have* the basic concepts of logic and mathematics, we can invent or choose a variety of systems and calculi. These can be seen as extensions of an already existing grammar – suburbs that may be grafted on to the existing 'ancient city' (cf. PI 18). But there is no standpoint from which we did or could invent or devise the original system. Given that we have certain concepts of number, for example, we may consider enlarging the system by the introduction of negative numbers; and this indeed happened in the history of the subject. But we could never have stood in this relation to the original use of numbers. For if we had no such concept, we would not be in a position to consider embarking on that use. Again, the standpoint of invention and choice has an evaluative aspect. It makes sense to ask whether a given choice was a good one compared to others.[12] Conventions, institutions, games and the like can all be assessed from an outside standpoint. But such questions cannot arise about 'rules of grammar' or propositions like 'two plus two equals four'. It makes no sense to ask whether these are, or were, 'a good choice'.

Whereas in the *Tractatus* Wittgenstein had regarded 'logical form' as the limit of our language, he now spoke of 'forms of life' as 'given'. 'What has to be accepted, the given, is – so one could say – *forms of life*' (PI p. 226). 'The language-game', he wrote in another work, 'is so to say something unpredictable. I mean: it is not based on grounds. It is not reasonable (or unreasonable). It is there – like our life' (OC 559). These references to 'life' and 'forms of life' show how he now regarded logic as intertwined with human needs and interests, in contrast to the earlier conception. The remark about 'forms of life' was expressed more fully in a previous draft, in which he spoke of

> the fact that we act in such and such a way, e.g. *punish* certain actions, *establish* the state of affairs thus and so, *give orders*, submit reports, describe colours, take an interest in the feelings of others. What has to be accepted, the given – one might say – are facts of living. (RPP I/630).

An example of taking 'an interest in the feelings of others' is that of pain. Observing that someone close to me is in pain, I react in suitable ways. But can I really know that he is in pain? A philosopher or scientist may try to persuade me that one cannot know this. But the relevant ways of speaking and behaving will not go away.

> 'I can only *believe* that someone else is in pain, but I *know* it if I am.' – Yes; one can make the decision to say 'I believe he is in pain' instead of 'He is in pain'. But that is all. . . .
> Just try – in a real case – to doubt someone else's fear or pain. (PI 303)

We could imagine a law being passed to prohibit the use of 'know' in regard to another person's pain; but this would not eliminate the concept or our need for it – the role it plays in our life. For we would still need, in real-life situations, to distinguish the case in which I *believe* he is in pain from that in which I *know* he is.

Similarly, the philosopher who tells us that a word like 'pain' may come to mean (or really does mean) a brain-process, would have to explain how a brain-process statement (which is based on observation) could replace the first-person 'I am in pain' (which is not). For it is essential to *this* statement, and to the role it plays in our lives, that it is independent of observation. Any complaint based on observation may, conceivably, be mistaken; but the complaint 'I am in pain' cannot be mistaken. If I complain that there is something wrong with my television, I am subject to correction – perhaps I pressed the wrong button or am wearing the wrong glasses. But the complaint 'I am in pain' is not subject to correction. The doctor who assures me, after careful examination, that there is 'nothing wrong' with me will not eliminate my pain or my need for sympathy; for my complaint was not based on a belief that there is something wrong with me – or any other belief.

This aspect of the concept of pain has also been regarded, and under Wittgenstein's name, as a matter of convention. 'Following Wittgenstein', writes Richard Rorty, 'we shall treat the fact that there is no such thing as "a misleading appearance of pain" . . . just as a remark about a language-game – the remark that we have a convention of taking people's word for what they are feeling' (*Philosophy and the Mirror of Nature*, 32). This convention, according to Rorty, is comparable to 'the fact that the [American] Constitution is what the Supreme Court thinks it is, or that the ball is foul if the umpire thinks it is'. Now it is easy to imagine ourselves living with a different constitution, or playing games with different rules from the existing ones. These things are not 'given', in the sense of Wittgenstein's 'forms of life'. But a philosopher who regards the logic of pain as no more than a convention owes us an account of what life would be like without that logic (and the same would be true of other concepts, such as knowledge and thinking).[13]

What belongs, in the relevant sense, to 'the given', may also involve quite sophisticated language, such as the terms 'inadvertently' and 'automatically'. The distinction between these was used in a famous controversy between Stanley Cavell and others, about the status of appeals to 'the actual use of language' in discussing philosophical issues.[14] The point was made that people use language in different ways, and that distinctions to which philosophers draw attention may not be observed in the vocabulary of less educated people. Thus to the philosopher who claims that the distinction between 'inadvertently' and 'automatically' is confirmed by actual usage, it may be replied that some people may use these words interchangeably, or not use them at all. This objection may seem to put the 'actual use' approach on a very precarious footing. Cavell, conceding that perhaps 'half the speakers of English' could not say what the distinction is, and might even use the words interchangeably, claimed that it would still be open to the philosopher to persuade the uneducated person ('the butcher and the baker') that his use of language was an 'impoverished' one; and that 'there is something you aren't noticing about the world'. But John Cook has shown that the distinction is not one that a normal person could *fail* to observe; nor, on the other hand, does the issue turn essentially on a choice of words. If the relevant situations are described with sufficient fullness, it can be seen that the distinction is an inescapable part of our form of life. Cook describes in detail two different situations in which a baker is let down by his assistant turning on the oven too early, in one case doing it (as we would say) inadvertently, and in the other automatically. The baker and his assistant, whether they are acquainted with these actual words or not, *would* observe the distinction in what they say to one another – the kind of excuses made by the assistant, and the kind of advice given by the baker to avoid similar let-downs in the future. It would not make sense to suppose that they might mistake the one kind of discourse for the other.[15]

On the other hand, it is a mistake to think, as some philosophers of religion have, that the religious 'language-game' can be regarded as a form of life in Wittgenstein's sense, and therefore not amenable to justification or criticism. For it is obvious that religion is not part of 'the given', so that we could not understand what human life would be like without it. If there is a sense in which religious belief is immune from criticism, it is not that of Wittgenstein's forms of life and language-games.[16]

F. RULES, GAMES AND LANGUAGE-GAMES

It is often thought that the concept of *following a rule* is central to

Wittgenstein's account of language. There is something right and something wrong with this view. It is true that the discussions of following a rule, obeying an instruction (such as '+ 2') and understanding the meaning of a word are interwoven in the *Investigations*. However, what he wanted to show was not that language is rule-governed, but, on the contrary, that rules, instructions and definitions are all equally impotent to explain why we (in general or as individuals) speak or calculate as we do, since any rule (like any definition) will only work if it is understood correctly.

He also saw an 'analogy between language and games' (PI 83); and he claimed that the 'rules of grammar' are constitutive of a language-game in the way in which the rules of chess are constitutive of chess. Someone who played by different rules would not be playing incorrectly; he would be *'playing another game'* (Z 320).

But these analogies must be treated with caution. In the case of games like chess, we refer explicitly to rules in deciding what may and may not be done. Is the same true of language? There are, of course, rules of grammar in the ordinary, non-Wittgensteinian sense, to which we may appeal, especially in the case of learning a foreign language. But this is not so with grammar in Wittgenstein's sense, such as the 'grammar' of arithmetical statements or the statement 'I am in pain', as described in the last section. We do not appeal to a rule (of grammar, or anything else) to confirm, for example, that 'I am in pain' is not based on an observation.

It has also been held that the connection between a colour word and the corresponding colour is established by a rule. According to A. J. Ayer, 'it is a meaning rule of English that anyone who observes something green will be describing it correctly if he says it is green'; and if there is any doubt, 'it is to be settled by looking up the rules' (*Philosophical Essays*, 120–2). But the use of the word 'green' is not to be justified in this way. If I am asked why I call something green, it would be no use citing Ayer's rule. Perhaps I would reply 'Because it *is* green', or 'Can't you see?' (cf. BB 131, 134, 148). A foreigner might perhaps need to look it up in a dictionary, but even this would not be a case of 'looking up the rules'; for the dictionary would define the word by examples, and these would be taken from the actual use of the word by native speakers.

In one of his lecture-notes Wittgenstein spoke of a colour-sample as a rule. In what circumstances am I entitled to say I see something red? 'The answer is showing a sample, i.e. giving a rule' ('Notes for a Lecture', *Philosophical Review*, 1968, 301). Now it is hardly normal usage to describe a colour-sample as a rule; but it may be said that the use of such a sample is akin to citing a rule, in that it provides a justification for what is said or done. But is the use of such samples ('rules') characteristic of the language-game of colours? There is a place for them when dealing with unusual shades or the latest concoctions of paint manufacturers. But it is not so with ordinary colours, as Wittgenstein pointed out in his more considered writings.

> How do I recognise that something is red? From the agreement of the colour with a sample? – With what right do I say: 'Yes, that's red'? Well, I say it; and it can't be justified. (RFM 406–7)

That it can't be justified does not mean, however, that I do *not* have the right to say it; for my use of a word may be justified even though no justification (by rule, sample or otherwise) can be produced. 'To use a word without justification does not mean that one is unjustified in using it' (RFM 406; PI 289).

An important aspect of language is that there are right and wrong ways of using words. Here is one way of making the distinction between the regularity of language and that of laws of nature. If something happened contrary to a law of nature, it would be surprising but not wrong; but when someone uses a word contrary to its normal usage, his use of it is wrong. Wittgenstein's objection to the sign 'S', as we saw in Chapter 5, was that it would *lack* the distinction between right and wrong. Now it may be thought that there would be no right and wrong without rules; so that if a use of language can be described as right or wrong, there must be a rule behind it. But this would be a mistake. An action, or a way of going on, may be right or wrong for a variety of reasons, some involving a rule and others not. If I take the wrong turning I act wrongly, but this does not mean that I have broken a rule; and similarly if I have chosen the right or wrong wallpaper for my room. Hence it was misleading for Wittgenstein to insert a remark about rules in the section immediately following his conclusion about the private language, that 'here we can't talk about right' (PI 258). 'Are the rules of the private language *impressions* of rules?', he asks in PI 259. This may seem to imply that what is wrong with the sign 'S' and what makes it different from the public language, is something to do with rules. But the argument of PI 258 and the ensuing sections can proceed perfectly well without the short remark about rules, and indeed the word 'rules' does not appear elsewhere in these sections. Of course there is an *analogy* between the private language and the case of someone who thinks he can follow a rule privately (in that sense of 'privately'). But an analogy is not an identity, and using a word correctly is only in some ways like following a rule correctly.

Another way in which rules have been introduced into the discussion of language is in connection with *when* it is appropriate to speak – to make a certain move in the language-game. Right and wrong are also important here. For example, a person who said 'that's red' whenever he observed something red would not be thought to have mastered the use of language. But do right and wrong in this context entail that there are rules? Some philosophers have tried to formulate sets of rules governing assertion and other speech-acts.[17] A limitation of this enterprise is that only someone who already had a mastery of speech-acts would be able to make anything of such rules. But in any case, there is no *use* for such rules in the performance of speech-acts. In such and such circumstances, it would, or would not, be appropriate for me to say 'that's red' when observing a red object. If someone asked me why I said it just then, I should be able to give a *reason*; but this would not, or not necessarily, involve a rule. (It might do so if I were taking part in a game in which we take turns at calling out the colours of things.)

In this matter there is a disparity between language and games. My reason for leaving the field is that I have been bowled out. Why is that a reason? Because it is a rule of the game that this is what one must do. My reason for saying 'That's red' is, or might be, that someone just asked me. Why is this a reason? Not because of the rules of a game. There is no rule that underwrites this reason, as in the case of the game.

The analogy that Wittgenstein draws between language and games is useful and fertile. But we should remember that it is only an analogy. Language is not literally a game or collection of games. When a child learns to speak, he is not learning to play a game; and when people have a conversation, they are not playing a game. There are language-games, in the literal sense, which might be played at parties or among children, in which people take turns in calling out particular words or some such thing; but these are not uses of language in the full sense.

The assimilation of language to games may lead to startling conclusions about the reality of the world outside language. According to one exponent of Wittgenstein, the language-game of colours is no more 'real' than the game of football. The existence of the colour red depends, he holds, on whether 'the language-game with this rule is played'; but 'we need not have this game', any more than the game of football.[18] But it is absurd to think that the existence of colours is dependent on games we play. Grass was green, and blood red, long before human beings appeared on the earth, and they would be so even if no human beings ever existed to say so. To deny this would be to interfere with well-established ways of talking, and Wittgenstein would be the last to do so.

Games, and the rules of games, can be invented, introduced, altered and abrogated at will; but this is not so with uses of language, except in a superficial verbal sense. Wittgenstein sometimes spoke of language as 'autonomous', contrasting it with such activities as cookery. The latter, he said, is 'defined by its end', and this is not so in the case of language. The purpose of cookery is to produce tasty food, and its success is measured by this criterion; but in the case of language, there is no such purpose (Z 320, PG 184). However, in this respect, again, there is a disparity between games and language; for the former are not autonomous, independent of an exterior purpose or criterion of success. We can ask, for example, whether chess is a *good* game; whether Monopoly is a better game than Careers; or whether chess would be improved if we altered one of the rules. These are perfectly good questions, and the answers to them are not given by the existing rules, but will depend on outside considerations. A game may be criticised for being too long or too short, not providing enough excitement; it may be dangerous, too expensive, difficult to supervise and so on. But these questions cannot arise about our language-games, such as those of pain, knowledge or inadvertent actions. There are no considerations, outside language, on which we can evaluate these language-games, and which might lead us to opt for different ones.

A similar point may be made about the choice of an individual in taking part in an activity. It is up to me whether to play chess or other games. It is also up to me whether to *learn* to play these games or not. On the other hand, I may live in a society in which one does not have this choice because the games are unknown there. But these possibilities do not exist in the case of language-games, such as those mentioned above. It was not up to me whether to take part in these, or learn to take part in them. And a society in which they are unknown would hardly qualify as a human society.[19]

G. CONCLUSION

We have examined certain views of language which may be regarded as alternatives to realism, and attributable to Wittgenstein in view of his rejection of realism. What, in a nutshell, was his view? Was he a pluralist, a conventionalist? Did he hold that language is a sort of game, or that its use is to be explained in terms of rules? Many commentators have foisted these and other theories on Wittgenstein, refusing to take seriously his renunciation of explanation and theory. Some have treated the expressions 'language-game' and 'form of life' as technical terms, introduced by Wittgenstein as essential components of his 'theory'. Others, finding no such theory in Wittgenstein's writings, regard him, for that reason, as hopelessly obscure. Some resort to the writings of 'Wittgensteinians' – real or alleged followers of Wittgenstein, who express views that are more clear-cut than those of their (alleged) master.[20] The truth is, however, that Wittgenstein did not intend to follow any of the standard theories, nor to put forward a rival one of his own. His descriptions, he said, were not meant as 'hints of explanations' (BB 125).

It would be surprising, after all, if something as fundamental and pervasive as language could be reduced or assimilated to something other than language. Language is not a convention, not a game, not a picture. We may get insights by comparing or contrasting it in various ways with these and other models. But we should not start with the assumption that some such model or theory will 'explain' what language is – or that language is in need of such explanation.

7

Knowledge, Certainty and Doubt

A. DO I *KNOW* I AM SITTING IN A CHAIR?

This book is concerned mainly with the philosophy of Wittgenstein's masterpiece, the *Investigations*, and associated writings. Among his other works, the most important are probably the notes *On Certainty*, which will be the main subject of this chapter. This work was written, as the editors tell us, in the last year and a half of the author's life (Preface, vi); the last remark in the volume is dated '27.4.[1951]', and he died two days later.

Wittgenstein had worked on the *Investigations* over many years, re-writing and re-arranging his material with infinite pains – though he was not satisfied, even then, that he had 'produced a good book' (PI, end of Preface).[1] By contrast, the remarks in *On Certainty* (some of them dated day by day as he wrote) may fairly be described as first-draft material, and this must be borne in mind in reading and discussing the work. In spite of his many insights, and frequent brilliance of expression, his remarks in this volume are sometimes unclear or at odds with one another, as we shall see.

In the *Investigations* Wittgenstein had chosen as his starting-point a quotation from Augustine, and his reaction to the view expressed there was a dominant theme throughout the book. A similar role is played in *On Certainty* by the writings of an important recent thinker, and friend of Wittgenstein's, G. E. Moore. In the first section of the book Wittgenstein cites one of Moore's statements, and much of the book is taken up with his reactions to Moore's position. The quotation from Augustine, and the main focus of the *Investigations*, had been on language; whereas Moore's concern, and the main theme of *On Certainty*, is about knowledge and doubt. But, as we shall see, there are also important continuities between the two works.

The statement with which *On Certainty* begins had been made by Moore in a remarkable lecture given to the British Academy in 1939, in which he took up a challenge that had been issued a century and a half earlier by Kant. It was, said Kant, 'a scandal to philosophy' that no-one could yet produce a 'satisfactory proof' of the existence of things external to the mind. Moore's 'proof' consisted in holding up his hands and saying, with suitable gestures, 'Here is one hand' and 'Here is another', and concluding from this that there are things external to the mind.

Moore was aware that this way of disposing of the problem might not satisfy everyone. Some philosophers, he thought, would demand a logical proof of his premises, 'Here is one hand' and 'Here is another'. Without this, they would argue, he could not *know* them to be true, and the way would still be open for sceptical doubt. Moore's reply was to admit that he could not give such a proof, but to claim that he could, nevertheless, know these statements to be true. There are some truths, he maintained, that a person can know without being able to give a proof.[2] In an earlier paper, 'A Defence of Common Sense', he had given an extensive list of propositions, of various kinds, all of them 'truisms' which, he said, he could '*know*, with certainty, to be true', contrary to what might be said by sceptical philosophers; for example, that he had a body, that there were other human beings besides himself, that the earth had existed long before he was born, and so on (*Philosophical Papers*, p. 32ff). These propositions, and Moore's use of them, are discussed in Wittgenstein's notes.

Wittgenstein's treatment has a negative and a positive aspect. His negative argument is that Moore's examples, so far from being paradigms of knowledge, are not proper examples of it at all. On the other hand, agreeing with Moore in assigning a special place to these propositions, he tries to give an account of their role in connection with our knowledge. Wittgenstein uses Moore's examples and similar ones of his own. I shall refer to both as 'Moore's propositions'.

Wittgenstein argues that when Moore speaks of 'knowledge', he is not using the word in accordance with its normal conditions. 'One says "I know" when one is ready to give compelling reasons'; if a person 'knows something, then the question "how does he know?" must be capable of being answered' (OC 243, 550). But it is not clear how these conditions could be met in the case of Moore's examples, such as 'Here is a hand'. If one tried to give reasons in such a case, one 'could give a thousand, but none that is as certain as the very thing it is meant to be a reason for' (OC 307). Such 'reasons' would not have the function of normal reasons. Hence, if the reasons for someone's assertion 'are no surer than his assertion, then he cannot say that he knows . . . ' (OC 243).

Wittgenstein also made the point (in the *Investigations*) that where we can speak of knowledge, it would also make sense to speak of believing or making certain. 'One says "I know" where one can also say "I believe" or "I suspect"; where one can convince oneself' (PI p. 221; cf. OC 58). But these possibilities, again, would not exist in the case of Moore's propositions.

It would seem that, in what he says about reasons, Wittgenstein is putting forward a general claim about the conditions of knowledge. According to a recent commentator, 'Wittgenstein concludes that, as a general matter, "whether I *know* something depends on whether the evidence backs me up or contradicts me" [OC 41]. When there is no possibility of evidence [doing this], the matter cannot be something that I know' (T. Morawetz, *Wittgenstein and Knowledge*, 92). Yet it would be surprising, in view of what he says elsewhere about generalisations and theories, if this were really Wittgenstein's settled view. It is also a claim that is hardly likely to be true if he is right in what he says about the fibre-to-fibre structure of our concepts. And indeed it is not difficult to think of counter-examples to this 'theory of knowledge' (as we may call it). I know that the Battle of Hastings took place in 1066, but would not be able to say how I know this. I know that two years ago I visited Castle Howard and enjoyed my visit, but there is no evidence that 'backs me up'.

Wittgenstein also says (OC 175) that whereas 'I know' requires a justification, this is not so in the case of belief. But this too is a mistake. Whether a justification is required depends on what the belief or knowledge is about, and on the context in which these terms are used. If I express a belief that so-and-so will win the election, then I *would*, in most circumstances, be expected to be able to say why I believe this. Finally, Wittgenstein seems to think, with many recent theorists of knowledge, that knowledge entails belief ('What I know, I believe' – OC 177). But such generalisations, apart from being open to refutation, are hardly in accordance with Wittgenstein's attitude to generalisation and theory, as expressed in the *Investigations* and elsewhere.[3]

But was Wittgenstein really committed to these views? Was he committed to denying that one could speak of knowledge or belief in the case of Moore's propositions? In a number of passages we find him using these and related words in regard to such propositions. His 'belief' that he has two hands is, he says, shared by 'every reasonable person' (OC 252); he is 'quite certain' that 'motor cars don't grow out of the earth' (OC 79); he 'knows' that the earth has existed long before his birth (OC 288). There are also passages in which he confesses his difficulty in trying to decide whether these are cases of knowledge or not. He asks himself: 'Haven't I got it wrong and isn't Moore perfectly right? . . . Of course I do not think to myself "The earth already existed some time before my birth", but does that mean I don't *know* it?' (OC 397). Again, 'Do I know that I am now sitting in a chair? – Don't I know it?! In the present circumstances no-one is going to say that I know this . . . . But even if one doesn't say it, does that make it *untrue*??' (OC 552).

The last passage draws attention to another reason that has been given for denying that these are cases of knowledge – namely, that there would be no *use* for the word 'know' in these cases; it would not perform the useful function that it performs in other, more usual cases. 'I would like', says Wittgenstein 'to reserve the expression "I know" for the cases in which it is used in normal linguistic exchange' (OC 260); and this would not include my knowledge that I am now sitting in a chair. But is there, after all, no context – no use, in any sense, for such expressions of knowledge?

> I am sitting with a philosopher in the garden; he says again and again 'I know that that's a tree', pointing to a tree that is near us. Someone else arrives and hears this, and I tell him: 'This fellow isn't insane. We are only doing philosophy.' (OC 467).

But is 'doing philosophy' a genuine use? 'If', writes a commentator, 'a "philosophical use" is just one in which a philosopher may give examples, then the issue is whether there is such a use. What is at issue is whether it makes sense to proceed as Moore does' (Elizabeth Wolgast, *Paradoxes of Knowledge* (Cornell, 1977), 73). But this is a curious sort of issue. Knowing that Moore used the expression 'I know' in that context, how can we ask 'whether there is such a use'? Here the last word would seem to be : 'This language-game is played' (PI 645).

But should Moore's use *count* as a use? May it not, after all, be devoid of sense? According to Norman Malcolm (in an early paper), Moore's use of 'I know' in the context of his argument was senseless in the same sort of way as the expression 'good-natured' in the context 'My desk is good-natured'.[4] But this cannot be right. Moore's audience would have been very puzzled if he had told them that his desk was good-natured; but they were not puzzled by his claims to know that he had two hands. Probably they thought: yes, of course; here is something we all know. Nor would they have been puzzled by the fact that Moore made his assertions in that context.

But perhaps it will be said that Moore and his audience were both deluded; that in spite of what they thought, the whole discussion was meaningless. It would be rash, no doubt, to conclude that there is a meaningful use of language wherever people take themselves to be participating in a discussion. But how else is the matter to be settled? To someone armed with a view of the essence of language, such as that of the *Tractatus* or the verification principle, this question will have a firm answer, and he will have a method of deciding any given case. But if the later Wittgenstein was right in his rejection of this conception of language, then the question will not be amenable to such treatment. In that case we shall still be able to point out how the philosophical use *differs* from ordinary uses; but this will not entail that it is not a use at all.

The same point may be made about other non-ordinary uses of language, for example in science, aesthetic judgement and religion. The latter is especially interesting here, for in his 'Lectures on Religious Belief' Wittgenstein made a point of bringing out the great differences that exist between the ordinary and religious uses of 'believe'. But he did not conclude that the latter was a misuse of the word, or that religious belief was not really belief. His conclusion was: ' . . . there is this extraordinary use of the word "believe". One talks of believing and at the same time one doesn't "believe" as one ordinarily does'.[5]

Perhaps it will be said that a crucial difference between religion and philosophy is that the former is a 'practice'. But cannot the same be said of philosophy? Again, if Moore's philosophising is ruled out because of lack of an ordinary context, should not the same rule apply to Moore's critics? If they say, for example, that the meaning of a word is its use in practice, then it may be pointed out that this remark would only be made in a philosophical context.

Perhaps they would accept that the remark is 'nonsensical', but only in a special *Tractatus* sense of that word. But if this is correct, should not a similar allowance be made for Moore's assertions?

There is a passage in which Wittgenstein speaks of Moore's propositions as 'grammatical'. Taken in a grammatical sense, he says, Moore's 'I know' would mean: 'There is no such thing as doubt in this case', or 'The expression "I do not know" makes no sense in this case' (OC 58); but if that is so, he claims, then ' "I *know*" makes no sense either'. Yet his next remark again shows him vacillating on this issue. ' "I know" ', he says, 'is here a *logical* insight' (OC 59). But, the reader may wonder, how can it be a logical insight if it makes no sense? I believe that Wittgenstein's talk of 'no sense' in the first remark was a hangover from his earlier, *Tractatus* self. The propositions of that work were (in the sense described in Chapter 2) 'nonsense', but this did not mean that they consisted of gibberish or lacked any point or context. They were intended to express a 'logical insight'.

A similar difficulty arises in the discussion of pain in the *Investigations*. We saw earlier (Chapter 5) how Wittgenstein dealt with the objector who said 'Only I can know whether I am really in pain', by drawing attention to the fact that, according to normal usage, other people frequently know that one is in pain. But he also took issue with the positive aspect of the objection, as follows:

> It can't be said of me at all (except perhaps as a joke) that I *know* I am in pain. What is it supposed to mean – except perhaps that I *am* in pain? (PI 246).

Now one thing it may mean, one way in which the statement would have a use, is as a 'grammatical' reminder; and, curiously enough, Wittgenstein himself indicates such a use in the very next section. Here he echoes the 'Only I can know . . . ' of PI 246 with the sentence 'Only you can know if you had that intention', on which he comments:

> One might tell someone this when one was explaining the meaning of the word 'intention' to him. For then it means: *that* is how we use it. (And here 'know' means that the expression of uncertainty is senseless.) (PI 247)

Now it is not clear in what circumstances one would actually 'explain' this word to anyone (presumably we do not learn it in such a way). But we can easily think of cases in which we might *remind* someone of this aspect of its use; and similarly in the case of pain. To a dithery patient, the doctor may say: 'You must know whether you have a pain', or 'Only you can tell me'. And an indecisive person may be told: 'You must know what you want.' The function of such remarks is grammatical. It is not that the person concerned happens to have particularly good evidence for what he wants, intends or feels; but that he has, in these matters, a special authority or a special right of decision; and these are not based on evidence. When the word 'know' is used in this (grammatical) way, it does not mean what the objector in PI 246 had intended; but it does mean something. (It is 'nonsense', but only in a *Tractatus* sense of this word.)

Now in drawing attention to the normal use of 'know' that occurs when other people know that I am in pain, Wittgenstein was on safe ground. For it is a fact, and a fact known to anyone who cares to reflect on the matter, that we use the word 'know' in this way. But the other claim, that *I* cannot be said to know this, is not so easily defended. It seems, indeed, only too easy to produce a refutation of it. All that is required is for someone to *say* 'He knows he is in pain'; this would disprove the claim that 'it can't be said'. To be sure, we would need to have a genuine example of *saying*; the speaker would have to understand what he is saying and not merely utter the words. Let us assume that he uses the words concerned ('know', 'pain') correctly in other contexts. This would not entail, of course, that he is using them so in this context. Perhaps their combination here does not make sense. But how is this to be proved? The statement 'He knows he is in pain' is grammatical in the ordinary sense. Nor does it contain a demonstrable incoherence, as in the case of 'five o'clock on the sun' (PI 350). What we can say is that this is a rather peculiar use of 'know'. We can also point out (as Wittgenstein did) that if we treat this as a normal example, perhaps even a paradigm, of knowledge, then we are liable to go wrong in matters of importance in philosophy. But this will not prove that 'it can't be said'. Perhaps someone who has listened to these points will no longer *wish* to say it. But perhaps he will still wish to say it. (Or perhaps he will refrain from saying it in the presence of his philosophy teacher but go on saying it elsewhere – for example, when asked to give examples of things he knows.)

It is unfortunate that Wittgenstein expressed himself on this issue in such a definite way; and the same is true of his denials of knowledge of Moore's propositions in *On Certainty* (though, as we have seen, he was not consistent about this). For this may divert attention from the main investigation, and lead to futile disputes about whether these are 'really' cases of knowledge or not. In reply to A. J. Ayer's 'proof' (against Wittgenstein) that one does know it when one is in pain, Malcolm pointed out that in this case ' "I know" cannot do any of its normal jobs', and concluded that this was 'a good and sufficient reason for excluding the combination of words "I know I am in pain" from language' (*Thought and Knowledge*, 127, 125). But what can it mean to exclude words from language? Would people be forbidden to utter this sentence? In this matter it is better to follow the methodology stated by Wittgenstein in another passage: 'Philosophy simply puts everything before us, and neither explains nor deduces anything' (PI 126). What needs to be put before us, and what is important in promoting understanding, is a proper view of the function of 'know' in the first- and other-person sentences (for example, that in the former it 'cannot do any of its normal jobs'). This, and not something that follows from it, is the important advance. (Cf. Z 314).[6]

B. THE 'PECULIAR LOGICAL ROLE' OF MOORE'S PROPOSITIONS

Moore's answer to scepticism was to produce propositions which, he said, he could '*know*, with certainty, to be true' (*Philosophical Papers*, 32). In this matter he was in the tradition of thinkers through the ages, and especially since the time of Descartes, who held that scepticism must be defeated, and knowledge rehabilitated, by confrontation with cast-iron items of knowledge about which one could not possibly be deceived. But this was not Wittgenstein's approach; as we saw, he questioned whether these were cases of knowledge at all. He did, however, attribute to these propositions a 'peculiar logical role in our system' (OC 136), which he characterised in a number of ways. They must be taken for granted if there is to be any doubting or questioning at all. 'The *questions* that we raise, and our *doubts*, depend on the fact that certain propositions are exempt from doubt; are, as it were, the hinges on which those turn' (OC 341). They are part of one's 'world-picture', 'the inherited background against which I distinguish between true and false' (OC 94). 'I cannot doubt [such a] proposition without giving up all judgement' (OC 494), cf. 308). Nor could I argue with someone who questioned (or appeared to question) such propositions. If he said that he doubted whether he had a body, 'I wouldn't know what it would mean to try to convince him that he has one' (OC 257). An argument is possible only with someone who regards such propositions as 'exempt from doubt'. This does not mean, however, that we have here straightforward (and especially strong) examples of knowledge; for, as we saw, they do not conform very well to the normal conditions for knowledge.

The 'peculiar logical role' of these propositions is also brought out if we try to fit them into the established dichotomy of empirical and a priori knowledge. That they are not *a priori* in the sense of mathematical demonstrations seems clear enough. We cannot prove by such methods that the earth exists, that there are other people besides myself, or that the object before me is my hand; nor is it self-contradictory if we suppose these propositions to be false. Can we, then, regard them as empirical?[7] On the face of it, the proposition 'The earth existed 100 years ago' has the same logical character as 'The earth existed a billion years ago'. The latter is a matter for empirical enquiry, but can the same be said of the former? It is not clear what would count as evidence for (as against) such a proposition. 'We don't', says Wittgenstein, arrive at such propositions 'as a result of investigation' (OC 138). (This is connected with the point that 'How does he know?' cannot be answered in these cases – see p. 153.) Hence 'not everything that has the form of an empirical proposition is an empirical proposition' (OC 308).

The propositions in question 'belong', says Wittgenstein, 'to the foundation of all operations of thought (of language)' (OC 401). His account should, however, be contrasted with traditional accounts of 'foundations of knowledge', given by philosophers of both the rationalist and empiricist traditions. According to Descartes, for example, the whole of our knowledge is based on a few self-evident truths, from which all the rest can be derived by deductive reasoning. Without this foundation the whole edifice would collapse before the onslaught of scepticism. Empiricists, on the other hand, have seen the foundation of knowledge as consisting of items of sense-experience. According to Locke, it is all built up from 'ideas' which are, in some sense, imprinted on the mind when we use our sense-organs. In our time, empiricists such as Carnap and Ayer have tried to analyse all genuine knowledge into 'basic propositions', or 'protocol sentences', concerning the speaker's immediate 'sense-data'.

Wittgenstein too speaks of fundamental propositions and beliefs. Commenting on the proposition 'I have two hands', he writes: 'At the foundation of grounded belief lies belief that is not grounded' (OC 252–3). A superficial reading of *On Certainty* might suggest that we are being offered yet another account of the foundations of knowledge, comparable with those just mentioned. But Wittgenstein did not mean foundations in the traditional sense. The propositions concerned were, rather, parts of an interdependent system: ' . . . one might almost say that this foundation-wall is carried by the whole house' (OC 248). We are not to think of them as a 'point of departure' (OC 105) – a kind of knowledge that we have, or could have, before any other. For example, that mountains have existed for a long time is presupposed by many of the things we say about mountains. But is it something that we learn, or could learn, first of all? A child, says Wittgenstein, 'doesn't learn *at all* that that mountain has existed for a long time; that is, the question whether it is so doesn't arise at all. It swallows this consequence down, so to speak, with what it *does* learn' (OC 143).

Wittgenstein did not believe that one could be in a position of having only a set of fundamental beliefs (whatever they might be) and then proceed to build the rest of one's knowledge on that basis. 'When we first begin to *believe* anything, it is not a single proposition, but a whole system of propositions. (Light dawns gradually over the whole)'; 'a totality of judgements is made plausible to us' (OC 141, 140). Descartes, by contrast, believed that a person might be certain of only one proposition – *cogito ergo sum* – and then, by using his powers of reason, construct a whole corpus of knowledge on the basis of this proposition. Empiricists, on the other hand, have looked to sense-experience, as opposed to reason, as the main source of knowledge; but here again, it was thought that the relevant items of knowledge ('impression', 'sense-data' and the like) come to us one by one, after which we combine and arrange them in various ways, so as to construct the knowledge we actually have. What we are 'given' are basic items of knowledge, which we have prior to the construction. Wittgenstein, by contrast, wrote: 'What has to be accepted, the given, is – one might say –

forms of life' (PI p. 226). The expression 'forms of life' is meant to convey the wholeness of the system, and also the fact that it includes action ('life') as well as passive observation or experience. (This point will be further discussed in Section C.)

Wittgenstein's 'fundamental' propositions, unlike the fundamental data of traditional epistemology, are of various types. Some are personal, others impersonal; some about objects in one's environment, others about one's body; some about mathematical truths, others about causal regularities, and others again about remembered facts. In a number of passages he discusses the differences between them and the different ways in which they fit into our world-picture.

Again, Wittgenstein's propositions do not have the permanence of the traditional ones. If 'cogito ergo sum' is the most fundamental item of knowledge, then this is a necessary and permanent part of the human condition; and similarly if the basis of knowledge consists of sense-data. Wittgenstein does speak of his propositions as a 'river-bed' which remains fixed relative to the flux of ordinary empirical propositions; but, he says, it may happen 'that this relation alters with time, so that fluid propositions become hard, and hard ones fluid (OC 96–9). To the suggestion that one could test 'I have two hands' by using one's eyes, he replies: 'Why shouldn't I test my *eyes* by observing whether I see two hands? *What* is to be tested by *what*? (Who decides *what* stands fast?)' (OC 125). (A nice example of a 'river-bed' proposition that has become fluid is 'no human being has ever been on the moon' (OC 108 and *passim*). Perhaps Wittgenstein was right – though this is debatable – in treating this as a river-bed proposition when he wrote; but if so, it has become 'fluid' since then.)

Finally, Wittgenstein makes the point that the logical status of a proposition may depend on the situation in which it is made. In certain circumstances (for example where an amputation is to take place) 'I have two hands' may function, not as a 'river-bed' proposition, but as an ordinary empirical statement for which evidence could be adduced. But this point, again, varies with different propositions. The question whether there are physical objects, for example, cannot be related to empirical circumstances in such a way (cf. OC 23).

Another characteristic of river-bed propositions is that they are not part of the 'traffic' of ordinary discourse; they are, 'so to speak, shunted on to an unused siding' (OC 210); and they 'lie apart from the road travelled by enquiry' (OC 88). What is 'presupposed' by the language-game is not part of it. Wittgenstein sometimes says that the facts concerned 'show' themselves in the language-game (OC 7, 501, 618), but are not stated in it. This reminds us of the distinction between 'saying' and 'showing' that he had drawn in the *Tractatus*, according to which the pictorial relation that was presupposed by language could not itself be stated in language.

But are such views compatible with the later Wittgenstein's identification of meaning with use? If there is (apart from philosophy) no use for these propositions, if they lie forever in a dead siding, must it not follow that they are meaningless? (This is similar to the issue about the use of 'I know', discussed in the last section.) It may be thought that in identifying meaning with use, Wittgenstein was laying down a criterion of meaningfulness – that an expression has meaning only if there is a use for it.[8] But such a criterion, which would be typical of philosophers of the verificationist school, is hardly to be expected from Wittgenstein. His aim was to investigate *what* the meaning of a word or sentence is (by paying attention to its actual use), rather than to eliminate some kinds of language as meaningless.

If such a criterion *were* adopted, would the requirement be for actual or for possible use? The former is hardly plausible. It is, after all, largely a matter of accident whether a given fact is ever stated or not. Suppose, for example, that there were four chairs in my room last Tuesday. Perhaps there will never be any point in stating this. Is the sentence therefore meaningless? (It would be easy to think of thousands of other examples, from more or less remote corners of history, geography and so on.) Similarly, there may never be any point in stating that the earth exists, but this would not entail that this sentence is meaningless or untrue. ('It seems to me that I have known something the whole time, and yet there is no sense in saying so, in uttering this truth' – OC 466.) But what if the criterion were about possible rather than actual use? It is easy to think of situations in which there *would* be a point in using the sentence about the chairs. But then, with a little ingenuity, the same can be done for sentences like 'The earth exists'. To a group of space-travellers this sentence might convey important information. And there is a considerable literature in which philosophers have shown that, with sufficient imagination, a suitable context can be provided for the most unlikely sentences.[9]

C. KNOWLEDGE, DOUBT AND ACTION

In traditional systems of epistemology, as we have seen, all our knowledge is based on fundamental items which must be taken as self-evident; and if this cannot be done, then the whole edifice is undermined. But this would also deprive us of our reasons for acting, for we act on the basis of knowledge (or belief). But which comes first, knowledge or action? Can knowledge exist prior to action? Of course it can do so in particular cases. I find out that a certain film is on at the cinema, and *then* proceed to act on this knowledge. But can the same be said for knowledge in general? Descartes, in the sceptical phase of his argument, tells us that he will not yet allow his doubt to affect his actions: 'I am not considering the question of action but only of knowledge'.[10] To be on the safe side, he will carry on as usual and not allow his doubt to subvert his activities. But the question of knowledge remains fundamental: his activities will lack justification unless and until he can, as he hopes, establish the truth of those 'ancient and commonly held opinions' (about the existence of the physical world and so on) that he has put into doubt. And if he cannot succeed in this, then he must, to be consistent, suspend his activities.

This priority of knowledge over action was turned on its head by Wittgenstein. The end-point of justification is not, he says, 'that certain propositions are seen immediately to be true . . . , but our *acting*, which lies at the bottom of the language-game' (OC 204). But what does this mean? Is Wittgenstein saying that we know because we act, rather than the other way round? This would be absurd. It makes sense to say I am going to the cinema because I know the film is on, but not vice versa. Yet this order of priorities is not there in the original learning-situation, in which we learn to take part in the language-game. We do not begin by learning that such and such is the case and then proceed to the relevant action. A child, says Wittgenstein, learns to *fetch* a book, to *sit* in a chair and so on; but he is not taught that these things exist. Again, one might teach him the word 'tree' by standing in front of a tree and saying 'lovely tree'. These activities presuppose the existence of trees and books. 'But can the child be said to *know*: that a tree exists?' (OC 480). Does he believe or know 'that milk exists? Does a cat know that a mouse exists?' (OC 478).

We learn the use and meaning of such words as 'book' and 'chair' in situations in which some action is being performed; and then we also learn to justify our actions, or some of them, by reference to knowledge (for example, that there is a book in the other room). But the propositions about existence are not part of the language-game, except in the 'background' sense. 'Are we to say', asks Wittgenstein, 'that the knowledge that there are physical objects comes very early or very late?' (OC 479). In one sense it comes very early, for we have here one of those propositions that 'show' themselves in our language-games even though they are not normally stated and have no use outside philosophy. But in another sense the answer is 'very late'. The very concepts of existence and 'physical object' are sophisticated ones which could not come first in the acquisition of language. Nor is it necessary to acquire them in order to be competent in the use of language. In this sense they belong to the superstructure of the conceptual system and not to its foundation.

In Descartes's writings we are invited to develop a system of knowledge from the standpoint of a disembodied mind (the existence of our bodies being, so far, unproved); and in the works of empiricists knowledge is treated as something that is 'given' to a passive receptacle, the mind. But a human child is an organism that *acts*, and reacts, in certain ways, and the language-game that he learns is built on to this behaviour. This point was made in the *Investigations*, as we saw in Chapter 5, about the language-game of sensations, in which 'they teach the child a new pain-behaviour' by means of words which are 'connected with the primitive, the natural' behaviour of crying (PI 244). The same kind of development, from the 'natural' to the 'new' (language-game) behaviour, occurs in connection with the child's interest in milk and other objects in its environment. The new behaviour will involve concepts of knowledge and justification (and also deception), but the 'background' propositions need not come into it at all. A philosopher might claim, for example, that in most of our actions we rely on the 'uniformity of nature' – that things will continue to behave in regular ways. But, says Wittgenstein, such principles do not enter into our language-games any more than into the behaviour of animals. 'The squirrel does not infer by induction that it is going to need stores next winter as well. And no more do we need a law of induction to justify our actions or predictions' (OC 287). We might say, paraphrasing PI 246, that if we are using the word 'justify' as it is normally used, then our actions are very often justified; and there is no need to appeal, in addition, to a 'law of induction' of the kind sought by philosophers. Similarly, we can explain a squirrel's behaviour by reference to its expectations, memory and so on (for example where it deposited its nuts), but we need not and would not ascribe to it any ideas about the philosophical principle. In the case of human beings, the philosophical question *can* be introduced, but this is not necessary in order for the activity or language-game to be conducted in the normal way and in accordance with normal standards of justification.

An objection sometimes made against Wittgenstein is that he makes too much of the original learning-situation, as if what is taught to the child is decisive in evaluating the claims of philosophers with regard to justification and other matters. Is it not absurd to regard a child's grasp of these matters as more authoritative than that of a sophisticated adult? Children are taught that babies are brought by a stork and that Father Christmas delivers presents in the night; but later it occurs to them to question and think critically about these beliefs. May not the same development take place in the case of ordinary beliefs versus philosophical doubt?

But this is a misleading comparison. For what the child is taught when he learns about chairs, trees and hands is not a belief (that these things, or physical objects in general, exist), but to participate in an activity, a language-game. Thus if we tell him 'This is your hand', we are not teaching him a belief, but the meaning of the word 'hand' – how to use this word in 'the innumerable language-games that are concerned with his hand' (OC 374). To the objector (in a passage in *Zettel*) who asks 'So does he have to begin by being taught a false certainty?', Wittgenstein replies: 'There isn't any question of certainty or uncertainty yet in their language-game. Remember: they are learning to *do* something' (Z 416). It is true that later they may proceed to raise questions about certainty or uncertainty, but the impact of these will not be like that of an adolescent's questioning of childish beliefs. In the latter case we have one belief competing against another. As the child learns more about the world, he gives up some of his early beliefs and lets others take their place. The question 'Where do babies come from?' is now given a different answer: they come from X and not Y. But this is not so in the other case. The doubts about physical objects or the 'law of induction' are not in competition with previously existing beliefs, for the child had neither beliefs nor doubts about these propositions. Nor is it a matter of competing language-games, as if one language-game (the philosophical) could drive out another (for example, that of fetching books and other objects when requested to do so). Hence the philosopher 'will teach his children the word "chair" after all, for of course he wants to teach them to do this or that, e.g. to fetch a chair' (Z 414). (By contrast, 'if someone does not believe in fairies', he can simply 'omit to teach them the word "fairy" ' (Z 413).) He will teach the word 'chair', not because he is able to refute the philosophical doubts, but because he and the child need to take part in the relevant language-games.

Such language-games should also be contrasted with religious beliefs. (Hence it may be misleading to regard religion as a language-game, as some philosophers have done.) A person may change his mind about a religious belief (either rejecting or adopting it) as a result of critical questioning of his existing beliefs: and then his behaviour would be affected accordingly. Here we have a case of competing beliefs, and behaviour dependent on these beliefs. But someone who takes part (as we all do) in the language-games of ordinary life, does not do so because he *believes* in the existence of physical objects.

It may be claimed, however, that if someone does proceed to the stage of philosophical doubt, then this *ought* to affect his behaviour in ordinary life. We may assume that this would have been Descartes's position, had he not hoped for a speedy resolution of his doubts. If the sceptic means what he says when he uses the word 'doubt', then we would expect his behaviour to be affected in suitable ways, for this is a criterion of doubting, as normally understood. If someone doubts, in the normal sense, that there is a chair in the other room, or whether the train will really be at the station, then he would act (or refrain from acting) in suitable ways; and similarly in the case of more substantial beliefs and doubts, as in the case of religion. Yet this does not happen in the case of philosophical doubt. We can, says Wittgenstein, imagine people who qualify all their statements with an expression of uncertainty; but '*how* would the life of these people differ from ours?' (OC 338). Again, a sceptic who has looked up the time of the train may insist: 'I have *no* belief that the train will really arrive' – but he will go to the station all the same. 'He does everything that the normal person does . . . ' (OC 339).

It may be thought that the sceptic behaves in these ways 'to be on the safe side', believing, perhaps, that the law of induction is at least probably true, even if there is no proof of it. But this is not a tenable position, for there is no more proof that the law is *probably* true than that it is certainly true. And if our actions were based on such laws and propositions, then the sceptical challenge must deprive us totally of any justification for action, and this should be reflected in the sceptic's own behaviour. Yet, as David Hume pointed out long ago, sceptical arguments *'admit of no answer and produce no conviction.* Their only effect is to cause that momentary amazement and irresolution and confusion, which is the result of scepticism' (*Enquiry Concerning Human Understanding,* ed. Selby-Bigge, 155).[11]

But may not the sceptic's continued behaviour be due merely to weakness of will? Could there not be a really consistent sceptic, who suits his actions to his words? Such a person, we may take it, would *not* go to the station; would not take measures to provide himself with food; would not bother to evade traffic when crossing the road; would just as soon put his hand in the fire as not do so, and so on. But such behaviour is beyond the will-power of normal human beings. Here is another sense in which it is 'our *acting* which lies at the bottom of the language-game' (OC 204). We cannot help doing these things, any more than the squirrel can help acting in accordance with its nature. 'Nothing could induce me to put my hand into a flame – although after all it is *only in the past* that I have burnt myself' (PI 472). Our certainty in these matters 'lies beyond being justified or unjustified; [it is,] as it were, something animal' (OC 359). Moreover, if someone did act, or try to act, in ways appropriate to scepticism, would we recognise his behaviour as an expression of doubt?

> If someone said that he doubted the existence of his hands, kept looking at them from all sides, tried to make sure it wasn't 'all done by mirrors', etc., we should not be sure whether we ought to call that doubting. We might describe his way of behaving as like the behaviour of doubt, but his game would not be ours. (OC 255)

Such a person, we might say, is unable to distinguish philosophical doubt from real doubt. And this would be a reason for regarding him as mad.

Wittgenstein's book is entitled *On Certainty,* and he takes his departure from Moore's propositions. Moore's approach to scepticism was in the confrontationist tradition – confronting the sceptic with items of knowledge which would be unshakeable. One might have expected something similar from Wittgenstein, but this, as we have seen, was not the case. One of his aims, indeed, was to discredit Moore's propositions from being genuine items of knowledge; and this may seem to strengthen the sceptic's position rather than to weaken it. What, in brief, was Wittgenstein's answer to scepticism?

Wittgenstein's approach, here as elsewhere, is to describe rather than to explain or justify (cf. OC 189, 192). 'In certain circumstances', he writes, 'we regard a calculation as sufficiently checked. What gives us the right to do so? . . . Somewhere we must be finished with justification, and then there remains the proposition that *this* is how we calculate' (OC 212). The sceptic will challenge us to produce a further proposition which would justify our practice of calculating, and this, as Wittgenstein agrees, cannot be done. Can it be said, he writes in another passage, that 'everything speaks for, and nothing against, the table's still being there when no-one sees it? But what does speak for it?' (OC 119). The sceptical challenge to these propositions is not refuted by Wittgenstein. What he denies is that our language-games are founded on such propositions. In the case of religion or science, a whole practice or way of doing things may be underpinned by some fundamental belief or theory, such as the theory of natural selection or a belief in God, and if these are given up, it will no longer make sense to proceed as before. But there is no such underpinning in the case of ordinary life; and the 'fundamental' propositions postulated by foundationalists and sceptics (who are partners in the same misconception) has no such role. It is only through a misdescription of the logical situation that the sceptical doubts and denials seem to pose a challenge to our ordinary ways of going on. The remedy is not to take issue with these denials but to attain 'a clear view of the aim and functioning of [our] words' (PI 5).

D. KNOWING WHAT WE MEAN

There is also an internal incoherence in the sceptical position to which Wittgenstein drew attention. 'If you tried to doubt everything', he wrote, 'you would not get as far as doubting anything. The game of doubting itself presupposes certainty'

(OC 115). The presupposed certainty is about the meanings of words. 'If you are not certain of any fact, you cannot be certain of the meaning of your words either' (OC 114, cf. 506).

If someone doubts, for example, that the object before him is a hand, then he must know the meanings of these words, for example, the word 'hand'. But to know the meaning of this word is to know that *'this*, for example', is a hand (OC 268; cf. 369). Again, 'I am not more certain of the meaning of my words than I am of certain judgements. Can I doubt that this colour is called "blue?"' (OC 126). If I cannot be sure of this fact, then I cannot be sure of the meanings of my words, in which I express my doubt or belief.

Here we are brought back to the point about 'agreement in judgements' (PI 242), discussed in Chapter 5 (see pp. 88–9). It may be thought that the knowledge of meaning (whether of 'blue', 'hand', 'pain' or 'two') is independent of one's *use* of these words, in judging, doubting and so on; so that, given the knowledge of meaning, one could use them to affirm or doubt any proposition whatever. But this is not so, for someone who doubts that the object before him is a hand or that a certain flower is blue would be held not to know the meanings of these words. Hence I cannot tell someone (or myself) that I doubt whether this is a hand without, by this very utterance, throwing doubt on the meaning of my statement.

This point also applies to the word 'doubt' itself. If someone says he doubts one of these propositions, then 'how do I know that he uses the words "I doubt it" as I do?' (OC 127). Similarly, 'if this deceives me, what does "deceive" mean any more?' (OC 507); and how, if such propositions are to be doubted, 'can I rely on what is meant by "true" and "false"?' (OC 515).

It might be thought that the sceptic could simply accept these points, and proceed to apply his doubt to the meaning of words as to everything else. He might, for example, ask himself whether he can really be sure of his meaning when he uses the words 'doubt', 'hand' or any others. But in doing this, he would again have to help himself, illegitimately, to a knowledge of meaning – in this case, the meaning of the question just mentioned. Normally such doubts about meaning – the meanings of ordinary words – do not arise, because our knowledge of them is daily confirmed and, so to speak, fine-tuned, by our dealings with other people. (This would not be so in the case of Robinson Crusoe, who might indeed become doubtful about his memory of meanings.) But this source of knowledge cannot be invoked by a consistent sceptic, for he would doubt whether there *are* any other people.

But could not the doubts occur without any use of language? Of course the sceptic must use language if he is to make his points in discussion; but may one not doubt privately, without using language? What would this mean? A person may think silently of the proposition 'Here is a hand', consider whether it might be denied and so on. But this thinking would still be in terms of words, so that the scepticism about meanings must still arise. Another form of doubt is 'dispositional'. I may doubt whether it will be fine weather tomorrow, without ever thinking about the matter. But then it must still be true that *if* someone asked me, I would express my doubt in words; and to do that, I must know what the words mean. It is true that we can also ascribe doubt to creatures incapable of verbal expression. A squirrel, for example, may be said to be in doubt as to where he buried last year's nuts, or a dog as to which person he ought to follow. But in these cases the doubt is expressed in behaviour; and it is the behaviour that makes us ascribe doubt to the animal. But this is not so in the case of the sceptic.

The sceptic must either 'cheat' by helping himself to the assumption that he knows what he means, or he must remain silent. His predicament, like that of the person in the private language argument, is at 'the point where one would just like to emit an inarticulate sound' (quoted on p. 116).

E. 'SHOULD I SAY "I BELIEVE IN PHYSICS"?' (OC 602)

One of the things we 'swallow down' in the course of our learning, and which may be described as part of our 'world-picture', is the belief in modern science. In our quest for knowledge about the world, and reliable predictions about the course of nature, we look to scientific evidence and scientific methods. But is this something we take for granted, as needing no justification? Or can we claim to know, on the basis of reasons, that the scientific view is correct? (Cf. OC 602) This issue is brought to a head when the scientific view comes into collision with an alternative one. Suppose, says Wittgenstein, we came into contact with people who did not acknowledge the force of scientific evidence. 'Instead of a physicist, they consult an oracle' (OC 609). Is this a difference that could be resolved by reasoning? Or would we merely be 'using our language-game as a base from which to *combat* theirs?' (OC 609). Reason, says Wittgenstein, can only take us a certain way.

> I said I would 'combat' the other man, – but wouldn't I give him *reasons*? Certainly; but how far do they go? At the end of reasons comes *persuasion*. (Think what happens when missionaries convert natives.) (OC 612)

Now it may be objected to this that reason and persuasion are not exclusive, for we often persuade someone to change his beliefs by *giving* him reasons – good reasons – for doing so. But it is also true that sometimes, at least, the reasons (or so-called reasons) that are given in such situations are not good; and various irrational procedures may be used to produce the desired change. Again, we may be mistaken in thinking that the 'primitive' people would be better off by changing their beliefs and their ways – a point that was illustrated in Chapter 6 with Wittgenstein's example of the people who said 'Our affairs went better before' when they had been persuaded away from their 'mistakes in counting' (RFM 105–6; see p. 132). Nevertheless there is such a thing as persuading the other people of the falseness of their view, and the superiority of scientific procedures, by rational means and without resorting to 'combat' or persuasion of an irrational kind. We may, for example, prove to them by demonstration that scientific methods and medicines are effective against disease. It may be said that, all in all, the scientific intrusion may do more harm than good, leading to a disruption of tribal values and so on; but this does not affect the point that it is possible to prove the effectiveness of the scientific approach.

There is an important difference between the status of the scientific view and the status of Moore's propositions. In describing the latter as belonging to our 'world-picture', as the 'hinges' on which all propositions turn, we are speaking about *human* thought and language, and not those of one society as against another. In the case of science, on the other hand, we know very well that this 'world-picture' is only a recent and local development. However, in justifying the scientific approach, we would be able to draw on universal values; we could appeal to that 'common behaviour of mankind [which] is the system of reference by means of which we interpret an unknown language' (PI 206, previously quoted p. 135). We saw in Chapter 6 that there were limits of Wittgenstein's pluralism. Though we could not prove to the people who calculated and measured in strange ways that their practices were wrong, there is a point beyond which we could not make sense of their activities at all; they would not be *different* ways of calculating, for we could not describe them in these terms at all. Some aspect of this 'common behaviour' were suggested on p. 136 (in connection with Quine's position): human beings desire food when they are hungry, express fear (and behave accordingly) when threatened with pain, and so on. It is only under these conditions that we can interpret their language and, indeed, regard them as human beings in the full sense. But this frame of reference, and common understanding, must also enable us to reason with them, and to prove by rational argument the advantages of the scientific view.

What, after all, is the scientific view? This is not the place for an examination of the various definitions of science that have been put forward and contested by philosophers in recent years; but we may take it that one essential aspect of it is a due respect for experience. But the practice of learning from experience is an essential part of rationality itself. It is not something peculiar to the scientific view or any other; for it is part of that frame of reference, and common behaviour of mankind, which are necessary if we are to make anything at all of the language and practices of people different from ourselves.[12] And by appealing to the universal frame of reference we could demonstrate the advantages of the scientific view, both in terms of results, and in terms of the rational procedures that lead to these results.

'Instead of a physicist, they consult an oracle. (And for that we consider them primitive.)' (OC 609). Are we wrong if we do so? Are they not equally entitled to describe the scientific view as primitive? But what would this mean? The difference between their view and ours is nor merely that they believe one thing and we another; there is also a sense in which our view *encompasses* theirs. 'I call him primitive because I have resources that are unfamiliar to him and because, let us suppose, he has no resources that are unfamiliar to me . . . . We can represent their beliefs and procedures to ourselves, but they cannot apprehend our own.'[13] Such a contrast is indeed made by Wittgenstein himself in another part of his book.

We say: these people do not know a lot that we know. And, let them be never so sure of their belief – they are wrong and we know it.

If we compare our system of knowledge with theirs, then theirs is evidently the poorer one by far. (OC 286)

The relationship is analogous to that between a modern scientist and his predecessors. The former can understand (and reject) the views of the latter, but the latter may have no inkling of the modern ideas. In this matter there is both continuity and discontinuity. The pre-scientific people are cut off from the richer system, but behind that system are those universal values of reason by means of which we can converse with them and introduce them to the richer system; and similarly in the history of the development of our own society.

8
Conclusion

Wittgenstein's notes *On Certainty*, as we have seen, are open to a number of objections, and seem sometimes to be at odds with one another. How he would have revised and re-drafted this material, had he lived to do so, must remain a matter for speculation and extrapolation from his more finished writings. But it is clear that, even in the state in which we have it, the work represents a major advance in epistemology, as well as exhibiting the kind of brilliance and originality that we find throughout its author's writings.

Originality is not, of course, a quality that is peculiar to Wittgenstein's work. It may be said of almost every philosopher of importance that he enriched the subject by contributing ideas that had not been thought of before. This is true, for example, of Moore's contribution to epistemology. His approach to scepticism was certainly something new and has proved to be of lasting importance in subsequent discussions of the subject. (In this book I have not tried to do justice to Moore's position, discussing it only from the point of view of *On Certainty*.) Even so, Moore's originality was not of the startling and, as we may say, disorienting kind that we find in Wittgenstein's work. Moore was addressing himself to a well-established question on the philosophical agenda, and his treatment may be described (as I claimed) as belonging to the 'confrontationist' type. But when we turn to Wittgenstein's writings here and elsewhere, we find that the established questions are not addressed in an easily recognisable way at all; one may feel, indeed, that they have been left unanswered, and that Wittgenstein's writings, fascinating as they may be, do not really get to grips with the important questions. In *On Certainty*, for example, he seems to approve neither of scepticism nor of the alternative view offered by Moore; and to confine himself, instead, to describing the relevant uses of language ('language-games'). But to regard this approach as a satisfactory way of unravelling philosophical problems calls for a radical re-orientation of the ideas with which we are likely to approach such problems, and with which they have been approached by philosophers in the past.

175

Wittgenstein himself said that his philosophy was no longer the *same subject* as the traditional one; it was 'one of the heirs of the subject which used to be called "philosophy"' (BB 28); and this was an appropriate remark. But it would be absurd to make this kind of claim about Moore's contribution, or even about some of the great innovators of the past, such as Descartes.

Wittgenstein was not, of course, the first to claim to be making a new start in philosophy, sweeping away old cobwebs with a new broom. Such a claim was made, notoriously, by the Logical Positivists of the Vienna Circle, but it soon turned out that their 'elimination of metaphysics' was really just another philosophy in the traditional mould, with such well-known positions as empiricism, idealism and foundationalism, and exposed to objections appropriate to these positions. But this is not true of Wittgenstein's 'descriptive' philosophy, though misguided attempts have frequently been made to fit his ideas into one of the traditional moulds or '-isms'; nor is it open to objections of the traditional kinds.

A curious feature of Wittgenstein's later philosophy is that many philosophers (myself included) accept what he said almost entirely. This is a very unusual state of affairs in philosophy, where even the greatest thinkers are freely criticised even by their most sympathetic exponents. For this reason supporters of Wittgenstein may be accused or suspected of being dogmatic – accepting what the great man said just because he said it. They may be suspected of being carried away by the brilliance of his writing or, in an earlier generation, by having fallen personally under his charismatic spell; and it must be admitted that some have been open to these accusations. There is a reason, however, why Wittgenstein's statements should be less liable to refutation than those of others. The reason is that he does not attempt to do any of the usual things that are exposed to the hazard of refutation; he offers no theories or explanations, and does not try to 'deduce anything' from the data before us (PI 126). The issue he puts before us is not whether some theory or generalisation is correct or can be defended against counter-examples, but whether the underlying descriptive method is the right one – whether 'the subject that used to be called "philosophy"' really ought to be superseded in that way. This method was such a radical departure that Wittgenstein thought it necessary to tell his readers, repeatedly and emphatically, what he was and was not doing – and even so, his disclaimers have been widely disregarded. Merely to introduce this method was an achievement of great originality, and for that very reason the question of accepting it will be difficult to get into focus and not amenable to established ways of criticism and objection.

Wittgenstein's new way of doing philosophy goes against the grain of tradition. But there is more to this than merely tradition. For, if Wittgenstein is right, the methods and views he is opposing are due to perennial features of language and the human mind. 'Language', he wrote in 1931, 'sets everyone the same traps; it is an immense network of easily accessible wrong turnings'. His task would be to 'erect signposts at all the junctions where there are wrong turnings so as to help people past the danger points' (*Culture and Value*, Blackwell, 1980, 18). According to the *Investigations*, philosophy was to be 'a struggle against the bewitchment of our understanding by means of language' (PI 109).[1] He also spoke of certain 'cravings' – 'our craving for generality' and the 'craving for a definition' (BB 18, 27); and claimed that 'the philosopher's treatment of a question is like the treatment of an illness' (PI 255). A suspicious reader may feel that Wittgenstein is here resorting to 'combat' and 'persuasion' as opposed to rational argument. But, as I hope has been shown in the course of this book, Wittgenstein's position, in general and in detail, is supported by arguments which the reader can and should evaluate for himself. But in doing so he must be prepared to open his mind to unaccustomed, and perhaps uncomfortable, ways of thinking about himself and the world.

Notes and References

1. INTRODUCTION

1. 'What makes a subject hard to understand – if it's something significant and important – is . . . the contrast [Gegensatz] between understanding the subject and what most people *want* to see. . . . What has to be overcome is a difficulty having to do with the will, rather than with the intellect' (*Culture and Value*, 17e). See also A. Kenny, 'Wittgenstein on the Nature of Philosophy' and B. McGuinness, 'Freud and Wittgenstein', in B. McGuinness (ed.), *Wittgenstein and His Times* (Basil Blackwell, 1982) pp. 14, 42.

2. THE *TRACTATUS* AND THE 'ESSENCE OF HUMAN LANGUAGE'

1. References to the *Philosophical Investigations* are to sections of Part I; for example, PI 1 refers to Part I section 1. References to Part II are given by page numbers; for example, PI p. 221. The above 'picture of . . . human language' is attributed in PI 1 to Augustine, and the section opens with a quotation from the latter's writings. But I agree with other commentators in treating it as reflecting Wittgenstein's own earlier view.
2. The German 'Satz' may be translated either way. There are philosophical reasons for distinguishing between the two words (and also, perhaps, 'statement'), but I shall ignore these for the sake of simplicity.
3. For a different reading of 3.1432 see P. M. S. Hacker, *Insight and Illusion* (Oxford University Press, 1986) 67ff. Here and elsewhere in this brief introduction to the *Tractatus* I do not attempt to do justice to the vast amount of debate that has taken place about the interpretation of particular sections of the work.
4. The wording is 'If the world had no substance. . .'. But the previous section (2.021) states; 'Objects make up the substance of the world'.
5. Strictly speaking, the supposition of 2.0211 itself makes no sense according to the *Tractatus* account of the truth. For what would the word 'true', at the end of the quoted sentence, mean if there were no objects?
6. Compare Russell in the opening remarks of his *Philosophy of Logical Atomism* 'You can, for instance, say: "There are a number of people in this room at this moment." . . . [But] what you have said is most fearfully vague and . . . you really do not know what you meant.'

(LK 179). But by 'reflection and analysis' we can pass from 'the vague thing that we start from' to 'the real truth of which that vague thing is a sort of shadow' (LK 179–80). In his preface, Russell said that his lectures were 'very largely concerned with explaining certain ideas which I learnt from my friend and former pupil Ludwig Wittgenstein', though he could not say whether the latter was alive or dead. Wittgenstein had joined the Austrian army and was taken prisoner by the Italians. His contact with Russell was resumed in 1919.

7. 'Some Remarks on Logical Form'. *Proceedings of the Aristotelian Society*, 1929.
8. The verification principle was in fact first propounded by Wittgenstein in the late twenties, when his ideas were in the course of change. At that time he had discussions with members of the Vienna Circle, where the new philosophy of Logical Positivism was being worked out. The verification principle became one of their main tenets, but Wittgenstein himself soon gave it up. See my *Logical Positivism* (Basil Blackwell, 1981) for further discussion.
9. In my discussion of a proposition showing its sense I have profited from Norman Malcolm's *Nothing is Hidden* (Basil Blackwell, 1986), chapter 5.

3. MEANING AND USE

1. 'I'll teach you differences' (from *King Lear* I, iv, 88) was a motto that Wittgenstein thought of using for the *Investigations*, according to his pupil M. O'C. Drury. See Rush Rhees (ed.), *Ludwig Wittgenstein: Personal Recollections* (Basil Blackwell, 1981), p. 171.
2. Where (in the case of long sections of PI) I have added letters, they denote paragraphs within the sections. Thus '47e' is the fifth paragraph of section 47.
3. 'Words in their primary and immediate signification stand for nothing but the ideas in the mind of him that uses them'. John Locke, *An Essay Concerning Human Understanding* (Oxford University Press, 1975), 3.2.2.
4. Here and in some other passages I have used my own translations of the German text.
5. Baker and Hacker, in their *Analytical Commentary* (Basil Blackwell, 1983, p. 99) dismiss as 'absurd' the idea that 'proper names when ostensively defined are an exception' to the remark about the explanation of meaning, on the ground that 'it would be pointless to introduce the principle [about meaning and use] into a discussion of proper names if such names were typically exceptions to it'. But Wittgenstein (rightly) says 'sometimes' and not 'typically'. Baker and Hacker suggest that Wittgenstein may have meant such cases of meaning as 'those clouds mean rain'. This is, indeed, a type of meaning that cannot be identified with use, but it seems clear from the wording of PI 43 that Wittgenstein had *word*-meaning in mind in that section.

6. The following passage from Kripke is typical: 'If there were a substance . . . which had a completely different atomic structure from that of water, but resembled water in [other] respects, would we say that water wasn't H_2O? I think not. We would say. . .' (This 'we would say' is meant to show that the 'scientific essence' of water – H_2O – is decisive in regard to the meaning of 'water'.) Saul Kripke, 'Naming and Necessity', in G. Harman and D. Davidson (eds), *Semantics of Natural Language* (Reidel, 1972), 323.

7. For a fuller discussion, see my 'Scientific Realism and Ordinary Usage' in *Philosophical Investigations*, 7 (1984), 187ff.

8. See, for example, J. A. Fisher, 'Aberrant Speakers', *Philosophical Investigations* (Fall 1981), 26.

4. 'EXPLANATIONS COME TO AN END'

1. It is doubtful, however, whether Wittgenstein actually held this view at the time of writing the *Tractatus*. The only remark about explanation of meaning in that work is in the difficult section 3.263. In the 'Theses', however, we are told that 'The sense of a proposition is the way it is verified' (WVC 244), and that this is achieved, in the last resort, by 'elementary propositions', which 'deal with reality immediately' (WVC 248). The 'Theses' can be seen as a kind of modified statement of some of the ideas of the *Tractatus*, in the light of Wittgenstein's current views (ca. 1930), as communicated to F. Waismann, for circulation among members of the Vienna Circle. The fascinating story of Wittgenstein's collaboration with Waismann is told by Gordon Baker in 'Verehrung und Verkehrung: Waismann and Wittgenstein' in C. G. Luckhardt (ed.), *Wittgenstein: Sources and Perspectives* (Ithaca, New York: Cornell University Press, 1979).

2. A. D. Woozley, *Theory of Knowledge* (London: Hutchinson, 1949), p. 49. Also see A. J. Ayer's proposals for defining the past and the present, in *The Problem of Knowledge* (Penguin, 1956), 152. For Locke's treatment, see the *Essay*, 2.14.2–4. By contrast, see Wittgenstein's account of 'how a child might be trained in the practice of "narration of past events"', BB 104–5.

3. Though I once heard of a child who thought her name was 'Letsgo', because her mother would address her with this expression when taking her out.

4. Zeno Vendler, *Res Cogitans* (Cornell University Press, 1972) pp. 139–40. Noam Chomsky claims that 'as a precondition for language learning, [the infant] must possess . . . a linguistic theory. . .' (*Aspects of the Theory of Syntax* (Massachusetts Institute of Technology Press, 1965), p. 25). According to J. A. Fodor, 'one cannot learn a language unless one has a language', and this applies also to the learning of one's native language. He postulates a 'language of thought'. (*The Language of Thought* (Harvester Press, 1975) 63–4). See the discussion by Norman Malcolm in *Philosophical Investigations*, 5 (January 1982).

5. Tolstoy, *What is Art?* (Oxford University Press, 1930), 87. For a history

of the concept of beauty since ancient Greek times, see W. Tatarkiewicz, *A History of Six Ideas* (Nijhoff, 1980).

6. In one of William Golding's novels, there is an amusing example involving the word 'rule'. The Pharoah ('Great House') is playing a primitive game with his 'Head Man'. ' "I've sometimes thought", said the Head Man, "that it might be interesting if we didn't let chance decide the moves but thought them out for ourselves." "What an odd game", said Great House. "It wouldn't have any rules at all"'. (*The Scorpion God*, Faber, 1973, 30.)

7. See, for example, W. E. Kennick, 'Does Traditional Aesthetics Rest on a Mistake?', *Mind* (1958), and B. R. Tilghman, *But is it Art?* (Basil Blackwell, 1984).

8. R. Bambrough, 'Objectivity and Objects', *Proceedings of the Aristotelian Society*, LXXII (1971/2).

9. Ibid.

10. A classic and amusing demonstration of this point was given by Lewis Carroll in 'What the Tortoise said to Achilles', in *Mind* (1895).

11. Richard Rorty, in his widely acclaimed *Philosophy and the Mirror of Nature*, accuses Wittgenstein (among others) of 'a prejudice against the notion of "mental entities" and "psychological processes"' (Basil Blackwell, 1980), 213.

12. Kripke's reading of Wittgenstein may be compared to a mistake that is often made about David Hume's account of cause and effect. It is said that Hume was sceptical about causality, or denied that there is such a thing. But Hume only denied a certain, widely held, conception of it. His aim was to give a correct account of causality and not to doubt or deny its existence. (Whether his account was correct is another question.) For further discussion of Kripke's views, see O. Hanfling, 'Was Wittgenstein a Sceptic?', *Philosophical Investigations*, 8 (1985).

13. 'Birds learning of tunes, and the endeavours one may observe in them, to hit the notes right, put it past doubt with me, that they . . . retain *ideas* in their memories, and use them for patterns. For it seems to me impossible, that they should endeavour to conform their voices to notes (as 'tis plain they do) of which they had no *ideas*'. (Locke, *Essay Concerning Human Understanding*, 2.10.10.)

5. LANGUAGE AND THE PRIVACY OF EXPERIENCE

1. Russell made a virtue of this necessity. Having declared that 'when one person uses a word, he does not mean by it the same thing as another person means by it', he went on: 'I have often heard it said that this is a misfortune. That is a mistake. It would be absolutely fatal if people meant the same things by their words. It would make all intercourse impossible, because the meaning you attach to your words must depend on the nature of the objects you are acquainted with, and since different people are acquainted with different objects, they would not be able to talk to each other unless they attached quite

different meanings to their words' (*Logic and Knowledge*, Allen & Unwin, 1956, 195). 'Acquaintance' was Russell's word for a peculiarly close and private relation that he held to exist in the case of knowledge by perception.

2. Here I disagree with Norman Malcolm, *Nothing is Hidden* (Basil Blackwell, 1986), 172.

3. 'It is conceivable', wrote Wittgenstein in another passage, 'that *all* the processes of understanding, obeying, etc, should have happened without the person having been taught the language' (BB 12). See also the discussion by G. P. Baker and P. M. S. Hacker in *Wittgenstein: Meaning and Understanding* (Basil Blackwell, 1983), 30ff. Wittgenstein himself conducted various thought-experiments with adaptations of Crusoe, in unpublished manuscripts. (MS 116, p. 117; MS 124, p. 213ff; MS 165, p. 116ff.)

4. According to Rorty, there is a way of 'avoiding the paradox' of PI 304 (which he expounds), whereby 'we can . . . let a sensation be as much a something as a table' (*Philosophy and the Mirror of Nature*, Basil Blackwell, 1980, 109). But the whole point of Wittgenstein's remark is that a pain is *not* 'a something' in the sense of a table.

5. For a discussion of Schlick's view, see my *Logical Positivism* (Basil Blackwell, 1981), section 5.6.

6. It appears that Wittgenstein himself held such a view at one time, See PR p. 84.

7. His argument for this remarkable view is quoted in note 1 above.

8. BB pp. 72–3; a similar suggestion is made in PI 273. See also Wittgenstein's '"Private Experience" and "Sense Data"', reprinted in O. R. Jones (ed.), *The Private Language Argument* (Macmillan, 1971) pp. 251–2, on 'lying *subjectively* but not objectively'.

9. Cf. D. Cockburn, 'The Mind, the Brain and the Face', in *Philosophy*, 60, October 1985.

10. 'The Homunculus Fallacy' is well exposed by A. Kenny in *The Legacy of Wittgenstein* (Blackwell, 1984), under that title. The view that 'each of us is precisely a brain' is held by John Searle in his *Intentionality* (Cambridge University Press, 1983), p. 230, and is well criticised in Norman Malcolm's *Nothing is Hidden*, 183ff.

11. See Richard Dawkins, *The Selfish Gene* (Oxford University Press, 1976).

12. Such feelings played a major role in Collingwood's account of art. According to this, the artist begins in a state in which he thinks 'I feel . . . I don't know what I feel' (p. 109). In finding an adequate 'expression' of the feeling, he creates a work of art. *The Principles of Art* (Oxford University Press, 1938).

13. The published translation has: 'produce a memory which is actually correct'.

14. R. J. Fogelin, *Wittgenstein* (Routledge & Kegan Paul, 1976), 162–3. An early version of the 'sceptical' reading was given by A. J. Ayer in *The Problem of Knowledge* (Penguin, 1956), 60, and a similar view is repeated in his *Wittgenstein* (Weidenfeld & Nicolson, 1985).

15. 'How then are we to tell a suitable "private language" story? – The answer is: Don't even try! . . . So if we ask "What are we to imagine

in connection with this diary case?", Wittgenstein's final answer is: "Nothing"'. (John W. Cook, in A. Ambrose and M. Lazerowitz (eds), *Ludwig Wittgenstein* (Allen & Unwin, 1972) 40, 42.) According to S. Candlish, 'we are not to think [of the diary example] as a possible or even ultimately intelligible case'. ('The Real Private Language Argument', *Philosophy*, 55 (1980) 87.)

16. A. Kenny, *Wittgenstein* (Allen Lane, 1973) 194.
17. R. J. Fogelin, *Wittgenstein*, 161.
18. In this section I have used material from my paper 'What does the Private Language Argument Prove?', *Philosophical Quarterly*, 84 (1984) 475–6.
19. *Essay Concerning Human Understanding*, 2.9.2. Locke uses 'perception' in a wider sense than usual, but this does not affect the point. A similar idea is rejected by Wittgenstein in PI 316: 'To get clear about the meaning of the word "think", let us watch ourselves while we think: what we observe will be what the word means! – But this concept is not used like that. . .'. (The published translation is misleading here.)
20. From the lectures 'Form and Content', *Philosophical Papers* II (Reidel, 1979) 306–7, 334. An extract from the lectures is reprinted in O. Hanfling (ed.), *Essential Readings in Logical Positivism* (Basil Blackwell, 1981). 131–149, and the matter is further discussed in my *Logical Positivism*, section 5.6. It is likely that Wittgenstein's ideas about private meaning were stimulated by his contact with Schlick.
21. In this section I have used material from my paper 'What does the Private Language Argument Prove?', *Philosophical Quarterly*, 84 (1984), 480–1.
22. R. A. Sharpe, 'How Having the Concept of Pain Depends on Experiencing It', *Philosophical Investigations*, 6 (1983), 143.
23. Gilbert Ryle, *The Concept of Mind* (1949) 193 (reprinted Penguin, 1970).
24. David Pears, *Wittgenstein* (Fontana, 1971) 148.
25. For further examples, see my paper 'What does the Private Language Argument Prove?', *Philosophical Quarterly*, 1984. Some material from this paper has been used in the last three or four paragraphs of this section.
26. W. H. Hudson, 'Two Questions about Religious Education', in R. Straughan and J. Wilson (eds), *Philosophers on Education* (Macmillan, 1987) 115.
27. According to Stanley Cavell, Wittgenstein thought that 'all our knowledge, everything we assert or question . . . is governed . . . by criteria' (*The Claim of Reason* (Oxford University Press, 1979), 14.) Peter Hacker, in *Insight and Illusion* (OUP, 1972), spoke of 'Wittgenstein's criterial semantics', claiming that, for Wittgenstein, 'the sense of an expression is given by a specification of its criteria' and that, accordingly, 'an expression without criteria lacks sense' (302, 292). Similar views are expressed by, for example, Newton Garver in *Philosophical Investigations*, 7 (1984), 214. In view of Wittgenstein's rejection of theory and generalisation, these are astonishing claims. Hacker has, however, repudiated his earlier views in the second (1986) edition of his book.

28. Saul Kripke in I. Block (ed.), *Perspectives on the Philosophy of Wittgenstein* (Basil Blackwell, 1981), 291. The term 'sceptical solution' is taken from Hume. I discuss Kripke's account of Wittgenstein in 'Was Wittgenstein a Sceptic?', *Philosophical Investigations*, 8 (1985).
29. G. Schlesinger, *Metaphysics* 187.
30. My account is based mainly on Wittgenstein's most authoritative work, the *Investigations*. I am aware of other uses of 'criterion' in his less finished writings, for example the 'Notes for Lectures' reprinted in O. R. Jones (ed.), *The Private Language Argument* (Macmillan, 1971).
31. J. W. Canfield, *Wittgenstein: Language and World* (University of Massachusetts Press, 1981), 31. Canfield expounds Wittgenstein's later thought largely in terms of criteria. Hacker also spoke of this as 'a term of art in Wittgenstein's later philosophy', in his first edition (p. 284).
32. H. L. Finch, *Wittgenstein: The Later Philosophy* (Humanities Press, 1977), 56.
33. G. P. Baker and P. M. S. Hacker, *Scepticism, Rules and Language* (Basil Blackwell, 1984), 111–12.
34. It is worth noting that in Wittgenstein's most extended work on epistemology, *On Certainty*, the word 'criteria' does not appear.
35. This is Wittgenstein's comment on the statement 'It is correct to say "I know what you are thinking", and wrong to say "I know what I am thinking"'.
36. In this section I have used material from my 'Criteria, Conventions and Other Minds', in Stuart Shanker (ed.), *Ludwig Wittgenstein: Critical Assessments*, vol. II (London: Croom Helm, 1986).

6. LANGUAGE-GAMES AND OBJECTIVITY

1. Berkeley's views are expounded in his *Principles of Human Knowledge* and *Three Dialogues*.
2. The English translation has 'pile up logs' – from the German 'verhaufen . . . Scheitholz'. But 'verhaufen' is not a German word; Wittgenstein must have meant 'verkaufen' – 'to sell'. Also 'firewood' seems a better translation of 'Scheitholz'.
3. Michael Dummett, 'Wittgenstein's Philosophy of Mathematics', in G. Pitcher (ed.), *Wittgenstein* (Macmillan, 1968)
4. Barry Stroud, 'Wittgenstein and Logical Necessity', in G. Pitcher (ed.), *Wittgenstein*, 488.
5. See, for example, Simon Blackburn, *Spreading the Word* (Oxford University Press, 1984), 78ff.
6. 'Bemerkungen über Frazer's *The Golden Bough*', *Synthese*, 1967, 237. Translated and published in book form by Rush Rhees, as *Remarks on Frazer's 'Golden Bough'* (Brynmill, 1979). Cf. Nigel Barley, *The Innocent Anthropologist* (British Museum, 1983): 'Dowayos would always speak as if they were staunch positivists. "How do you tell one kind of *zepto* [magic plant], for example, from another?" I would ask. "How can I tell whether this is the kind that stops adultery or the kind that heals

headaches?" They stared at me in sheer disbelief at such simplicity. "By trying them", they would answer. "How else?"' (107; see also 109–10).

7. This example may be compared with Plato's reservations about the introduction of writing into philosophy. 'The living word of knowledge . . . has a soul. . . , of which the written word is properly no more than an image'. *Phaedrus* 276a, p. 295 (Sphere Books, 1970), Jowett's translation. Another interesting example is H. G. Wells's story 'The Country of the Blind', in which a sighted man arrives in a society of blind people, living in a remote valley. He tries, unsuccessfully, to prove that his way of dealing with the world is superior to theirs.

8. 'Handlungsweise' is a somewhat broader term than 'behaviour'; it might be translated as 'way of behaving' or 'way of acting'.

9. Wittgenstein mostly spoke of language-games in the plural, especially when (as in PI 23) he was concerned to stress their variety. But in some passages (when what is at issue is the autonomy of language vis-à-vis a non-linguistic reality) he may have meant *the* language-game, in a singular sense. Thus he speaks of 'the human language-game' in OC 554, and 'the whole language-game' in BB 108; and in PI p. 200 he writes that 'the primitive language-game which children are taught needs no justification'.

10. Jean Ennals, on the BBC World Service, 29 November 1981. A nice example of the questioning kind of philosophy is that of the doctor and nurse in PI p. 179. I have criticised Kripke's bold interpretation of this in 'Was Wittgenstein a Sceptic?', *Philosophical Investigations* (January 1985), 15.

11. Of the RFM, Part I may be regarded as more authoritative than the rest. The first two sections are almost identical with PI 189–90, and the rest was included in an early version of the *Investigations*. But he decided, for reasons which are not given, against its inclusion in later drafts. (See Editors' Preface to RFM, and G. H. von Wright, 'The Origin and Composition of the *Philosophical Investigations*' in von Wright (ed.), *Wittgenstein* (Basil Blackwell, 1982).

12. On the arguments that took place about the introduction of negative numbers, see Morris Kline, *Mathematics,: The Loss of Certainty* (Oxford University Press, 1980), 115.

13. Rorty's description of the language-game is, in any case, careless; for of course we do not always 'take people's word for what they are feeling'.

14. Cavell's 'Must We Mean What We Say?', and other relevant papers, are reprinted in C. Lyas (ed.), *Philosophy and Linguistics* (Macmillan, 1971).

15. John W. Cook, 'The Illusion of Aberrant Speakers', *Philosophical Investigations*, 5 (1982). The 'facts of living' approach can also be used for such long-disputed concepts as knowledge and promising. See my 'Promises, Games and Institutions', *Proceedings of the Aristotelian Society*, LXXV (1974/5), and 'A Situational Account of Knowledge', *The Monist*, 68 (1985).

16. An example of the misunderstanding occurs in the recent 'Attitudes

to Evidence and Argument in the Field of Religion' by R. W. Hepburn: 'A language-game, wrote Wittgenstein, "is not based on grounds. . . . It is there – like our life". Religious belief, Norman Malcolm claimed, paraphrasing Wittgenstein, "does not rise or fall on the basis of evidence or grounds: it is 'groundless' "'. (in R. Straughan and J. Wilson (eds), *Philosophers on Education* (Macmillan, 1987) 129. For Malcolm's claim, see S. C. Brown (ed.), *Reason and Religion* (Cornell University Press, 1977) 148.) But Hepburn and Malcolm are both mistaken. Malcolm's 'paraphrase' is not justified by Wittgenstein's text (cf. OC 459, 509, 559); and Hepburn's 'A language-game . . .' replaces Wittgenstein's '*The* language-game . . .' (OC 559). Wittgenstein is talking about human language and life as a whole, and not making a case for particular language-games.

17. See John Searle, *Speech Acts* (Cambridge University Press, 1969), 66–7; cf. William Alston, *Philosophy of Language* (Prentice-Hall, 1964), 42–3.

18. J. Canfield, *Wittgenstein: Language and the World* (Amherst, 1981), 16.

19. The last two paragraphs, and some other passages in this section, are adapted from my paper, 'Does Language Need Rules?', *Philosophical Quarterly*, 30 (July 1980).

20. 'I know what the (several) views of *Wittgensteinians* are, even if I do not know for sure which, if any, was Wittgenstein's', writes Hilary Putnam. He goes on, however, to speak of *Wittgenstein's* views, attributing to the latter the idea that 'mathematical facts . . . are *explained* by our "natures" or "forms of life"'. See 'Analyticity and Apriority: Beyond Wittgenstein and Quine' in H. Putnam, *Realism and Reason* (Cambridge University Press, 1983).

7. KNOWLEDGE, CERTAINTY AND DOUBT

1. For details of its composition, with many comparisons with earlier drafts, see the commentaries by G. P. Baker and P. M. S. Hacker, published by Blackwell since 1980.

2. G. E. Moore, *Philosophical Papers*, 127 and 145–50.

3. I have criticised these and other claims made by recent theorists of knowledge in my paper 'How is Scepticism Possible?', *Philosophy*, 63 (1987). See also 'A Situational Account of Knowledge', *The Monist*, 68 (1985).

4. Norman Malcolm, 'Defending Common Sense', *Philosophical Review*, 58 (1949), 218.

5. Ludwig Wittgenstein, *Lectures and Conversations on Aesthetics, Psychology and Religious Belief*, edited by Cyril Barrett (Basil Blackwell, 1966) 59. Also compare the following: 'Anything that I normally call evidence wouldn't in the slightest influence me.' 'No matter what might happen I shouldn't call it evidence against. . . .' In the first passage (*Lectures and Conversations*, 56) Wittgenstein is commenting on religious belief, in the second (Malcolm's *Memoir*, Oxford University Press, 1958, 89) on an assertion of the type that Moore had put forward.

6. In this section I have used or adapted material from my paper 'On

the Meaning and Use of "I know"', *Philosophical Investigations*, 5 (1982).
7. Moore himself claimed that they were empirical, in a retrospective essay, replying to critics who regarded them otherwise. See P. A. Schilpp, *The Philosophy of G. E. Moore* (Open Court, 1952) 672.
8. Cf. John W. Cook, 'Notes on Wittgenstein's *On Certainty*', *Philosophical Investigations*, 3 (Fall 1980), 26.
9. See also A. C. Ewing's argument that sentences like 'Quadratic equations go to race-meetings' should be described as false rather than meaningless, in 'Meaninglessness', *Mind* (1937).
10. *The Philosophical Works of Descartes*, vol. I, edited by Haldane and Ross (Cambridge University Press, 1911), 148.
11. Hume also wrote that 'it is not reasoning which engages us to suppose the past resembling the future' (*Enquiry Concerning Human Understanding*, 39), and used the example of putting one's hand in a fire in this connection. Although Wittgenstein had not read Hume, the resemblance between their views is extensive and remarkable, in spite of deep differences in other respects. See my 'Hume and Wittgenstein' in G. Vesey (ed.), *Impressions of Empiricism* (Macmillan, 1976).
12. Cf. p. 132 and p. 184 n. 6.
13. Thomas Morawetz, *Wittgenstein and Knowledge* (London: 1988), 128, 131. In this section, I have profited from Morawetz's discussion, p. 123ff.

8. CONCLUSION

1. This remark is usually taken to mean that our understanding is bewitched by language. But it (and the German original) could also be read in the sense that the *remedy* is 'by means of language'. The two readings could, of course, both be true.

Index of Names and Subjects

feelings
  in animals, 103, 104, 105–6
  cause *v.* object of, 98–9
  Hume on, 99–100
  simulation of, 104
  see also sensations
Fogelin, R. J., 114
'forms of life', 144, 162
formulae, understanding of, 74–6
Frazer, J. G., 132
fundamental beliefs, 161–3
fundamental names
  demonstratives as, 10–13
fundamental propositions, 128, 161–3,
  165

games
  analogy with language, 136–7, 149–51
  as example of 'family resemblance',
    64, 65, 71, 72
genes
  moral qualities attributed to, 106–7
grammar (in ordinary sense), 41–2
grammar (in Wittgenstein's sense), 42,
  147, 157–8

Hobbes, Thomas, 78
Hume, David, 99–100, 168

ideas
  words standing for, 78, 117
images, *see* mental images; pictures
induction
  and justification of action, 165–6
inexpressible, the, 22
intention, 21
interpretation
  and ostensive definition, 57–8

James, William, 113
Jones, O. R., 118
judgements
  agreement in, *see* agreement;
    common behaviour; common
    language
justification, 62–3, 165–6, 169

Kant, Immanuel, 153
knowledge, 49, 52–3
  and belief, 154–5
  evidence for, 154
  Moore's propositions on, 153–9
  of pain, *see* pain
  of physical objects, 165

Kripke, Saul, 80–1

language, 177
  common, 88–9, 135–7
  foreign, learning of, 60
  human context of, 21, 27
  learning of, 55, *see also* ostensive
    definition
  native, learning of, 61–2
  ordinary *v.* philosophical use of, 156
  practical usage of, 31–2
  rules and, 146–9
  sounds counting as, 134
  translatability of, 134–6
language-games, 32, 33, 110, 136, 150
  and fundamental propositions, 163,
    165
  and learning process, 165, 166–7
language skills
  innateness of, 60–2
learning process, 165, 166–7
  see also ostensive definition
legal definitions, 67
limits
  of language and world, 23
linguistic idealism, 129
Locke, John, 25, 56–7, 78, 90, 100–1,
  117, 160–1
logic, *see* truth-functions
logical constants, 26
logical form
  representation of, 22–3
logical objects, 26
logical positivism, 24, 43, 176

machines
  and consciousness, 107
Malcolm, Norman, 13, 156, 159
mathematical propositions
  truth of, 27, 138, 237
mathematical rules, 74
mathematics
  and agreement in judgements, 127
  discovery *v.* invention in, 139–41,
    143–4
meaning
  agreement and, 127–8
  changes in, 66–7
  and context of use of words, 49
  correlation theory of, 4–9, 89–90, 98
  and essence, 39–40, 46
  identical with use, 44–5
  and mental images, 43
  multiple, 28–9

Index to Wittgenstein's Works